EFFICIENCY AND COMPETITION IN CHINESE BANKING

Elsevier

Asian Studies Series

Series Editor: Professor Chris Rowley,
Cass Business School, City University, London, UK;
Institute of Hallyu Convergence Research, Korea University, Korea
Griffith Business School, Griffith University, Australia
(email: c.rowley@city.ac.uk)

Elsevier is pleased to publish this major Series of books entitled Asian Studies: Contemporary Issues and Trends. The Series Editor is Professor Chris Rowley of Cass Business School, City University, London, UK and Department of International Business and Asian Studies, Griffith University, Australia.

Asia has clearly undergone some major transformations in recent years and books in the Series examine this transformation from a number of perspectives: economic, management, social, political and cultural. We seek authors from a broad range of areas and disciplinary interests covering, for example, business/management, political science, social science, history, sociology, gender studies, ethnography, economics and international relations, etc.

Importantly, the Series examines both current developments and possible future trends. The Series is aimed at an international market of academics and professionals working in the area. The books have been specially commissioned from leading authors. The objective is to provide the reader with an authoritative view of current thinking.

New authors: we would be delighted to hear from you if you have an idea for a book. We are interested in both shorter, practically orientated publications (45,000+ words) and longer, theoretical monographs (75,000–100,000 words). Our books can be single, joint or multi-author volumes. If you have an idea for a book, please contact the publishers or Professor Chris Rowley, the Series Editor.

Dr Glyn Jones
Email: g.jones.2@elsevier.com

Professor Chris Rowley
Email: c.rowley@city.ac.uk

EFFICIENCY AND COMPETITION IN CHINESE BANKING

YONG TAN

ELSEVIER

Amsterdam • Boston • Heidelberg • London
New York • Oxford • Paris • San Diego
San Francisco • Singapore • Sydney • Tokyo
Chandos Publishing is an imprint of Elsevier

CP
CHANDOS
PUBLISHING

Chandos Publishing is an imprint of Elsevier
50 Hampshire Street, 5th Floor, Cambridge, MA 02139, USA
The Boulevard, Langford Lane, Kidlington, OX5 1GB, UK

British Library Cataloguing-in-Publication Data
A catalogue record for this book is available from the British Library

Library of Congress Cataloging-in-Publication Data
A catalog record for this book is available from the Library of Congress

ISBN: 978-0-08-100074-8 (print)
ISBN: 978-0-08-100102-8 (online)

Publisher: Glyn Jones
Acquisition Editor: Glyn Jones
Editorial Project Manager: Harriet Clayton
Production Project Manager: Debasish Ghosh
Designer: Vicky Pearson Esser

CONTENTS

ABOUT THE AUTHOR

Yong Tan, PhD, was a Lecturer in Economics at the University of Huddersfield Business School from 2013; after two years, he was promoted to Senior Lecturer in Economics. Before joined the University of Huddersfield Business School, Yong was a part-time Lecturer in Economics at the University of Portsmouth Business School. Yong has experience in teaching a number of modules in different areas of economics and finance for both undergraduate and postgraduate levels. Yong is the series editor of International Economics for Henry Stewart Talks. Yong is a Fellow of United Kingdom Higher Education Academy.

Yong's research interest lies in the area of the Chinese banking industry. His research investigates various issues in the Chinese banking industry including bank performance (bank profitability, bank efficiency, as well as bank productivity), bank competition, and risk-taking behavior of Chinese commercial banks. Yong has published a number of research articles in various high-quality academic journals such as the Journal of International Financial Markets, Institutions, and Money; Journal of Developing Areas, Economic Issues; Journal of Emerging Market Finance; Studies in Economics and Finance; Journal of Chinese Economics and Business Studies; and Journal of Economics Studies. In addition, in 2014, Yong published one research monograph by himself entitled "Performance, Risk and Competition in the Chinese Banking Industry" by Elsevier. Furthermore, he is a member of the editorial board for the Eastern European Business and Economics Journal. Yong also works as a reviewer for a number of economics and finance journals on a regular basis and has experience reviewing book proposals for Elsevier.

PREFACE

The Chinese economy has experienced tremendous growth during the last decade, and, without any doubt, the banking sector plays a vital and consistent role in promoting the economic growth in China. How to create a sustainable, healthy, and well-performed banking sector is the most important issue for the Chinese government as well as for banking regulatory authorities. Several rounds of banking reforms in China since the Third Plenary Session of the Eleventh Central Committee has aimed to improve the performance, increase the competitive condition, as well as reduce the risk-taking behavior of Chinese commercial banks. A number of research studies are investigating the profitability of the Chinese banking industry, which is a very important aspect of bank performance. In addition, a growing number of publications are examining the efficiency of the Chinese banking industry, most of which focus on either technical efficiency or profit and cost efficiencies of Chinese commercial banks.

A handful of research studies are evaluating the competitive condition in the Chinese banking industry, most of which use the Panzar–Rosse H-statistic, whereas a few more studies during recent years have assessed the competitive condition in the Chinese banking industry using the Lerner index. No publication comprehensively and systematically examines the efficiency and competition of the Chinese banking industry.

This book examines different types of efficiencies in the Chinese banking industry over the period 2003–13. Three different types of Chinese commercial banks are considered which include the state-owned commercial banks, the joint-stock commercial banks, as well as the city commercial banks. These three types of Chinese commercial banks are the largest three bank types according to the size of the assets held. More specifically, both the non-parametric Data Envelopment Analysis as well as the parametric stochastic frontier approach have been used to measure the technical efficiency, pure technical efficiency, scale efficiency, cost efficiency, revenue efficiency, as well as profit efficiency in the Chinese banking industry.

With regard to the measurement of the competitive condition in the Chinese banking industry, the most traditional idea is derived from the structure–conduct–performance hypothesis. In other words, this book will first use the banking sector concentration ratio to measure the competition in the Chinese banking industry. In addition, the Panzar–Rosse H-statistic, which has the ability to the classify the degree of competition in the banking sector into monopoly, monopolistic competition, or perfect competition, is also be used in this book. Furthermore, this book uses the Lerner index to measure the competition in the Chinese banking industry; the Lerner index has the ability to measure competition as well as the market power of Chinese commercial banks for different ownership types. Finally, this book is the first book using the Boone indicator to measure the competition in the Chinese banking industry. This book significantly contributes and fills the gaps of the empirical literature in banking sector competition worldwide and, in particular, in Chinese banking sector competition by using the Boone indicator to investigate the competitive condition in different banking markets. This book focuses on three Chinese banking markets, which are the loan market, the deposit market, as well as the non-interest income market.

To test the impact of competition on different types of efficiencies in the Chinese banking industry, bootstrapped truncated regression is used, whereas to check the robustness of the results, alternative econometric techniques are also used including the Tobit regression analysis as well as the Ordinary Least Square estimator. The book will be structured as follows:

Chapter "Introduction" will give a general introduction on the whole book and in particular with focus on a number of issues such as aims and objectives of the book, methodology, and data, as well as the content/structure of the book.

Chapter "Chinese Banking Sector and Reforms" will focus on discussing the reforms and structure in the Chinese banking industry. To be more specific, this chapter will firstly discuss the banking reforms in China which are divided into four different stages according to period which are between 1949 and 1978, between 1978 and 1992, between 1992 and 2001, and between 2001 and 2013. The second part of this chapter will concentrate on discussion of the structure in the Chinese banking industry. Specifically, the five large-scale commercial banks will be introduced, which will be followed by the introduction of 12 joint-stock commercial banks on a one-by-one basis. This chapter will also discusses the city commercial banks, other banks, and non-financial institutions and finally a conclusion is provided.

Chapter "Theory of Bank Efficiency and Bank Competition" will focus on discussing relevant theories in bank efficiency and bank competition. The theories of different types of efficiencies will be discussed including technical efficiency, pure technical efficiency, scale efficiency, cost efficiency, revenue efficiency, as well as profit efficiency. In addition, the theories related to the estimation of efficiencies will also be reviewed. Two main streams of methods will be discussed which include the non-parametric method and parametric method. With regards to the non-parametric method, two analyses will be evaluated which are Data Envelopment Analysis as well as Free Disposal Hull. In terms of the parametric methods, three specific methods will be discussed including the stochastic frontier approach, the thick frontier approach, and the distribution-free approach. The third part of this book will focus on discussing related theories in bank competition and theories related to the concentration ratio, the Panzar—Rosse H-statistic, the Lerner index, and the Boone indicator will be discussed on a one-by-one basis. Finally, the chapter will give a conclusion.

Chapter "Literature Review on Bank Efficiency and Bank Competition" will give a literature review on bank efficiency and bank competition. More specifically, the first part of the literature review will be focused on bank efficiency, which will be followed by reviewing related studies in bank competition. Both the review of efficiency and competition will focus on China as well as other countries. The third part of this chapter will review the research investigating the impact of competition on efficiency in the banking industry; finally, this chapter will also provide a conclusion.

Chapter "The Measurement of Bank Efficiency and Bank Competition in China" will mainly discuss the methodologies used in this book. In particular, the first part of this chapter will discuss the methodologies used to estimate the bank efficiency, which is followed by the discussion of methods used to evaluate different competition indicators. The third part of this chapter will discuss the modeling with regard to the impact of competition on efficiency in the Chinese banking industry, the chapter will be ended with a conclusion.

Chapter "Empirical Results on the Impact of Competition on Bank Efficiency in China" will report the results of the estimations. Firstly, this chapter will discuss the findings of different types of efficiencies and, then, the findings with regard to different competition indicators will be presented and discussed. The results in terms of the impact of competition on bank efficiency in China will also be described and explained and then the chapter will be summarized and concluded.

Chapter "Conclusion," which is the final chapter of this book, will be divided into three parts. The first part will be an overall introduction and summarization of the findings of this book. The second part of this chapter will provide some policy implications for the Chinese government and banking regulatory authorities, and the final part will discuss the limitations inherent to this book and point out areas for future research.

ACKNOWLEDGMENT

I would like to thank Harriet Clayton, George Knott from Elsevier for all the support and valuable comments during my writing process. I would also like to thank all the staff in the production team from Elsevier for their effort to make this book published.

I would like to thank Professor Tim Coelli, Professor Sunil Kumar, as well as Professor Rachita Gulati for granting me copyright permissions to use relevant materials.

Finally, I would like to express deep gratitude to my father, Lianmin Tan, my mother, Jie Liu, for their consistent patience, support, encouragement, and love during my 10 years of living in the United Kingdom. In particular, I would to give special thanks to my wife, Pengtong Liu, for her support and love. This book is not mine—it belongs to the three of you.

CHAPTER 1

Introduction

1.1 INTRODUCTION

The banking sector in China plays an important role in the development of the country's economy. According to statistics from the World Bank, at the end of 2012, the domestic credit provided by the banking sector in China accounted for 155.1% of Gross Domestic Product (GDP)[1]. Therefore, the performance of Chinese banks has attracted great attention from the government, banking regulatory authorities and academic researchers. Technical efficiency, as one important indicator of bank performance, measures the extent to which banks have the power to minimize the volume of inputs used in producing a certain volume of output or use particular numbers of inputs to maximize output production. Two components of technical efficiency, namely pure technical efficiency and scale efficiency, provide more information with regard to the source of efficiency. More specifically, pure technical efficiency relates to the ability of bank managers to utilize banks' given resources. Higher ability is reflected by higher pure technical efficiency, whereas scale efficiency refers to exploiting scale economies by operating at a point at which the production frontier exhibits constant returns to scale. Lower-scale efficiency indicates that banks have more room to adjust their scale of operation, whereas the resulting increase in scale efficiency contributes to the overall improvement of technical efficiency.

Technical efficiency measures performance from the perspective of volume of production, whereas, in the normal operation, banks and different companies focus more on minimizing the cost; thus, the analysis of cost efficiency is to some extent much more important than the analysis of technical efficiency. Cost efficiency is defined as the distance between a specific bank's cost and the best practice bank's cost given the assumption that they produce the same output under the same environmental conditions (Isik and Hassan, 2002).

Besides examining the cost efficiency, the final goal for the bank is to maximize revenue as well as profit. Thus, in other words, evaluating

[1] The data is from http://data.worldbank.org.

Efficiency and Competition in Chinese Banking
ISBN 978-0-08-100074-8

revenue efficiency and profit efficiency has become a favourite model amongst researchers for evaluating the overall performance of banks in recent years. Both revenue efficiency and profit efficiency account for the errors on both the output and the input sides. Berger et al. (1993) argue that input inefficiency might be smaller than output inefficiency. However, the cost efficiency, no matter whether measured by parametric or non-parametric methods, assumes that input prices and output quantities are givens, and banks try to minimize cost through allocating the optimal level of input. Two sources lead to cost inefficiency. One is attributed to using an excess volume of input which is related to technical inefficiency, whereas the other is derived from a sub-optimal mix of input, which is related to allocate inefficiency. However, a bank can be inefficient under the consideration that too few outputs or a non-optimal mix of outputs are being produced given the input they use and the input prices they pay. Thus, the inefficiency not only derives from the cost perspective, but also from the revenue/profit perspective. DeYoung and Nolle (1996) argue that ignorance of the output side in estimating efficiency biases the cost efficiency model in evaluating the performance of banks. For example, extra cost will be incurred for a higher quality of financial products and services being offered. The cost efficiency model will regard this bank as inefficient because the output is ignored and only the input side has been considered. However, a bank with cost inefficiency can be profit efficient when the customers pay more money for higher-quality goods and services.

Several rounds of banking reforms in China have increased competition in the Chinese banking sector. The traditional Structure–Conduct–Performance (SCP)[2] theory uses the concentration ratio as the measure of bank competition. According to the China Banking Regulatory Commission (CBRC), the share of the five state-owned commercial banks' (SOCBs) assets in total banking sector assets in China decreased to 43.3% between 2003 and 2013. However, joint-stock commercial banks (JSCBs) and city commercial banks (CCBs) have kept increasing in size, and, by 2013, they held 17.8% and 10.03%, respectively, of total banking sector assets. This shows that competitive conditions in the Chinese banking sector have increased. Table 1.1 summarizes the assets of SOCBs, JSCBs, CCBs and total banking institutions in China over the period 2003–13.

[2] The Structure–Conduct–Performance (SCP) theory argues that in a highly concentrated banking market in which competition is low, the banks tend to collude with each other to obtain super-normal profits.

Table 1.1 Total assets of state-owned commercial banks (SOCBs), joint-stock commercial banks (JSCBs), and city commercial banks (CCBs) and all banking institutions over the period 2003–13 (renminbi [RMB] 100 million)

	2003	2004	2005	2006	2007	2008	2009	2010	2011	2012	2013
SOCBs	160,512	179,817	210,050	242,364	285,000	325,751	407,998	468,943	536,336	600,401	656,005
JSCBs	29,599	36,476	44,655	54,446	72,742	88,337	118,181	149,037	183,794	235,271	269,361
CCBs	14,622	17,056	20,367	25,938	33,405	41,320	56,800	78,526	99,845	123,469	151,778
Banking institutions	276,584	315,990	374,697	439,500	531,160	631,515	795,146	953,053	1,132,873	1,136,224	1,513,547

The banking sector concentration measures the competitive condition in a less precise way compared to the Panzar—Rosse H statistic, which has the ability to classify the banking market into different types of competition, such as Monopoly, Oligopoly, Monopolistic competition as well as perfect competition. In addition, another competitive indicator, namely the Lerner index, not only measures competitive conditions but evaluates the market power of specific banks or specific ownership types of commercial banks. Finally, the newly invented Boone indicator further extends the previous competition indicator and has the advantages of assessing the competitive condition of different banking markets such as the loan market, the deposit market and the non-interest income market.

Competition has a significant impact on efficiency in the banking industry according to the competition-efficiency and competition-inefficiency hypotheses. These hypotheses have been widely tested in the European and US banking sectors (Brissimis et al., 2008; Casu and Girardone, 2009; Ariss, 2010); however, they have not been tested in the Chinese banking industry[3]. Testing these hypotheses in the Chinese banking industry will produce policy implications for the Chinese government, as well as the banking regulatory authorities, concerning the enhancement of the performance of Chinese commercial banks.

1.2 AIMS AND OBJECTIVES OF THE BOOK

This book pursues several aims and objectives. Firstly, this book will help the reader acquire a better understanding of the structure and reforms of the Chinese banking sector.

Secondly, this book provides a systematic introduction and explanation on the theory of bank efficiency and bank competition which will be useful for students as well as academic researchers.

Thirdly, this book evaluates efficiency in the Chinese banking industry using recent data, thus providing a general picture of the Chinese banking operation to Chinese government, banking regulatory authorities, academic researchers as well as the general public who are interested in the Chinese banking industry. To be more specific, this book aims to evaluate comprehensively the efficiency of Chinese commercial banks, ie, assess the

[3] There are a number of research studies investigating the competitive conditions in the Chinese banking industry (see Tan and Floros, 2013; Fu, 2009; Tan, 2014, 2016, amongst others).

efficiency in the Chinese banking industry from the different perspectives of banking production such as the cost, technical, revenue and profit perspectives.

Fourthly, this book aims to examine the condition of competition in the Chinese banking industry in an extensive manner to provide a broad and clear view to government officials, banking managers as well as academic researchers and to do so on a yearly basis. More specifically, the book will classify the types of bank competition in China each year over the examined period. In addition, this book aims to provide information on the market power of different types of ownership of commercial banks, thus provide the competitive condition of the Chinese banking industry from a different angle. Furthermore, this book will be the first one to estimate the competitive condition of different banking markets in China, ie, deposit, loan and non-interest income markets using the newly developed Boone competition indicator.

Fifthly, this book aims to perform a robust analysis on the impact of competition on efficiency using different modern econometric techniques, namely the ordinary least square estimator, the Tobit regression as well as Bootstrapped truncated regression.

Finally, this book aims to provide some policy implications derived from the findings to government as well as banking regulatory authorities.

1.3 METHODOLOGY AND DATA

The methodology used in this book will be mainly focussed on three aspects, namely, the methods used to measure efficiency, examine the competition as well as test the impact of competition on bank efficiency in China. With regard to the method used to measure different types of bank efficiency (technical, cost, revenue and profit efficiency), both a non-parametric Data Envelopment Analysis and a parametric stochastic frontier approach will be used. For the method used to examine the condition of competition in the Chinese banking industry, the book will use the bank concentration ratio, the Panzar–Roose H statistic, the Lerner index as well as the Boone indicator. Finally, with regard to obtaining robust results on the impact of competition on bank efficiency in China, three modern econometric methods will be used, including the ordinary least square estimator, the Tobit regression as well as the Bootstrapped truncated regression.

The data used in this book includes 100 Chinese commercial banks (5 large-scale commercial banks, 12 joint-stock commercial banks and 83 city commercial banks) and the input and output variables used to measure technical efficiency will be explained. The variables used to measure the cost, revenue, and profit efficiencies and the different competition indicators, such as Panzar—Rosse H statistics, Lerner index and Boone indicator will be discussed as well. In the estimation of the impact of competition on bank efficiency, this book also controls for comprehensive bank-specific, industry-specific and macroeconomic variables. The bank-specific variables include bank size, liquidity, capitalization, risk, and non-traditional activity. The industry-specific variables mainly include banking sector development and stock market development. Two macroeconomic variables are considered in this book, which are the annual inflation rate and annual GDP growth rate. The bank-specific variables are from the Bank-scope database, which is considered the most comprehensive database for research in banking. Finally, the data related to industry-specific variables and macroeconomic variables arises from two main sources, the China Banking Regulatory Commission and the World Bank DataBank.

1.4 STRUCTURE OF THE BOOK

The structure of the book can be organized as follows:

Chapter 2: Chinese banking sector and reforms

Several rounds of banking reforms in China have aimed to improve performance, increase the competitive condition as well as reduce the risk-taking behaviour of commercial banks. This chapter divides Chinese banking reform into different stages. The first stage covers the period beginning in 1949, the official establishment of Peoples' Republic of China, until 1978, which is a milestone in Chinese history because 1978 was when the policy of reform and opening-up began in China. The second period covers the era from 1978 to 1992. Beginning in January 1992, Deng Xiaoping, the Chief Architect of Chinese reforms and the opening up of China to world markets, announced the beginning of China's socialism-based market economy. This period mainly focusses on creating the two-tier banking system. The third period of Chinese banking reform started from January 1992 and ended in 2001. This period mainly concentrated on establishing policy banks, asset management companies, and passing relevant laws to regulate the banking industry in China. This period also resulted in the creation of a number of joint-stock commercial banks. The most recent stage of banking reform covers the period from 2001 to 2013. In 2001, China joined the World Trade Organization (WTO), thus an important event for not only the Chinese banking industry, but also the entire Chinese economy. Successful admission to the WTO opened the Chinese banking industry to much stronger competition from all over the world. This stage has introduced several measures in Chinese banking reform, such as the establishment of the China Banking Regulatory Authority, capital injection, non-performing loan write-off, attracting foreign strategic investors, initial public offering (IPO) as well as gradually releasing the restrictions imposed on foreign banks.

This chapter not only discusses the Chinese banking sector reform, but also the structure of the Chinese banking sector. To be more specific, five large-scale commercial banks will be introduced, which include the Agricultural Bank of China, the Industrial and Commercial Bank of China, the Bank of China, China Construction Bank as well as the Bank of Communication. After introducing of these large-scale commercial banks, this chapter will introduce the joint-stock commercial banks on a one-by-one basis. Twelve joint-stock commercial banks are introduced in this book; they are the China Merchant Bank, China CITIC Bank, Hua Xia Bank, China Everbright Bank, Shanghai Pudong Development Bank, China Minsheng Bank, Industrial Bank, China GuangFa Bank, Ping An Bank, Zheshang Bank, Bohai Bank as well as Evergrowing Bank. Besides the large-scale commercial banks and joint-stock commercial banks, this chapter will also briefly introduce the city commercial banks as well as other banks and non-bank institutions. These include policy banks, rural commercial banks, rural cooperative banks, urban credit cooperatives, rural credit cooperatives, non-bank financial institutions, foreign banks as well as new types of rural financial institutions and a postal savings bank.

Chapter 3: Theory of bank efficiency and bank competition

This chapter mainly focusses on three aspects. Firstly, this chapter will discuss the framework of efficiency. More specifically, the theories of cost efficiency, technical efficiency, revenue efficiency and profit efficiency will be discussed one by one. Secondly, this chapter will introduce and systematically discuss the methods used to measure efficiency; the methods will be divided mainly into twoaspects, the parametric and the non-parametric methods. In the parametric method, three specific techniques will be explained including stochastic frontier approach, distribution-free approach and thick frontier approach. On the other hand, two non-parametric techniques will be discussed: Data Envelopment Analysis and the Free Disposal Hull model.

Finally, this chapter will review the theory regarding bank competition. To be more specific, the concentration ratio as reflected in the traditional structure—conduct—performance paradigm will be discussed first which is followed by reviewing the theory of another competition indicator, Panzar—Rosse H statistics, which has the ability to divide the competitive condition into different types such as monopoly, oligopoly, monopolistic competition and perfect competition. Then the third competition indicator, namely the Lerner index, will be explained which not only measures the competitive condition, but captures the market power held by banks. Finally, the Boone indicator, which measures the competitive condition in different banking markets, such as the loan market, the deposit market and the non-interest income market, will be discussed.

Chapter 4: Literature review on bank efficiency and bank competition

This chapter first reviews the international studies on bank efficiency which is followed by reviewing the empirical literature on bank efficiency focussing on individual countries. More specifically, this chapter reviews relevant studies investigating efficiency in the Chinese banking industry. The chapter then reviews the literature about the theory of bank competition and its measurement, which is followed by reviewing relevant literature testing the competitive condition in the Chinese banking industry. Finally, this chapter reviews the empirical studies evaluating competitive condition internationally. The last part of this chapter reviews the competition-efficiency and competition-inefficiency hypotheses and relevant literature studying the impact of competition on efficiency in the banking industry.

Chapter 5: Methodology to estimate bank efficiency and bank competition in China

The chapter will introduce and discuss the method used to measure bank efficiency. Specifically, the non-parametric data envelopment analysis will be used to measure technical efficiency. With regard to the inputs and outputs used in the efficiency estimation, three inputs will be considered, total cost, price of fund and price of capital, whereas four outputs will be considered, total loans, security, non-interest income and total deposits. In terms of the estimation of cost, revenue as well as profit efficiencies, the parametric stochastic frontier approach will be used.

The next section of this chapter will introduce and discuss the method used to measure different competition indicators including bank concentration ratio, Panzar–Rosse H statistics, Lerner index and Boone indicator. Finally, this chapter will model the impact of competition on efficiency in the Chinese banking industry.

Chapter 6: Empirical results on the impact of competition on bank efficiency in China

This chapter is mainly divided into three parts. Part one will focus on presenting and discussing the efficiency of Chinese commercial banks. To be more specific, the results will be further divided into four different types of efficiency, namely cost efficiency, technical efficiency, revenue efficiency as well as profit efficiency, whereas the second part of this chapter will concentrate on describing and discussing the competitive condition in the Chinese banking industry. The results of competitive condition, measured by different competition indicators, will be discussed on a one-by-one basis, which include the bank concentration ratio, Panzar–Rosse H statistic, Lerner index as well as the Boone indicator. Finally, in the third part, the results with regard to the impact of competition on efficiency in the Chinese banking industry will be presented and discussed. To check the robustness of the result, several modern econometric techniques will be used, which include the ordinary least square estimator, Tobit regression as well as the Bootstrapped truncated regression.

Chapter 7: Conclusion

This final chapter is also mainly divided into three subsections. In subsection 7.1, the importance of the current study will be summarized and, more importantly, the results with regard to the impact of competition on efficiency in the Chinese banking industry will also be summarized. In subsection 7.2, policy implications derived from the results of the current study will be discussed which is important for the Chinese government as well as banking regulatory authorities. In subsection 7.3, the limitations of the current study will be discussed and areas of future research will be recommended.

REFERENCES

Ariss, R.T., 2010. On the implications of market power in banking: evidence from developing countries. Journal of Banking and Finance 34, 765–775.

Berger, A.N., Hancock, D., Humphrey, D.B., 1993. Bank efficiency derived from the profit function. Journal of Banking and Finance 17, 317–347.

Brissimis, S.M., Delis, M.D., Papanilolaou, N.I., 2008. Exploring the nexus between banking sector reform and performance: evidence from newly acceded EU countries. Journal of Banking and Finance 32, 2674–2683.
Casu, B., Girardone, C., 2009. Testing the relationship between competition and efficiency in banking: a panel data analysis. Economics Letters 105, 134–137.
DeYoung, R., Nolle, D., 1996. Foreign-owned banks in the US: earning market share or buying it? Journal of Money, Credit and Banking 28, 622–636.
Fu, M., 2009. Competition in Chinese commercial banking. Banking Finance Review 1 (1), 1–16.
Isik, I., Hassan, M.K., 2002. Cost and profit efficiency of Turkish banking industry: an empirical investigation. The Financial Review 37, 257–280.
Tan, Y., Floros, C., 2013. Market power, stability and performance in the Chinese banking industry. Economic Issues 18 (2), 65–89.
Tan, Y., 2014. Performance, Risk and Competition in the Chinese Banking Industry. Chandos Publishing, Oxford.
Tan, Y., 2016. The impacts of risk and competition on bank profitability in China. Journal of International Financial Markets, Institutions and Money 40, 85–110.

CHAPTER 2

Chinese Banking Sector and Reforms

2.1 INTRODUCTION

The sustainable and healthy development of banking sector plays an important role in the economic growth of the country. China, during recent years, has undergone consistent economic growth; it is no doubt that this economic growth to a certain extent is attributed to the well-developed banking sector. This chapter will focus on the banking reforms in China. The periods of banking reform in China are divisible into four stages. The first stage started in 1949 when the Peoples' Republic of China (PRC) was officially established; this stage ended in 1978, when the third Plenary session of the 11th Central Committee of the Communist Party of China was held, which officially started China economic and financial reform. The second-stage reform covers the period 1978–92. This period of reform mainly focussed on creating a two-tier banking system as well as a more competitive banking environment through the establishment of a number of joint-stock commercial banks (JSCBs). The third stage covers the period 1992–2001. This purpose of this stage of reform was to further increase competition through establishment of different types of bank ownership such as rural and urban credit cooperatives and city and rural commercial banks. Another principal aim in this stage of reform was to reduce the influence of government on the operation of state-owned commercial banks and further reduce the risk-taking behaviour of Chinese commercial banks through establishing policy banks and asset management companies. This stage of reform ended in 2001, when China officially joined the World Trade Organization (WTO). China's admission to WTO took Chinese financial and banking reform to a new level. The last stage of reform in China covered the period 2001–13. This most recent stage of reform has focussed on increasing the competitiveness of Chinese commercial banks through capital injection, reducing the volume of non-performing loans of Chinese commercial banks through write-offs by asset management companies, improving corporate governance, increasing external monitoring through

Efficiency and Competition in Chinese Banking
ISBN 978-0-08-100074-8

initial public offerings (IPOs), improving risk management and enhancing technology through the introduction of foreign strategic investors.

The second part of this chapter will focus on the structure of the Chinese banking sector. Discussion addresses the five large-scale commercial banks including the Bank of China (BOC), China Construction Bank (CCB), Agricultural Bank of China (ABC), Industrial and Commercial Bank of China (ICBC) and Bank of Communication (BOCOM). This will also introduce the 12 JSCBs on a one-by-one basis. JSCBs include the China International Trust and Investment Corporate (CITIC) Bank, China Merchant Bank, Minsheng Bank, China Everbright Bank, Evergrowing Bank, Shanghai Pudong Development Bank, Ping An Bank, Industrial Bank, China Bohai Bank, Hua Xia Bank, China Guangfa Bank and China Zheshang Bank. As the third largest bank ownership in China, city commercial banks and other banking and financial institutions in China will be discussed.

2.2 CHINA'S BANKING REFORMS

2.2.1 China's Banking Reform 1949–78

After 1949, when the PRC was established, the banking sector in China was administrated by two government institutions which were the People's Bank of China (PBOC) and the Ministry of Finance. These two government institutions reported directly to the state council which is the chief administrative authority of the PRC. The PBOC served as both the central bank and a commercial bank, while it controlled about 93% of the total financial assets of the country and handled almost all financial transactions. The main role of the PBOC was to fulfil the national production plan directed by the state council. The cash flows in consumer markets and transfer flow from bank branches were controlled by the PBOC using both a 'cash-plan' and a 'credit-plan'.

2.2.2 China's Banking Reform 1978–92

Before undertaking reforms, the Chinese banking sector had a mono-bank system based on the Soviet Grosbank system between the formulation of the PRC in 1949 and the late 1970s. The PBOC served as both a central bank and a commercial bank. It engaged in taking deposits and lending activities in accordance with the central plan of the government. The commercial bank function of the PBOC ended in 1979. Three state-owned commercial banks were established, namely the BOC, the People's Construction Bank of China (PCBC) and the ABC. The PBOC then started to serve as a central bank and regulatory authority for the banking sector, supervising the operation of these banks, whereas the newly established state-owned commercial banks took over the commercial business from the PBOC. Each of these three state-owned commercial banks was asked to provide financial services to a specific economic sector. The BOC focussed its business by engaging in deposits and loans for foreign exchange and international transactions, whereas fixed-asset transactions were mainly handled by the PCBC. The ABC concentrated on receiving deposits in rural areas and providing loans to agricultural production projects. The fourth state-owned commercial bank, the ICBC was established in 1984, which took over all the commercial business from the PBOC, and the ICBC centred its business on financing commercial and industrial activities. After the formation of ICBC, the structure of Chinese banking sector transformed from a mono banking system to a two-tier banking system. The four state-owned commercial banks were referred to as the Big Four; besides the establishment of these Big Four, a number of joint-stock commercial banks were found in 1987—1988 including Bank of Communication; China Merchants Bank; China Citic Bank; Shenzhen Development Bank; Industrial Bank as well as Guangdong Development Bank.

2.2.3 China's Banking Reform 1992—2001

Three policy banks were established in 1994, the purpose of which was to take over the lending responsibilities undertaken previously by the four state-owned commercial banks. These three policy banks were the China Development Bank, the Agricultural Development Bank of China, and the Export—Import Bank of China. The main mission carried out by the China Development Bank of China included: (1) supporting the development of national infrastructure, basic industry, key emerging sectors and national priority projects; (2) promoting coordinated regional development and urbanization by financing small business, agricultural/rural investment, education, healthcare and environment initiatives; (3) facilitating China's cross-border investment and global business cooperation. The main purposes of the Agricultural Development Bank of China have been to promote development of agriculture and rural areas through the following activities: (1) to raise the funds for agricultural policy businesses in accordance with the laws, regulations and policies; (2) to undertake the agricultural policy credit businesses specified by the central government, agriculture-related commercial businesses approved by the regulators; (3)

to serve as an agent for the state treasury to allocate the special funds for supporting agriculture. Finally, the main mandate of the Export–Import Bank of China has been to facilitate the export and import of Chinese mechanical and electronic products, complete sets of equipment and new and high-tech products, assist Chinese companies with comparative advantages in their offshore-project contracting and outbound investment and promote international economic cooperation and trade.

Two important laws were enacted in 1995 which are the Law of the PRC on the PBOC and the Law of the PRC on commercial banks. The Law of PRC on the PBOC was enacted to define the status and functions of the PBOC, ensure the correct formulation and implementation of monetary policy, establish and improve the macroeconomic management system of the central bank and maintain financial stability. Under the leadership of the state council, The PBOC is the Central Bank of the PRC. It is responsible for: (1) formulating and implementing monetary policy in accordance with law; (2) issuing the currency and administering its circulation; (3) regulating and supervising the inter-bank lending market and inter-bank bond market; (4) administering foreign exchange, regulation and supervising the inter-bank foreign exchange market; (5) regulating and supervising the gold market; (6) holding, administering and managing the state foreign exchange reserves and gold reserves; (7) managing the state treasury; (8) ensuring normal operation of the payment and settlement system; (9) guiding and arranging antimoney-laundering work in the financial sector and monitoring the fund movement for antimoney-laundering purposes; (10) performing statistical analysis, survey, analysis and forecasts of the financial industry; and (11) participating in related international financial activities in the capacity of the central bank of the state.

The Law of the PRC on Commercial Banks is formulated to protect the legitimate rights and interest of commercial banks, depositors and other clients, standardize the behaviour of commercial banks, improve the quality of funds, strengthen supervision and administration, ensure safety and soundness of commercial bank, maintain a normal financial order and promote the development of the socialist market economy. The law further stipulates that a commercial bank may engage in a number of businesses including: (1) receiving money deposits from the public; (2) extending short-, medium- and long-term loans; (3) providing domestic and international settlement services; (4) discounting bills; (5) issuing financial bonds; (6) acting as agent of issuing, cashing and underwriting government bonds; (7) dealing in government bonds; (8) inter-bank call-money business; (9)

dealing or acting as agent in foreign exchange transactions; (10) providing letter of credit service and guarantee; (11) acting as agent in collection and payment and insurance business; (12) providing safe deposit box service.

The bank's credit allocation was still largely influenced by the PBOC until 1997. In other words, the four state-owned commercial banks still acted as the lending arms for the government and they mainly allocated the credit to specific industries or state-owned enterprises. Due to the characteristics of state-owned enterprises, the ownership of which belonged to the government, the managers of the enterprises had little incentive to improve firm performance which led to losses on their operation. It made paying back the loans taken from the state-owned commercial banks difficult. Thus, large volumes of non-performing loans accumulated in state-owned commercial banks (Kumbhakar and Wang, 2007). To deal with this large volume of non-performing loans, four asset management companies (AMCs) were established in 1999, namely Huarong AMC; Great Wall AMC; Oriental AMC and Cinda AMC. The original idea was that each of the AMCs was mainly responsible for writing-off the non-performing loans from the specific state-owned commercial bank. Specifically, Oriental AMC was responsible for BOC; Great Wall AMC was mainly oriented to the ABC; Huarong AMC mainly wrote-off non-performing loans from ICBC and Cinda AMC dealt with the non-performing loans from CCB. During the period 1999–2000, the four AMCs wrote-off non-performing loans from the four state-owned commercial banks with a value of PRC Renminbi (RMB) 1.4 trillion, this non-performing loans write-off significantly reduced the non-performing loan ratio of state-owned commercial banks by 10% (Shirai, 2002).

Over the period 1992–96, a number of JSCBs have been established, including the Everbright bank, the Shanghai Pudong Development Bank as well as the Hua Xia bank. Different from the commercial banks which are wholly owned by the government, the shares of JSCBs are made up by central and local government, state-owned enterprises and at the current stage with some foreign banking institutions as well. Due to the fact that compared to the state-owned commercial banks, JSCBs have more freedom in allocating the credit, the loan portfolio is much healthier than the one for state-owned commercial banks (Cousin, 2007). At the same time, according to the requirement of the PBOC, urban credit cooperatives have been gradually transferred to city commercial banks. The JSCBs expanded their business nationwide on a regulator basis, whereas, in comparison, the business of the city commercial banks was restricted to within the city where they were established.

2.2.4 China's Banking Reform 2001–13

The Second National Financial Work Conference was held by the State Council in February 2002, following the admission of China to the WTO in December 2001. The purpose of the conference was to discuss the issues regarding how to stabilize China's financial system, also find ways to improve the efficiency and strengthen the competitive power of China's financial system.

To deal with these issues, a number of steps have been taken by the Chinese government to reform the Chinese banking sector. Firstly, a new regulatory organization, The China Banking Regulatory Commission (CBRC), was established in 2003. The CBRC carries out a number of functions including: (1) formulating supervisory rules and regulations governing the banking institutions; (2) authorizing the establishment, changes, termination and business scope of the banking institutions; (3) conducting on-site examination and off-site surveillance of the banking institutions, and taking enforcement actions against rule-breaking behaviours; (4) conducting fit-and-proper tests on the senior managerial personnel of the banking institutions; (5) compiling and publishing statistics and reports of the overall banking industry in accordance with relevant regulations; (6) providing proposals on the resolution of problems from deposit-taking institutions in consultation with relevant regulatory authorities; (7) being responsible for the administration of the supervisory boards of the major state-owned banking institutions.

The Chinese government started injecting capital to state-owned commercial banks and JSCBs with the purpose of promoting financial stability and improving the competitiveness of commercial banks. In December 2003, fresh capital worth United States dollars (USD) 22.5 billion and USD 20 billion were injected into BOC and CCB. In April and June 2004, the Chinese government injected fresh capital of USD 15 billion and RMB 2.5 billion to ICBC and BOCOM, respectively. As one of the largest JSCBs in China, the Chinese government injected capital of RMB 10 billion and RMB 20 billion to the China Everbright Bank in September 2005 and December 2006, respectively. In October 2008, the ABC was injected capital worth RMB 130 billion.

To further reduce the volume of non-performing loans in state-owned commercial banks and promote financial stability, the four AMCs wrote-off the non-performing loans another two times in 2004 and 2005. In 2004, Cinda AMC purchased doubtful loans from BOC and CCB worth RMB

278.7 billion, and the loss loans from BOC, CCB as well as BOCOM worth RMB 263.3 billion were dealt with by Cinda AMC as well as Oriental AMC. In 2005, doubtful loans worth RMB 450 billion from ICBC were purchased by all four AMCs, whereas the loss loans worth RMB 246 billion were dealt with by Huarong AMC. These two types of non-performing loan write-offs significantly reduced the volume of non-performing loans of Chinese state-owned commercial banks.

To improve the corporate governance and enhance the skill risk management and further promote bank efficiency, Chinese commercial banks started attracting the foreign strategic investors. The first one actually happened in 1997, when Asian development bank purchased shares from China Everbright bank worth USD 20 million, becoming the first Chinese commercial bank with foreign bank shares. By the end of 2003, five Chinese commercial banks successfully attracted seven foreign strategic investors. In 2004, Hong Kong and Shanghai Banking Corporation (HSBC) purchased a 19.9% share from the BOCOM, becoming the largest foreign bank purchase of domestic bank shares at that time. Is the purchase was below the maximum shareholding percentage by foreign strategic investors required by the CBRC by only 0.1%. Over the period 2004–05, the number of foreign strategic investors kept increasing; there were nearly 20 foreign strategic investors in 14 Chinese commercial banks. This number further increased with 33 foreign strategic investors purchasing shares from 25 domestic commercial banks at the end of 2007; by the end of 2011, the total number of foreign investors was 57 and the number of domestic commercial banks involved was 36.

To improve corporate governance and increase the degree of external monitoring, this period has seen a large number of Chinese commercial banks offering their IPOs on the stock exchange. With regard to the large-scale commercial banks, the first bank listed on the stock exchange was BOCOM, which offered its IPO on the Shanghai Stock Exchange and Hong Kong Stock Exchange on 15 May 2005 and 23 June 2005, respectively, followed by CCB listed on the Hong Kong Stock Exchange on 27 October 2005. BOC was listed on the Shanghai Stock Exchange on 5 July 2006, on the Hong Kong Stock Exchange on 1 June 2006. ICBC was listed on both Shanghai and Hong Kong Stock Exchanges on 27 October 2006. The list of ICBC-raised funds was worth USD 21.9 billion, becoming the largest IPO at that time. CCB was listed on the Shanghai Stock Exchange on 25 September 2007. The last large-scale commercial bank listed on a stock exchange was the ABC. It was successfully listed on Shanghai and Hong Kong Stock Exchanges on 15 July and 16 July 2010, respectively. The volume of funds raised by this IPO was USD 22.1 billion, breaking the record made by the ICBC in 2006 and becoming the new largest IPO at that time.

A number of JSCBs are listed on stock exchanges including Minsheng Bank, Hua Xia Bank, China Merchants Bank, Industrial Bank, Ping An Bank, China Everbright Bank as well as China CITIC Bank. On 26 November 2009, China Minsheng Bank was listed on Hong Kong Stock Exchange.[1] Hua Xia bank was successfully listed on the Shanghai Stock Exchange on 12 September 2003. China Merchants Bank was successfully listed on the Shanghai and Hong Kong Stock Exchanges on 9 April 2002 and 22 September 2002, respectively. Industrial bank was successfully listed on the Shanghai Stock Exchange on 5 February 2007. China Everbright Bank offered its initial public offerings on Shanghai and Hong Kong Stock Exchanges on 18 August 2010 and 20 December 2013, respectively. China CITIC Bank was successfully listed on both Shanghai and Hong Kong Stock Exchanges on 27 April 2007; it was also the second Chinese commercial bank listed on both stock exchanges on the same day after the ICBC.[2]

Among the 124 city commercial banks, there were only three listed on a stock exchange. They are Bank of Ningbo, Bank of Beijing and Bank of Nanjing. Bank of Ningbo was successfully listed on the Shanghai Stock Exchange on 17 July 2007, whereas Bank of Beijing offered its IPO on Shanghai Stock Exchange on 19 September 2007. Bank of Nanjing was listed on the Shanghai Stock Exchange on 19 July 2007.

This period has also seen the effort made by the Chinese government as well as the banking regulatory authority to increase competition in the Chinese banking industry by introducing and gradually releasing the restriction on foreign banks in engaging in banking activities in China. Staring in 2001, foreign banks were allowed to engage in foreign currency business to Chinese and foreign enterprises and individuals all over the country, although they were only allowed to offer local currency business to foreign enterprises and overseas individuals at specific cities/areas in China; this restriction was gradually released. The number of cities/areas, in which foreign banks were allowed to conduct local currency business, kept increasing on a year-by-year basis and also foreign banks were allowed to

[1] It was successfully listed on Shanghai Stock Exchange on 19 December 2000.

[2] Shanghai Pudong Development Bank was listed on Shanghai Stock Exchange on 10 November 1999. The predecessor of Ping An bank was Shenzhen Development Bank, which was listed on Shenzhen Stock Exchange on 3 April 1991, and it finished its merger with Ping An bank in 2012; thus, from 2 August 2012, the new bank was named Ping An bank.

provide local currency business to domestic Chinese enterprises as well as Chinese individuals. By the end of 2006, the foreign banks were treated exactly the same as the domestic Chinese commercial banks. This equal treatment significantly improves the competitive condition in Chinese banking industry.

2.3 STRUCTURE OF CHINESE BANKING SECTOR

By the end of 2013, China's banking sector consisted of a variety of different ownership types of banking and non-banking financial institutions, among which large scale commercial banks, joint-stock commercial banks and city commercial banks have the largest amount of assets. To be more specific, by the end of 2013, the total assets of these three different ownership types of Chinese commercial banks were RMB65600.5 billion, 26936.1 million and 15177.8 billion, respectively. Table 2.1 has a detail description with regard to the number of different ownership types of banking and non-banking financial institutions by the end of 2013 (CBRC, 2013).

Type of banking or non-banking financial institutions	Number
Policy banks	3
Large-scale commercial banks	5
Joint-stock commercial banks	12
City commercial banks	145
Rural commercial banks	468
Rural cooperative banks	122
Rural credit cooperatives	1803
Postal saving bank	1
Asset management companies	4
Locally incorporated foreign banking institutions	42
Sino-German Bausparkasse	1
Trust companies	68
Finance companies of corporate groups	176
Financial leasing companies	23
Money brokerage firms	5
Auto-financing companies	17
Consumer financial companies	4
Village and township banks	987
Lending companies	14
Rural mutual cooperatives	49

2.3.1 Large-Scale Commercial Banks

There are five large-scale commercial banks in China including ABC, CCB, ICBC, BOC and BOCOM. As reported previously, the total assets of this banking ownership by the end of 2013 reached RMB 656,005, with a growth rate of 9.3% compared to the previous year, whereas the total liabilities of this banking ownership at the end of 2013 were RMB 611,611, increasing by 9% compared to the previous year. The total owner's equity of this banking ownership by the end of 2013 was RMB 44,394; compared to the previous year, it increased by 12.33%. The profit after tax achieved by this banking ownership by the end of 2013 was RMB 8382.3, with an increase rate of 11.1% compared to the previous year, whereas the number of staff working in the large-scale commercial banks by the end of 2013 reached 1,720,705 (CBRC, 2013).[3] The large-scale commercial banks are introduced on a one by one basis as follows.

2.3.1.1 Agricultural Bank of China (ABC)

The Agricultural cooperative Bank established in 1951 is the predecessor of ABC. Since the late 1970s, the bank has undergone a series of transformations. It evolved from a state-owned specialized bank to wholly state-owned commercial banks and gradually transformed to a state-controlled commercial bank. In January 2009, the bank was restructured into a joint-stock limited liability company. In July 2010, the bank was successfully listed on the Shanghai and the Hong Kong Stock Exchanges, which indicated that the bank has successfully become a public shareholding commercial bank. By the end of 2013, the biggest three shareholders of the bank were Huijin, Ministry of Finance as well as Hong Kong Securities Clearing Company (HKSCC) Nominees Limited, which held the shares of 40.28%, 39.21% and 9.04%, respectively.

[3] The RMB values are in 100 million.

As one of the major integrated financial service providers in China, the bank is committed to catering to the needs of 'Sannong[4]' and capitalizing on the synergy between the urban areas and county areas. To become a first-class modern commercial bank, it also strives to expand into the international market and provide diversified services. Corporate and retail banking products are provided by the bank for a wide range of customers, and treasury operations are conducted by the bank on behalf of customers. With regard to the business scope, the bank engages in investment banking, fund management, financial leasing and life insurance, among others. By the end of 2013, the total assets of the bank achieved RMB 14,562,102 million, whereas the total deposits and total loans reached RMB 11,811,411 million and RMB 7,224,713 million, respectively. The capital ratio and non-performing loan ratio of the bank were 11.86% and 1.22%, respectively. The net profit achieved by the bank in 2013 was RMB 166,211 million. By the end of 2013, the number of domestic branch outlets was 23,547; the bank also had seven overseas branches as well as three overseas representative offices. There were 12 subsidiaries which included nine domestic subsidiaries and three overseas subsidiaries. Among the companies listed in Fortune's Global 500, the bank was ranked No. 64 in 2013 and the Banker's 'Top 1000 World Banks' list ranked the bank No. 10 in terms of Tier 1 capital for the year 2012 (ABC, 2013).

2.3.1.2 Industrial and Commercial Bank of China (ICBC)

ICBC 中国工商银行

The ICBC was established on 1 January 1984. The bank was restructured to a joint-stock limited company on 28 October 2005. The bank was successfully listed on both Shanghai and Hong Kong Stock Exchanges on 27 October 2006. Because of its continuous endeavour and sustainable development, the bank has evolved into the top large listed bank in the world with an excellent customer base, a diversified business structure, strong innovative capacity as well as strong market competitiveness. The bank's overseas network has expanded to 40 countries and regions. The financial products and services are provided through 17,245 domestic institutions, 329 overseas institutions and 1903 correspondent banks worldwide.

[4] Sannong means rural areas, farmer and agriculture.

In 2013, the bank issued loans worth RMB 8.7 trillion; compared to the previous year, it increased by RMB 974 billion. Although the balance of customer deposits was RMB 14.62 trillion, it increased by 7.2% or RMB 77,915 million compared to the previous year. The amount of deposits continued to lead the banking industry. In 2013, the bank realized a net profit of RMB 262,965 million, with an increase rate of 10.2% compared to the previous year. The earnings per share were RMB 0.75, increased by RMB 0.07 compared to 2012. The cost-to-income ratio fell by 0.44% to 28.8%, maintaining the leading position among comparable banks. The non-performing assets rose slightly by 0.09% point to 0.94%. In 2013, the bank ranked in the first place among Top 1000 world banks by The Banker. Among the Global 2000 listed by the US magazine Forbes, the bank became the largest enterprise in the world and was selected as one of the global systemically important banks for the first time. The Bank was named the world's largest corporate and the biggest bank in terms of Tier 1 capital by Forbes and The Banker. The Bank was also recognized by Fortune as the largest commercial bank by revenue (ICBC, 2013).

2.3.1.3 Bank of China (BOC)

中国银行
BANK OF CHINA

The BOC was formally established in February 1912. From 1912 to 1949, the Bank served consecutively as the country's central bank, international exchange bank and specialized international trade bank. After 1949, the Bank became responsible for managing China's foreign exchange operations and providing vital support to the nation's foreign trade development and economic infrastructure through its offering of international trade settlement, overseas fund transfer and other non-trade foreign exchange services. After 1978, when the Chinese government initiated the opening-up policy, the Bank became the country's key foreign financing channel by building up its competitive advantages in foreign exchange business. In 1994, the Bank was transformed into a wholly state-owned commercial bank, but then in August 2004, the Bank was transformed to a joint-stock limited company. The bank successfully offered its IPOs on the Hong Kong and Shanghai Stock Exchanges in June and July 2006, respectively. In 2013, BOC was recognized again as the Global systemically important bank, becoming the sole financial institution from emerging economies recognized for three consecutive years.

The BOC is the most international and diversified bank in China. It provides a comprehensive range of financial services to customers in mainland China, Hong Kong, Macau, Taiwan and 37 countries. The core business engaged in by the Bank includes corporate banking, personal banking and financial market services. The Bank has five wholly owned subsidiaries. BOC International Holdings Limited is responsible for investment banking. The insurance business is run by another two wholly owned subsidiaries which are BOC Group Insurance Company Limited and BOC Insurance Company Limited. The fourth wholly owned subsidiary, BOC Group Investment limited, is responsible for the Bank's direct investment and investment management business. The final wholly owned subsidiary, BOC Aviation Pte. Ltd, is responsible for the Bank's aircraft leasing business. The Bank also has one controlled subsidiary, BOC Investment Management Co. Ltd, which focusses on operating the Bank's fund management business.

By the end of 2013, the total assets of the bank reached RMB13.87 trillion, with an increase rate of 9.41% compared to the previous year. The value of total loans of the bank was RMB 7.61 trillion, which increased by RMB 0.7 trillion and with a growth rate of 10.82% compared to 2012. The amount of total deposits of the bank was RMB 10.1 trillion, increasing by RMB 0.92 trillion compared to the previous year. In other words, it increased by 10.07% compared to 2012. The net profit achieved by the bank reached RMB 0.16 trillion with a growth rate of 12.35% compared to the previous year. The non-performing loan ratio increased by 0.01% to 0.96% by the end of 2013. The Tier 1 core capital ratio, Tier 1 capital ratio and capital adequacy ratio were 9.69%, 9.70% and 12.46%, respectively, by the end of 2013 (BOC, 2013).

2.3.1.4 China Construction Bank (CCB)

The predecessor of CCB is the PCBC, which was founded in 1954. It was a wholly state-owned bank under the direction of the Ministry of Finance of the PRC to administer and disburse government funds for construction- and infrastructure-related projects under the state economic plan. In 1979, the

PCBC became a financial institution under the direction of the state council and gradually acquired more commercial banking functions. In 1996, the PCBC changed its name to CCB. CCB Corporation was established as a state-controlled commercial bank in 2004. The Bank successfully listed on the Hong Kong and Shanghai Stock Exchanges on 27 October 2005 and 25 September 2007, respectively. The Bank provides a comprehensive range of commercial banking products and services such as corporate banking, personal banking and treasury operation. The Bank has the leading position in the market in providing products and services including infrastructure loans, residential mortgage and bank cards.

By the end of 2013, the market capitalization of the Bank reached US $176.7 billion, ranking fifth among listed banks in the world. The Bank has 14,925 branches and sub-branches in Mainland China, 10 overseas branches in Hong Kong, Singapore, Frankfurt, Johannesburg, Tokyo, Seoul, New York, Ho Chi Ming City, Sydney and Taipei. The Bank also owned a number of subsidiaries such as CCB Principal Asset Management, CCB Financial Leasing, CCB Trust, CCB Life, Sino–German Bausparkasse, CCB Asia, CCB London, CCB Russia, CCB Dubai and CCB International. At the end of 2013, the Bank's total assets increased by 9.95% to RMB 15,363,210 million compared to 2012; gross loans and advances to customers increased by 14.30% to RMB 8,590,057 million; deposits from customer rose by 7.76% to RMB 12,223,037 million; net profit increased by 11.12% to RMB 215,122 million. The cost and expenses were effectively controlled with the cost-to-income ratio standing at 29.65%. The assets quality remained stable with non-performing loan ratio standing at 0.99%. The capital adequacy ratio and Tier 1 capital ratio were 13.34% and 10.75%, respectively. The Bank ranked fifth in the 'Top 1000 World Banks' with regard to Tier-1 capital and ninth in 'Top 1000 World Banks' in terms of total assets by The Banker. The Bank ranked second in 'Forbes Global 2000 Leading Companies' and 50th in the 'Fortune Global 500' (CCB, 2013).

2.3.1.5 Bank of Communication (BOCOM)

BOCOM, which was founded in 1908, is one of the four oldest banks in China and one of the earliest note-issuing banks in China. In 1958, although the Hong Kong Branch continued to operate, the mainland business of BOCOM merged with PBOC and the PCBC on BOCOM's foundation. To operate in line with economic reforms and development, BOCOM was restructured on 24 July 1986 with approval from the state council and began operation anew on 1 April 1987. Thus, it became China's first state-owned shareholding commercial bank. Its head office was in Shanghai. In June 2004, with the banking reform in China well under way, the state council approved BOCOM's general plan on deepening the reform of its shareholding structure in a bid to further develop BOCOM into a modern banking enterprise under a century-old national brand with improved corporate governance, adequate capital, strict internal control, safe operations, excellent services and return and strong international competitiveness. Through the reform, BOCOM has completed financial reorganization by successfully introducing mainland and overseas strategic investors such as HSBC, the National Social Security Fund and China SAFE Investment Ltd. On 23 June 2005, BOCOM was listed on the Hong Kong Stock Exchange, the first China-based commercial bank to get listed outside of the Chinese mainland, and on 15 May 2007, BOCOM was successfully listed on the Shanghai Stock Exchange.

The Bank has 30 provincial branches all over China, altogether 2690 outlets in 215 cities and 159 counties nationwide. In addition, the Bank has set up 12 overseas institutions, comprising branches in Hong Kong, New York, Tokyo, Singapore, Seoul, Frankfurt, Macau, Ho Chi Minh City, Sydney, San Francisco, Taipei and Bank of Communications (UK) Co., Ltd. The Bank has 99,919 employees. The Bank provides diversified and comprehensive professional services in the areas of corporate banking, personal banking, international banking and fee-based business. BOCOM Shroders Fund Management Co., Ltd, a joint venture with Shroders, was established in August 2005 as one of the first batch of fund management subsidiaries of banks. In 2007, the Bank acquired Hubei International Trust and Investment Co., Ltd, established BOCOM Financial Leasing Company, and set up BOCOM International Holdings Limited in Hong Kong. In 2008, the Bank invested in Changshu Rural Commercial bank and founded Dayi BoCom Rural Bank. In 2009, the Bank took a leading step in acquire stakes in domestic insurance companies, and the subsidiary BocommLife Insurance was set up in January 2010. At the same time, Anji Bocom Rural Bank in Zhejiang province, Shihezi Bocom Rural Bank in Xinjiang Province and Qingdao Laoshan Bocom Rural Bank were set up in April 2010, May 2011 and September 2012, respectively. At the end of 2013, the total assets of the bank reached RMB 5.96 trillion, with an increase rate of 13.04% compared to the previous year, whereas the total deposits and loans of the bank were RMB 4.16 trillion and RMB 3.27 trillion, with a growth rate of 11.52% and 10.83%, respectively. The net profit of the bank achieved RMB 62.3 billion with an increase rate of 6.73%. The non-performing loan ratio was 1.05%, increased by 0.13% compared to 2012. The cost-to-income ratio was 29.30%, declined by 0.36% compared to 2012, whereas the capital adequacy ratio and core Tier 1 capital ratio by the end of 2013 were 12.08% and 9.76%, respectively (BOCOM, 2013).

2.3.2 Joint-Stock Commercial Banks (JSCBs)

As the second largest banking ownership type in China according to total assets, the JSCBs play an increasingly important role in the development of the country's economy. By the end of 2013, the total assets of this banking ownership reached RMB 100 million, with a growth rate of 14.49% compared to the previous year, whereas the total liability of this banking ownership type by the end of 2013 was RMB 253,438, compared to the previous year, it increased by 14.09%. Total owner's equity of this banking ownership type by the end of 2013 was RMB 15,922, with an increase rate of 21.15% compared to the previous year. The profit after tax achieved by this banking ownership by the end of 2013 was RMB 2945.4, compared to 2012, it grows at a rate of 16.59%.[5] The number of staff working for the JSCBs by the end of 2013 was 364,103. The JSCBs are introduced on a one-by-one basis in the following (CBRC, 2013).

2.3.2.1 China Merchant Bank

招商银行
CHINA MERCHANTS BANK

As China's first JSCB, China Merchants Bank was established in 1987. Through its continuous development over the past 24 years, China Merchants Bank has grown from a small bank with a capital of 100 million Yuan, one branch and over 30 employees into a national JSCB that has a total net capital of 305.7 billion Yuan, total assets of 4.02 trillion, over 1000 branches and 68,000 employees. The bank was listed on Shanghai

[5] The RMB values are in 100 million.

Stock Exchange in April 2002 and Hong Kong Stock Exchange in September 2006. In 2013, the bank was awarded for the ninth consecutive time the 'Best joint stock retail bank in China' by the Asia Banker Magazine. At the 2013 global private banking awards ceremony organized by Financial Times of the United Kingdom, the bank was awarded the best private bank in China for the fourth consecutive year. The bank provides customers with various wholesale and retail banking products and services and maintains treasury business for proprietary purposes and on behalf of customers. It provides a wide range of innovative products and services including 'all-in-one card', 'all-in-one net' and 'sunflower wealth management', which have been widely recognized by customers in China.

By the end of 2013, the bank had 113 branches, 934 sub-branches, 1 exclusive branch-level operation centre, 1 representative office, 2330 self-service centres and 9492 cash self-service machines in more than 110 cities of mainland China. Furthermore, the bank had two wholly owned subsidiaries, namely China Merchants Bank Financial Leasing and China Merchants Fund as well as one joint venture, CIGNA (The merger of Connecticut General Life Insurance Company and Insurance Company of North America) and China Merchant Bank Life Insurance. The bank has also a number of wholly owned subsidiaries including Wing Lung Bank Ltd, and China Merchants Bank International in Hong Kong, and a branch in Hong Kong and a branch and a representative office in New York, a branch in Singapore and representative offices in London and Taipei.

At the end of 2013, the total assets of the bank amounted to RMB 4.02 trillion, increasing by 17.85% compared to the beginning of the year, total deposits from customers reached RMB 2.78 trillion, with a growth rate of 9.59% compared to the beginning of the year. Total loans and advances to customers was RMB 2.2 trillion, increasing by 15.37% from the beginning of the year. The cost-to-income ratio was 34.23%, decreasing by 1.62% compared to the previous year. The capital ratio of non-performing loan ratio were 11.14% and 0.83%, respectively (China Merchants Bank, 2013).

2.3.2.2 China CITIC Bank

中信银行
CHINA CITIC BANK

By the end of 1984, as the Chinese economy continued to develop, the Board of Director of CITIC group, Mr YiRen Rong sent suggestions to the central government of China to establish a separate bank under the group, which would be responsible for foreign exchange business. Both the state council and PBOC approved that the banking department can be established within the group to expand the group's foreign exchange business, which provided the basis for establishing the separate bank. In April 1985, the CITIC group established the banking department on the basis of the previous finance department to expand the business into areas such as foreign financing, foreign currency transactions, international settlement, granting of loans, financial leasing, deposit-taking, etc. The banking department of the group had obtained substantial help and support from the PBOC as well as the State Administration of Foreign Exchange. Its business developed very quickly, and the banking department accumulated experience in attracting RMB and foreign currency deposit, granting loans, issuing letter for import and export, securities and foreign currency transactions as well as foreign currency exchange, which met the condition of establishing a separate bank.

By the end of May 1986, the CITIC group asked for approval from PBOC to establish CITIC Industrial bank on the basis of the banking department. At the beginning of 1987, the CITIC Industrial Bank was established after the official approval from the state council and PBOC. The name of the bank changed to China CITIC Bank by the end of 2005, and its headquarters is in Beijing. The main shareholder of the bank is CITIC group. Banco Bilbao Vizcaya Argentaria, SA (BBVA) bought 5% stake of the bank worth of Euro zone currency (Euro) 0.5 billion. On 27 April 2007, China CITIC Bank successfully offered its initial public offering on the Shanghai Stock Exchange. By the end of 2013, the bank set up 189 new outlets, increasing the total number of outlets to 1073, with an annual growth rate of 21.2% compared to the previous year, covering 116 large and medium cities nationwide. As of the end of 2013, the total assets of the bank reached RMB 3.64 trillion, with a growth rate of 23.02% compared to 2012, the total deposits and loans were more than RMB 2.6 trillion and RMB 1.9 trillion, respectively and the net profit of the bank achieved RMB 39.18 billion, with a growth rate of 26.24% compared to the previous year (China Citic Bank, 2013).

2.3.2.3 Hua Xia Bank

HUA XIA BANK 华夏银行

Hua Xia Bank started operation in Beijing in October 1992 when China ushered in the programme of opening up and reform led by the chief architect Deng Xiaoping. The bank became a nationwide JSCB after restructuring in March, 1995. In September 2003, Hua Xia Bank went public as the fifth of Chinese banks listed on the Shanghai Stock Exchange. In October 2005, Hua Xia Bank entered into an agreement with the international strategic investor, Deutsche Bank, and completed two rounds of private placement of new shares in October 2008 and April 2011, respectively.

The company continuously furthered the building of the exclusive mechanism for small enterprises. By the end of 2013, 33 Tier-1 branches and 14 Tier-2 branches established regional sub-departments of small and medium enterprise credit departments, and small enterprises exclusive service network had basically covered the whole bank.

By the end of 2013, the bank's total assets reached RMB 1,672,447 million, an increase of RMB 183,587 million or 12.33% compared to the previous year. Total loans increased by RMB 103,001 million or 14.30% to RMB 823,169 million. Total deposits increased by RMB 141,592 million or 13.67% to RMB 1,177,592 million. The volume of non-performing loans by the end of 2013 was RMB 7443 million, increasing by RMB 1104 million compared to the previous year, whereas the non-performing loan ratio of the bank by the end of 2013 was 0.90%, increasing by 0.02% compared to 2012. The cost-to-income ratio achieved by the bank by the end of 2013 was 38.93%, declining by 1.02% compared to the previous year. The capital adequacy ratio, Tier-1 capital adequacy ratio and core Tier-1 capital adequacy ratio achieved by the bank in 2013 were 9.88%, 8.03% and 8.03%, respectively. With regard to profitability, the bank achieved return on assets of 0.98% in 2013, which increased by 0.04% compared to the previous year. By the end of the 2013, Hua Xia Bank ranked 94th among '1000 Bank' By 'The Banker' according to the asset size, whereas among 'the biggest 500 enterprises in China', Hua Xia Bank ranked 152, whereas it ranked 52 among 'biggest 500 service enterprises in China' (Hua Xia Bank, 2013).

2.3.2.4 China Everbright Bank

Bank 中国光大银行 CHINA EVERBRIGHT BANK

China Everbright Bank was established in August 1992. It is headquartered in Beijing and is a financial institution that is found under the approval of the state council and the PBOC. The bank has made outstanding achievements through the years and has cultivated a strong competitive edge in its corporate, investment banking, wealth management and mortgage businesses. The bank launched a series of financial restructuring in 2007. On 30 November, under the approval of the CBRC, the bank received a capital injection equivalent of RMB 20 billion by Central Huijin Investment Ltd in USD and thus increased its registered capital to RMB 28 billion. Central Huijin Investment Ltd, is now the largest shareholder of the bank, and Central Huijin's investment has substantially enhanced the bank' overall capital strength. In an effort to replenish its capital, the bank successfully got listed on the Hong Kong Stock Exchange on 20 December 2013, issuing 6244 million shares and raising proceeds of Hong Kong dollars (HKD) 24.852 billion. The H share listing has significantly improved the bank's capital strength.

By the end of 2013, the total assets of the bank reached RMB 2415.086 billion, up by 5.96% compared to the previous year, whereas total loans and advances were RMB 1,166,310 million, representing an increase of 13.99% compared to the previous year. The cost-to-income ratio by the end of 2013 was 31.84%, representing a year-on-year increase of 1.65%, the non-performing loan ratio was 0.86%, increasing by 0.12% compared to the previous year. The profit before tax achieved at the end of 2013 was RMB 34.421 billion with the net profit of RMB 26.754 billion, increasing by 13.27% compared to 2012. In 2013, one Tier-1 branch in Hong Kong, eight Tier-2 branches in Jinzhou, Nanyang, Baotou, Huizhou, Yanbian, Nantong, Weifang and Yulin and 70 outlets commenced operation. By the end of 2013, the bank had opened 853 branches outlets in 91 economically developed cities in 29 provinces, autonomous regions and municipalities across the country including 37 Tier-1 branches, 47 Tier-2 branches and 769 outlets. In 2013, the bank focussed on its retail banking business, small and micro finance business and E-banking business. The bank won a number of awards such as the most innovative bank of the year, the most respected banks and the best E-banking of the year (China Everbright Bank, 2013).

2.3.2.5 Shanghai Pudong Development Bank

上海浦東發展銀行
SHANGHAI PUDONG DEVELOPMENT BANK

Shanghai Pudong Development (SPD) Bank was established on 28 August 1992 under the approval of the PBOC. It was officially opened on 9 January 1993. As one of the JSCBs in China, it was listed on the Shanghai Stock Exchange in 1999 and is headquartered in Shanghai. At present, SPD Bank's registered capital stands at RMB 10.653 billion. SPD Bank has developed a good standing in China's financial markets with its outstanding performance, sound reputation and rapid growth.

With the core value of 'sticking to integrity and striving for excellence', and the vision of 'becoming the leading financial service provider with competitive advantages', the bank has actively focussed on financial innovation. It has continuously developed its various businesses and enhanced its overall business strength. By the end of 2013, the bank has established 39 Tier-1 branches and 915 stores across the country except in Ningxia and Tibet, building up a nationwide service network. Recently, SPD Bank has accelerated its footprint in the internationalization and diversification of business operation. The start of a Hong Kong branch and a London representative office and the investment in Shanghai Pudong Rural banks, AXA Shanghai Pudong Development Bank investment managers Co., Ltd, SPD Bank financial leasing Co., Ltd and Shanghai Pudong Silicon Valley bank were the milestones on the bank's way to become a group with comprehensive range.

In 2013, SPD Bank, for the first time, became a member of Fortune 500, ranking the 460th. The bank also ranked the 125th on the Forbes Global 2000, and the 53rd in terms of Tier-1 capital among 1000 world banks of the Banker magazine. Since its public listing at the stock market, SPD Bank has been rated among Top 100 listed companies in China by Asian weekly for a number of consecutive years. Meanwhile. SPD Bank was ranked the 15th on the list of China's best brand value 2013 with a brand value of RMB 14.791 billion. By the end of 2013, SPD Bank achieved total assets of RMB 3.68 trillion, a year-on-year increase of 16.99% and the operating income of RMB 100.015 billion, which was first time to exceed RMB 100 billion. The net profit attributed to the shareholders of the bank was RMB 40.922 billion, a year-on-year increase of 19.70%. The total loans of the bank achieved by the end of 2013 was RMB 1.767 trillion, with a growth rate of 14.44% compared to the previous year. The cost-to-income ratio of the bank in 2013 was 25.83%, declining by 2.88% compared to 2012, whereas the non-performing loan ratio of the bank by the end of 2013 was 0.74%, increasing by 0.16% compared to the previous year (SPD, 2013).

2.3.2.6 China Minsheng Bank Corp. Ltd

Established on 12 January 1996 in Beijing, China Minsheng Banking Corp., Ltd, is a national JSCB with investment mainly from non-state-owned enterprises (NSOEs), and is a standard joint-stock financial institution founded in strict compliance with the rules and regulations under the company law and the commercial banking law. The company differentiates itself from other state-owned banks and commercial banks as a combination of involvement of diversified economic sectors in the financial sector in China and application of normative modern enterprise system. As a pilot programme of China's banking reform, the company forges ahead with unremitting efforts to explore its businesses, expand its asset size, improve its profitability and maintain rapid and healthy growth. It has made proactive contributions to the reform and innovation of the Chinese banking industry.

On 19 December 2000, the A-share stock of China Minsheng Bank was listed on the Shanghai Stock Exchange. On 18 March 2003, RMB 4 billion in convertible corporate bonds of the company were traded at the Shanghai Stock Exchange. On 8 November 2003, the company, as the first commercial bank in China, successfully issued RMB 5.8 billion subordinated bonds in the inter-bank bond market through private placement. On 26 October 2005, the company became the first commercial bank in China that completed the shares reform of China's capital market. On 26 November 2009, the company was listed at the Hong Kong Stock Exchange. At a new historical starting point, the company reset its market positioning as a bank for NSOEs, small and micro enterprises and high-end retail customers and carried out adjustments on management framework, organization structure, business structure and establishment of Information Technology platform.

By the end of 2013, the total assets of the bank reached RMB 3.23 trillion, increasing by RMB 14.21 billion, compared to the previous year, and the total loans of the bank were RMB 1.57 trillion, with a growth rate of 13.70%. The total deposits of the bank amounted to RMB 2.15 trillion, increasing by 11.45% compared to 2012. The net profit attributable to shareholders by the end of 2013 achieved RMB

42.28 billion, with a growth rate of 12.55%, whereas the cost-to-income ratio was 32.75%, declining by 1.26% compared to the previous year. The non-performing loan ratio of the bank in 2013 was 0.85%, increasing by 0.09% compared to the previous year. The capital adequacy ratio, Tier-1 capital adequacy ratio and core Tier-1 capital adequacy ratio by the end of 2013 were 10.69%, 8.72% and 8.72%. In 2013, the bank was awarded the best bank for providing banking services to small and medium enterprises by the Asian Banker (China Minsheng Bank, 2013).

2.3.2.7 Industrial Bank Co. Ltd

兴业银行
INDUSTRIAL BANK CO.,LTD.

Industrial Bank was established in August 1988 and headquartered in Fuzhou city, Fujian province. It is one of the first batch of JSCBs approved by the state council and the PBOC. On 5 February 2007, Industrial Bank was listed on the Shanghai Stock Exchange with total registered capital of RMB 10.786 billion.

The main business scope of the bank includes: deposit taking; provision of short, medium and long-term loans; domestic and international settlement; bill acceptance and discounting; issuing financial bonds; agency issuing; cashing and underwriting of government bonds; trading of government bonds and financial bonds; agency issuing quoted securities except equity; trading and agency trading of quoted securities except equity; asset custody business; inter-bank borrowing and lending; trading or agency trading of foreign exchange; settlement and sales of foreign exchange; bank card business; letter-of-credit services and guarantee; agency collections and payments; safe-deposit-box services; financial consulting; credit investigation; consulting; witness business and other banking activities approved by the CBRC.

By the end of 2013, the total assets of the bank achieved RMB 3.68 trillion, increasing by 13.12% compared to the previous year, whereas the total deposits and total loans of the bank reached RMB 2.17 trillion and 1.36 trillion with growth rates of 19.69% and 10.40%, respectively. The volume of non-performing loans was RMB 10.33 billion, and non-performing loans ratio of 0.78%, increasing by 0.33% compared to the previous year. The net profits attributable to the shareholders achieved

RMB 41.21 billion, with a growth rate of 18.70% compared to 2012. The cost-to-income ratio was 26.71%, declining by 0.02% compared to the previous year. The core Tier-1 capital ratio, Tier-1 capital ratio and capital adequacy ratio were 8.68%, 8.68% and 10.83%, respectively.

The bank has set up 98 branches and 826 sub-branches in major cities and has a wholly owned subsidiary – Industrial Bank Financial Leasing Co. Ltd, two controlling subsidiaries – Industrial International Trust Ltd and CIB Fund Management Co., Ltd. In 2013, the bank's market position and brand image were steadily improved. The bank successfully enlisted in the world's top 50 banks ranked by 'The Banker', the Fortune 500 enterprises ranked by 'The Fortune' and global top 200 listed enterprises ranked by 'The Forbes' (Industrial Bank, 2013).

2.3.2.8 China Guangfa Bank

Established in July 1988, China Guangfa Bank is one of the earliest-incorporated JSCBs in China. Its headquarter is located in Guangzhou, Guangdong province with registered capital of RMB 11.41 billion. On 8 November 1993, China Guangfa bank opened a subsidiary in Macau, becoming the first JSCBs establishing subsidiary abroad. In 2006, following the reform and restructure, China Guangfa bank successfully attracted a number of foreign as well as domestic investors such as Citi Bank Corporation, China Life, State Grid Corporation of China, etc., which not only improve corporate governance and control, but improves the ability of the bank to innovate and manage. On 24 August 2006, China Guangfa bank signed a memo with Asia development bank on stock subscription and strategic cooperation which specified that China Guangfa bank will increase the amount of shares held by Asia development banks by issuing an extra 66 million shares; thus, China Guangfa bank became the bank in China with foreign investor holdings with the largest proportion of shares.

By the end of 2013, the total assets of the bank reached RMB 1.47 trillion, whereas the total loans and total deposits of the bank were RMB 714.7 billion and RMB 994.9 billion, increasing by 16.07% and 16.21%, respectively, compared to the previous year. The volume of non-performing loans in 2013 was RMB 6.2 billion, declining by RMB

2.91 billion compared to 2012. The non-performing loan ratio of the bank by the end of 2013 was 0.87%, decreasing by 0.61% compared to the previous year, whereas the net profit achieved by the bank by the end of 2013 was RMB 11.08 billion. The cost-to-income ratio by the end of 2013 was 41.92%, increasing by 1.09% compared to 2012, whereas the capital adequacy ratio, the Tier-1 capital adequacy ratio and the core Tier-1 capital adequacy ratio in 2013 were 9%, 7.5% and 7.5%, respectively, in 2013. Among the top 1000 banks around the world by the Banker, China Guangfa bank ranked 118 with regard to the Tier-1 capital. By the end of 2013, China Guangfa bank had 34 branches, 661 business outlets, 114 small enterprises banking centres and 13 smart banks in 71 cities at prefecture level or above in 16 provinces. The bank has over nine million banking customers, over 27 million credit cards issued and correspondent bank partnerships with 1687 bank headquarters and their branches in more than 128 countries and regions. It is the first financial institution to establish the strategic cooperation of multi-channel and multi-application e-payment with China Unionpay. The bank continues to provide customers with efficient, quality and comprehensive financial services. In 2013, with regard to the Tier-1 capital, the bank ranked 118 among '1000 banks' by 'The Banker' (CGB, 2013).

2.3.2.9 Ping An Bank

Ping An Bank was formed after the merger of former Shenzhen Development Bank and former Ping An Bank through absorption. Ping An bank, headquartered in Shenzhen, was China's first national JSCB offering shares to the public for trading. Ping An Insurance company of China, together with its subsidiaries, hold in total approximately 6.734 billion shares or approximately 59% of the total share capital of Ping An Bank and is therefore the controlling shareholder of Ping An Bank. As of the end of 2013, the total assets of the bank amounted to RMB 1891.741 billion, representing a growth of 17.75% compared to the previous year. The total loans of the bank by the end of 2013 reached RMB 847.289 billion, representing an increase of 17.55% compared to 2012. Total deposit balance of the bank in

2013 was RMB 1,217.002 billion, representing a growth of 19.18% compared to the previous year. The net profit for 2013 amounted to RMB 15.231 billion, representing an increase of 12.72% from the previous year. The basic earnings per share recorded RMB 1.86, representing an increase of 13.14% compared to the previous year. The cost-to-income ratio for the bank by the end of 2013 was 40.77%, increasing by 1.36% compared to the previous year. The non-performing loan ratio of the bank by the end of 2013 was 0.89%, declining by 0.06% compared to 2012. The capital adequacy ratio, Tier-1 capital adequacy ratio and core Tier-1 capital adequacy ratio of the bank by the end of 2013 were 9.9%, 8.56% and 8.56%, respectively. The bank actively engages in providing various financial products and services focussing on retail business, treasury and inter-bank business, investment bank business as well as corporate business. By the end of 2013, the bank had a total of 38 branches and 528 other outlets. In the past two years, Ping An bank received a various honours including the 'Best Bank in Supply Chain Financial service'; the "Best Bank for Small and Medium Enterprises'; the 'Wealth Management Bank with Excellent Competitiveness'; the 'Most Innovative Bank'; the 'Joint-stock Commercial Bank of the Year'; the 'Award for Best Corporate Social Responsibility' and the 'Most Respected China-Funded Bank in China' (Ping An Bank, 2013).

2.3.2.10 China Zheshang Bank

As one of the JSCBs in China, China ZheShang Bank started its operation on 18 August 2004 under the approval from the CBRC. Its headquarter is located in Hangzhou, Zhejiang province. The predecessor was Zhejiang commercial bank, which was a Sino—foreign joint venture bank established in Ningbo in 1993. On 30 June 2004, under the approval from CBRC, the bank was re-named, moved and restructured to the current bank.

By the end of 2013, the bank had 114 branches across 12 cities in the country. As of the end of 2013, the total assets of the bank reached RMB 488.12 billion, whereas the total deposits and total loans of the bank were

RMB 319.8 billion and RMB 216.7 billion, respectively, with growth rates of 23.94%, 19.94% and 19.17% compared to the previous year. The bank kept emphases on business with small and micro enterprises in China. By the end of 2013, the amount of loans granted to small and micro enterprises was RMB72.25 billion, increasing by 23.24% compared to the previous year, accounting for 33.34% of the total loans granted by the bank. The service fee charged for investment business provided increased by 60.45% in 2013 compared to 2012. The non-performing loan ratio by the end of 2013 was 0.64%, increasing by 0.18% compared to the previous year. The net profit achieved by the bank at the end of 2013 was RMB 4.9 billion, increasing by 21.75% compared to the previous year. The capital adequacy ratio, Tier-1 capital adequacy ratio and the core Tier-1 capital adequacy ratio by the end of 2013 were 11.53%, 9.17% and 9.17%, respectively. The cost-to-income ratio by the end of 2013 was 32.11%, with an increase rate of 0.07% compared to the previous year.

The bank has received a number of awards during recent years including 'the best bank for providing financial services to small and micro enterprises in China' in 2012; 'the most competitive bank with regard to providing investment bank business in China' in 2013. Among the top 1000 banks around the world published by the Banker, the bank was ranked 235 in 2013 (Zheshang Bank, 2013).

2.3.2.11 China Bohai Bank

渤海银行
China Bohai Bank

China Bohai Bank is the first national JSCB founded with the approval of the state council since 1996. It is also the first Chinese-funded commercial bank introducing overseas strategic investors at the establishment stage and the first national JSCB headquartered in Tianjin, the Bank was set up by its seven shareholders, namely, Tianjin Economic-Technological Development Area (TEDA) Investment Holding Co., Ltd, Standard Chartered Bank (Hong Kong) Limited, China Ocean Shipping (Group) Company, State Development and Investment Corporation, Baosteel Group Corporation, Tianjin Trust Co., Ltd, and Tianjin Shanghui Investment (Holding) Co., Ltd, with total registered capital of RMB 8.5 billion. The bank was established on 30 December 2005 and was officially opened in

February 2006. As of 31 December 2013, the bank had 14 Tier-1 branches, six Tier-2 branches and 77 sub-branches in 22 key cities nationwide.

As of the end of 2013, the bank's total assets and total liabilities amounted to RMB 568, 211 million and RMB 544,014 million, respectively, representing a respective increase of 20.36% and 20.28% over the beginning of the year. Net profit stood at RMB 4562 million, up by 36.63% over the previous year. Non-performing loan ratio stood at 0.26% by the end of 2013, increasing by 0.12% compared to the previous year. The cost-to-income ratio of the bank by the end of 2013 was 34.74%, declining by 3.84% compared to 2012. The capital adequacy ratio, Tier-1 capital adequacy ratio as well as core Tier-1 capital adequacy ratio in 2013 were 11.06%, 8.70% and 8.70%, respectively. The bank ranked 278th in overall strength among top 1000 world banks issued by The Banker, up by 21 places; ranked by 74th in overall strength and 52nd in competitiveness among Asian banks in the Asian Banker Top 500, up by 44 and 14 places, respectively, and ranked 36th among Asian banks in comprehensive competitiveness at the 2013 Asian Financial Annual Conference. In addition, the bank was granted the '2013 Innovation Award for Corporate Governance Model'; '2013 Best Bank in Wealth Management'; '2013 Best E-Banking'; '2013 Most Promising Debit Card'; and '2013 Best Mobile Banking' by 21st century Business Herald, National Business Daily, Money Week and Investor's Business Daily (China Bohai Bank, 2013).

2.3.2.12 Evergrowing Bank

Evergrowing Bank Co., Ltd is one of the nation-wide JSCBs in China. Its predecessor was YanTai House Saving Bank established on 29 October 1987 and formally operated on 1 December. In 2013, the bank finished restructuring after the official approval from PBOC. The headquarters of the bank is located in YanTai, Shandong province. By the end of 2013, the bank had 11 Tier-1 branches, 14 Tier-2 branches and more than 110 sub-branches. The total assets of the bank by the end of 2013 reached RMB 0.77 trillion, with a growth rate of 25% compared to the previous year, the total deposits of the bank were RMB 0.37 trillion, increasing by 21% compared to 2012. The total loans of the bank by the end of

2013 achieved RMB 0.21 trillion, with an increase rate of 21% compared to the previous year. The net profit was RMB 6.92 billion by 2013, increasing by 18.9% compared to 2012. The non-performing loans ratio in 2013 was 0.95%, increasing by 0.28% compared to the previous year. The capital adequacy ratio in 2013 was 10.61%, declining by 0.77% compared to the previous year, whereas the cost-to-income ratio by the end of 2013 was 24.35%, increasing by 0.03% compared to 2012. Five of the biggest shareholders hold more than 5% of the total shares of the bank. They are Yantai Blue Sky Investment Shareholding Co., Ltd, which is the biggest shareholder of the bank holding 20.55% of the total shares; United Overseas Bank is the second biggest shareholder of the bank, with 14.26% of total shares; the third shareholder is Nanshan Group Co., Ltd, with 7.25% of total shares; Jiangsu Huijin Shareholding Group Co., Ltd is the fourth shareholder with 7.25% of total shares. The last shareholder is Fuxin Group Co., Ltd, which holds 6.04% of the total shares (Evergrowing Bank, 2013).

2.3.3 City Commercial Banks

City commercial banks are the third largest banking ownership type in China according to total assets. The total assets of this banking ownership in China by the end of 2013 was RMB 151,778, with a growth rate of 22.93% compared to the previous year, whereas the total liabilities of this banking ownership type by the end of 2013 were RMB 141,804, compared to the previous year, it increased by 22.89%. The total owner's equity achieved by this banking ownership type at the end of 2013 was RMB 9974, with an increase rate of 23.53% compared to the previous year. The profit after tax of this banking ownership type by the end of 2013 reached RMB 1641.4, compared to 2012; it grows at a rate of 20%. The number of staff working for the city commercial banks by the end of 2013 was 278,470 (CBRC, 2013).[6]

2.3.4 Other Banks and Non-financial Institutions

Other banks and non-financial institutions mainly include policy banks, rural commercial banks, rural cooperative banks, urban credit cooperatives, rural credit cooperatives, non-bank financial institutions, foreign banks as well as new-type rural financial institutions and a postal savings bank.

[6] The RMB values are in 100 million.

By the end of 2013, the total assets of this category was RMB 100 million, increasing by 15.73% comparing to the previous year, whereas the total liabilities of this banking category reached RMB 404,784 million, with a growth rate of 15.34% comparing to 2012. The total owner's equity of this banking category at the end of 2013 was RMB 31,402, with an increase rate of 21.01% comparing to the previous year. The total profit after tax achieved by this banking category by the end of 2013 was RMB 404,784, comparing to 2012, it increased by 15.34%. The number of staff working in this banking category by the end of 2013 was 1,187,149.[7]

The rural cooperative banks were financial institutions with shares held by farmers, rural individual business, enterprise entity as well as other economic organizations. The purpose of this non-banking financial institution is to provide financial services to farmers, agriculture as well as rural economic development. One of the main differences among rural credit cooperatives, rural cooperative banks and rural commercial banks lies to the fact that the first one was mainly established in an area with a very high degree of agriculture, with the latter two rural financial institutions mainly serving the areas with a relatively lower degree of agriculture (more-developed areas). The urban credit cooperatives were established in China since the late 1970s, the funds raised by the urban credit cooperatives were mainly from the individuals living in the city areas and the purpose of this financial institution was mainly to provide loans to collectively owned enterprises, individual and private small enterprises as well as individuals. Although because this type of financial institution has the characteristics of lower operational performance, higher risk-taking behaviour as well as lower risk absorption abilities, according to the requirement from Chinese banking regulatory authority, this financial institution has been gradually transformed to city commercial banks. Main ownership of this financial institution is city-level government, and the purpose was to provide loans to small- and medium-size enterprises within the city and promote the local economic development.

Other non-banking institutions mainly include trust companies, finance companies of corporate groups, financial leasing companies, money brokerage firms, auto-financing companies, lending companies as well as consumer-financing companies. Trust companies are operated on the basis of trust; its main objects include both money as well as property. There are three parties in the trust business, they are trustor, trustee and beneficiary.

[7] The RMB values are in 100 million.

The trustor is the owner of the money or property, he/she entrusts them to trustee who is responsible to manage the money or property, whereas the beneficiary is the party who will receive the benefit through the operation of trustee. The beneficiary can be the same as trustee or other persons. The profit of trust companies is mainly from the commission paid by the trustor. The types of companies engaging in trust business mainly include Security Company, Fund Company as well as trust company.

Financial leasing companies are non-banking financial institutions. They purchase relevant equipment according to the specific requirement of companies and lease it to the companies, whereas the companies pay a certain amount of leasing fees on a regular basis to the financial leasing companies, over certain period of time (ie, 5 or 10 years), the equipment belongs to the companies. In other words, this kind of non-banking financial institutions solve the company's problems of short of funding for purchasing relevant equipment, and financial leasing companies make a profit through the payment of leasing fees from the companies.

Auto financial companies are non-banking financial institutions established according to the approval from CBRC, the purpose is to provide financial services to domestic citizens purchasing or selling autos. Consumer financing companies do not take deposits, they make small loans to domestic citizens with regard to personal consumption on durable goods. Taking loans out from consumer financing companies does not need any guarantee or mortgage, thus, these non-banking financial institutions have relatively higher risk. Lending companies are another type of non-banking financial institution established according to the approval from CBRC and other relevant laws. They are established by domestic commercial banks or rural cooperative banks in the rural area and provide loan services to farmers, agriculture and economic development of the local area. Unlike commercial banks, they do not take deposits. Financial companies of corporate groups are different from normal financial companies, they are non-banking financial institutions mainly engaged in providing financial management services to the members within the corporate groups. The main businesses engaged in by these financial institutions include taking deposits from the members, accepting checks and discounting, making settlements among members within the corporate groups, providing guarantees for the members, making loans and financial leasing for members, etc. The purpose of this financial institution is to enhance the fund management and also improve the efficiency of fund use. Money brokerage firms are a kind of financial intermediary; they provide intermediate financial services to customers, and the business mainly involves the products in the money market, capital market and foreign exchange market. The main products offered by the money brokerage firms include inter-bank borrowing, short-term commercial notes, spot and forward exchange transactions, currency and interest rate swaps, options, futures, government and company bonds, etc.

New-type rural financial institutions mainly include village and township banks as well as rural mutual cooperatives. The village and township banks are financial institutions established according to the approval from CBRC, the shareholders of this financial institution include domestic and foreign financial institutions, domestic non-financial enterprise entities and domestic citizens. They are banking financial institutions mainly providing financial services to farmers, agriculture and the economic development of local rural areas. They have several characteristics: (1) they provide small loans to farmers; (2) they mainly focus on providing financial services to small- and medium-size enterprises locally. Rural mutual cooperatives are banking financial institutions established according to the approval from relevant banking regulatory authorities; the shareholders include farms as well as small rural enterprises (as members in the cooperative), and they mainly provide financial services to their members with regard to loans, deposits and settlements.

Sino—German Bausparkasse was established on 2014 by two parties which are CCB and German Schwäbisch Hall Housing Saving Banking Corporation, in which the former holds 75.1% of total shares. This financial institution mainly attracted funds from depositors who have the advantage of taking out housing loans from this financial institution with a relatively lower interest rate compared to interest rates offered by other banks. At the beginning of the operation, the financial institution had the registered capital of RMB 0.15 billion. Its services were just to provide their deposit loan services to purchase houses. In 2008, both of these shareholders injected capital; the new capital of this financial institution reached RMB 1 billion. Furthermore, the financial institution expanded the business to introduce a number of different businesses such as taking deposits from and making loans to the public and making loans to support housing construction. It also issues financial security and works as an agent to issue government bonds.

One postal savings bank in China was established in March 2007. It has comprehensive coverage across different areas in China and has the largest number of consumers compared to other types of commercial banks. It provides comprehensive types of financial services including company deposits and loans, company settlements and assets operations. It also offers individual loan business, syndicate loans as well as banking card business. Its business has the characteristics of providing small loans and also focusses on agriculture.

2.4 SUMMARY AND CONCLUSION

This chapter mainly reviews the reforms in the Chinese banking sector. The reforms have been divided into four stages. The first stage covers the period of 1949–1978, whereas the second stage covers 1978–92, the third stage covers 1992–2001, and the last stage of Chinese banking sector reform covers the period of 2001–2013.

The main purposes of Chinese banking sector reform can be summarized as follows: (1) increase competition; (2) reduce risk-taking behaviour and the number of non-performing loans; (3) improve corporate governance and enhance external monitoring; (4) increase competitiveness; and (5) enhance risk management skills and improve banking operation technology.

The measures taken by the Chinese government in banking sector reform mainly include: (1) establishing different ownership types of Chinese commercial banks to increase competition; (2) establishing policy banks and asset management companies to reduce the number of non-performing loans; (3) injecting capital and IPOs to increase competitiveness; (4) entering WTO to further increase competition by treating foreign banks exactly the same as domestic Chinese commercial banks; (5) establishing China Banking Regulatory Commission to supervise banking operations and further reduce risk-taking behaviour; and (6) introducing foreign strategic investors to further improve risk management as well as technology in Chinese banking operations.

The second part of this chapter mainly focusses on explaining the structure of the Chinese banking sector. A number of different banking ownership types exist in the sector. This book focusses on a detailed discussion of three different ownership types which are large-scale commercial banks, JSCBs as well as city commercial banks. These three different ownership types are the three largest banking ownerships in China according to total assets. Five large-scale commercial banks as well as 12 JSCBs are explained on a one-by-one basis. In addition, besides the city commercial banks, other banking and non-banking financial institutions in China are also explained in this book.

SOURCES OF FURTHER INFORMATION

ABC, 2013. Agricultural Bank of China annual statement, 2013. http://www.abchina.com/en/investor-relations/performance-reports/annual-reports/.

BOCOM, 2013. Bank of Communication annual statement, 2013. http://www.bankcomm.com/BankCommSite/shtml/zonghang/en/3182/3195/3196/34403.shtml?channelId=3195.

BOC, 2013. Bank of China annual statement, 2013. http://www.boc.cn/en/investor/ir3/201403/t20140326_3099448.html.

CGB, 2013. China Guangfa Bank annual statement, 2013. http://www.cgbchina.com.cn/Info/15988702.

CCB, 2013. China Construction Bank annual statement, 2013. http://www.ccb.com/en/newinvestor/20140508_1399536163.html.

China Bohai Bank, 2013. China Bohai Bank annual statement, 2013. http://www.cbhb.com.cn/bhbank/S101/attach/2013ywnb.pdf.

CBRC, 2013. China Banking Regulatory Commission annual report, 2013. http://zhuanti.cbrc.gov.cn/subject/subject/nianbao2013/1.pdf.

China Citic Bank, 2013. China Citic Bank annual statement, 2013. http://bank.ecitic.com/download/investorrelation_en/e20140620H.pdf.

China Everbright Bank, 2013. China Everbright Bank annual statement, 2013. http://www1.cebbank.com/Info/140277592.

China Merchants Bank, 2013. China Merchants Bank annual statement, 2013. http://file.cmbchina.com/cmbir/3bb3ed4f-e3f0-4a9a-b96f-e5a0410e0367.pdf.

China Minsheng Bank, 2013. China Minsheng Bank annual statement, 2013. http://www.cmbc.com.cn/cs/Satellite?c=Page&cid=1375342063640&currentId=1356495496292&pagename=cmbc%2FPage%2FTP_InvestorRelationsLayout&parentId=1356495496292&rendermode=preview.

Evergrowing Bank, 2013. Evergrowing Bank annual statement, 2013. http://www.egbank.com.cn/images/jrhf/tzzgx/2014/06/19/hfyhygfyxgs2013ndbg.pdf.

Hua Xia Bank, 2013. Hua Xia Bank annual statement, 2013. http://res.hxb.com.cn/resource/830/1147/1164/217260/217668/217797/500717/1403612240303212024 5468.pdf.

ICBC, 2013. Industrial and Commercial Bank of China annual statement, 2013. http://www.icbc-ltd.com/icbcltd/investor%20relations/financial%20information/financial%20reports/2013annualreport.htm.

Industrial Bank, 2013. Industrial Bank annual statement, 2013. http://download.cib.com.cn/netbank/download/en/20140918en.pdf.

Ping An Bank, 2013. Ping An Bank annual statement, 2013. http://resources.pingan.com/app_upload/file/bank/b5cce65e5a6e423884462b22ba26ba00.pdf.

SPD, 2013. Shanghai Pudong Development Bank annual statement, 2013. http://www.spdb.com.cn/chpage/c530/.

Zheshang Bank, 2013. Zheshang Bank annual statement, 2013. http://www.czbank.com/czbank/UserFiles/File/2013report.pdf.

REFERENCES

Cousin, V., 2007. Banking in China. Palgrave Macmillan, UK.

Kumbhakar, S., Wang, D., 2007. Economic reforms, efficiency and productivity in Chinese banking. Journal of Regulatory Economics 32 (2), 105–109.

Shirai, S., 2002. Banking Sector Reforms in the Peoples' Republic of China: Progress and Constraints in Rejuvenating Bank Finance for Development in Asia and the Pacific United Nations. New York, pp. 49–97.

CHAPTER 3

Theory of Bank Efficiency and Bank Competition

3.1 INTRODUCTION

Efficiency is a commonly used measure in the production process. There are inputs and outputs in production. Higher efficiency mainly means any unit/company has the ability to use the same amount of input to generate a higher volume of output, whereas on the other hand, higher efficiency can also be interpreted as any unit/company has the ability to minimize the input to produce the same volume of output. This interpretation of efficiency purely considers the volumes of input and output, whereas, in the production process, not only is the volume of output and input being considered by the managers and regulators, but more attention has also been given to minimize cost as well as maximize profit and revenue. Thus, it is important to analyse efficiency in technical terms as well as evaluate efficiency from a cost, profit and revenue perspective. More specifically, managers and regulators are greatly concerned about how to use a certain amount of input to minimize the cost and maximize the profit and revenue.

The chapter mainly explains the theories of bank efficiency as well as bank competition. Specifically, this chapter is organized as follows: Section 3.2 discusses the framework of efficiency and is divided into four sub-sections which explain cost efficiency, technical efficiency, profit efficiency and revenue efficiency on a one-by-one basis. With regards to bank competition, four indicators to measure bank competition will be explained which include Concentration ratio, Panzar–Rosse H-statistic, Lerner index and Boone indicator.

3.2 THE FRAMEWORK OF EFFICIENCY

3.2.1 Technical Efficiency

A simple measure of firm efficiency is defined by Farrell (1957), whose work is derived from Debreu (1951) and Koopmans (1951). He argued that technical efficiency reflects a firm's ability to obtain maximal output from a

Efficiency and Competition in Chinese Banking
ISBN 978-0-08-100074-8

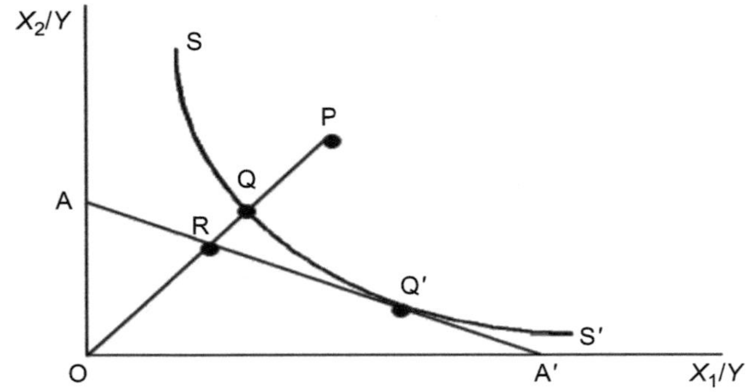

Figure 3.1 The measurement of technical efficiency. *(Coelli, T., 1996. A Guide to DEAP Version 2.1: A Data Envelopment Analysis (Computer) Program. CEPA working paper, 1996/08.)*

given set of inputs. Farrell explained his idea by making the assumption that firms use two inputs (X_1 and X_2) to produce one output (y), and the production is under the assumption of Constant Return to Scale (CRS) (see Fig. 3.1). In other words, an increase (decrease) in the inputs leads to the same proportional increase (decrease) of the output. The unit isoquant SS′ describes the technological set to produce the certain amount of output using the combination of the inputs (X_1 and X_2). In other words, SS′ shows the minimum number of inputs needed to produce one unit of output. All the production along this curve SS′ is supposed to be perfectly efficient, whereas any other points above or located at the right of the curve, such as the point P, are regarded as inefficient production due to the fact that the number of inputs used in the production to produce one unit of output is more than the efficient production.

The distance QP represents the technical inefficiency of the firm. It also represents the number of inputs which can be reduced without any influence on the output production. In other words, it represents the number of inputs which can be reduced without any decrease in the output. The percentage of the input reduction/technical inefficiency level for the point P can be represented by the ratio QP/OP, whereas the technical efficiency of a firm can be measured by the ratio OQ/OP. The value of technical efficiency ranges from 0 to 1. The value of 1 means that the firm is fully technically efficient.

The condition for the assumption of constant return to scale (CRS) is that all the firms operate at the optimal scale, which is impossible sometimes because of imperfect competition. The variable return to scale (VRS)

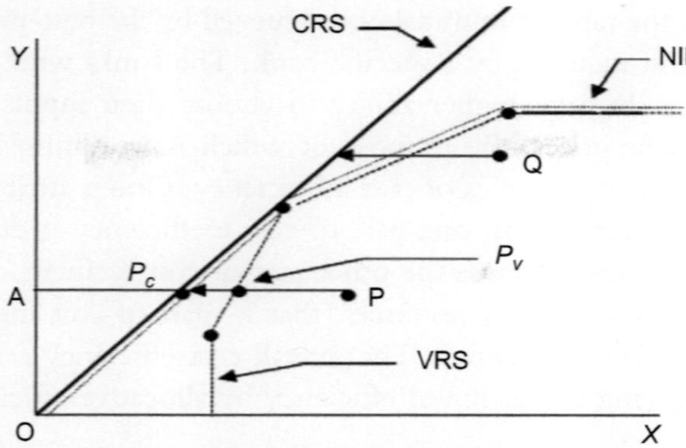

Figure 3.2 The measurement of pure technical efficiency and scale efficiency. *CRS*, Constant Return to Scale; *NIRS*, non-increasing returns to scale. *(Coelli, T., 1996. A Guide to DEAP Version 2.1: A Data Envelopment Analysis (Computer) Program. CEPA working paper, 1996/08.)*

further decomposes the technical efficiency into pure technical efficiency (PTE) and scale efficiency (SE). In Fig. 3.2, we make another assumption, which is that firms use one input X to product one output Y. The constant return to scale frontier is represented by CRS, firm's production can be laying on the curve or located to the right side, the technical inefficiency for the firm P is PP_c over AP, whereas the technical efficiency can be represented by the ratio AP_c/AP.

The SE considers the possibility that firms do not operate at the optimal size. The CRS assumption is replaced by the VRS assumption to measure the SE. The variable return to scale frontier is represented by VRS, under which the technical inefficiency for firm P is PP_v over AP, the PTE for the firm P can be represented by the ratio AP_v/AP, whereas the SE can be represented by the ratio AP_c/AP_v. If the firm operates under CRS, the value of scale efficiency equals 1, whereas the value of SE will be less than 1 in a VRS situation. In other words, firms have scale inefficiency.

3.2.2 Cost Efficiency

Rather than focussing on manipulating the inputs and outputs in banking operations which is reflected by technical efficiency, more practically, bank managers and banking regulatory authorities emphasize minimizing the cost of banking operations, one of the indicator used to measure this performance is cost efficiency. It is also called economic efficiency. It can be represented by the ratio of minimal cost achieved by the best-practice bank to the actual cost incurred by a specific bank. The banks with higher cost efficiency normally have higher ability to choose their inputs and mixes according to their prices, the purpose of which is to minimize the cost, whereas there are two sources of cost inefficiency. One is attributed to the technology, in other words, one part of cost inefficiency is derived from technical inefficiency, whereas the other part of cost inefficiency is due to the suboptimal allocation of resources, that is, part of cost inefficiency is related to allocative inefficiency. The overall cost efficiency can be calculated by multiplying the technical efficiency by allocative efficiency.

3.2.3 Revenue Efficiency

Berger and Mester (1997) argue that revenue efficiency measures the change in a bank's revenue adjusted for a random error, relative to the estimated revenue obtained from producing an output bundle as efficiently as the best-practice bank. Revenue efficiency emphasizes the fact that the banking operation aims to maximize revenue, and revenue efficiency is measured by the ratio of actual revenue to maximum revenue. There are two sources of revenue inefficiency. More specifically, revenue inefficiency can be attributed to output-oriented technical efficiency or output-oriented allocative inefficiency. The technical inefficiency can be interpreted as producing too few outputs given the input quantities, whereas the allocative inefficiency means non-optimal combination of outputs are produced given their prices.

The following figure (Fig. 3.3) explains revenue efficiency in the frontier methodological framework. We assume that the bank uses input X to produce two outputs, y_1 and y_2. TT′ represents the production possibility curve. Under the output-oriented assumption, a bank can be regarded as technically efficient if the operation point is located on TT′. Thus, we can say banks B, C, D and E are technically efficient under the output-oriented assumption. Due to the fact that Bank A locates below the frontier, it is regarded as inefficient. In other words, compared to revenue-efficient banks, the bank which is located at point A has the potential to increase the production levels of both outputs to point A′ located on the production possibility frontier. Therefore, for Bank A, the distance AA′ represents the output-oriented technical inefficiency. The output-oriented technical efficiency (TE) is measured by the ratio of actual output to maximum output of the bank. Using the above diagram, the output-oriented TE can be represented by the ratio of OA/OA′. It is assumed that the iso-revenue line is represented by PP′. Bank D is regarded as revenue efficient. Because the

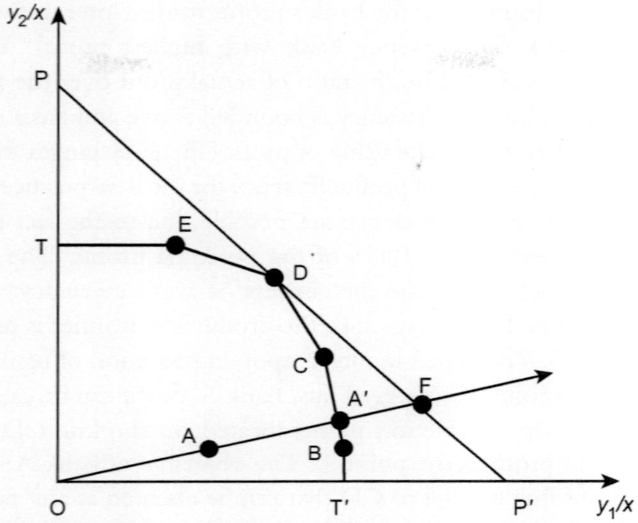

Figure 3.3 Revenue efficiency. *(Kumar, S., Gulati, R., 2013. Regulation and Efficiency of Indian Banks. Springer, India.)*

cost at point D equals the revenue at point F, the output-oriented allocative efficiency can be measured by the ratio of OA′/OF. If it is assumed that the production is located at the point A′, the increase in revenue can be represented by the distance A′F. Finally, the revenue efficiency of the bank can be represented by the ratio of OA/OF. Due to the fact that revenue efficiency includes both output-oriented TE and allocative efficiency, it is considered as a composite efficiency measure. The revenue inefficiency for Bank A can be represented by the distance AF. The relationship between revenue efficiency, TE and allocative efficiency can be expressed as

Revenue efficiency = technical efficiency × allocative efficiency.

3.2.4 Profit Efficiency

Profit efficiency is a more comprehensive type of efficiency concept which considers both cost and revenue performance. The profit efficiency assumes that both revenue and cost are controlled by managers. In empirical research, the analysis of profit efficiency is preferred to cost efficiency due to the fact the operating revenues and loan losses are ignored by cost efficiency. The profit efficiency can be defined as how close a bank is able to produce the maximum possible profit given the levels of input and output process and other exogenous conditions. Under the given conditions, profit efficiency can be improved if the bank's profits move closer to the profit of a benchmark bank (best-practice bank with highest profit). The profit efficiency can be measured by the ratio of actual profit over the maximum profit. The score of profit efficiency is bounded above and has a maximum value of 1. In other words, the value of profit efficiency ranges from minus (—) infinity to 1. The value of profit efficiency for the best-practice bank is 1. Negative values of profit efficiency are possible due to the fact that banks can throw away more than 100% of the potential profits. The following figure is used to better illustrate the concept of profit efficiency:

In the following figure (Fig. 3.4), the production frontier is represented by the curve OQ. The actual input—output combination of bank A which is represented by point A is x_A, y_A. Thus, Bank A′ profit can be calculated as: $q_A y_A - p_A x_A$. All the production points located on the line CD yield the same amount of profit as the point A. The objective of bank A is to reach highest isoprofit line parallel to CD that can be attained at any point on or below the curve OQ. Point B will be the highest point which is also the tangency of EF and OQ. If it is assumed that the input—output combination for point B is x^* and y^*, line OE represents the maximum profit achieved, and Bank A is able to achieve the maximum profit as long as it reaches one point on Line EF (Say, point A*). The calculation of maximum profit can be expressed as: $q_A y_A^* - p_A x_A^*$; this also equals $q_B y_B - p_B x_B$. The profit efficiency of bank A can be calculated by the ratio of actual profit divided by the maximum profit.

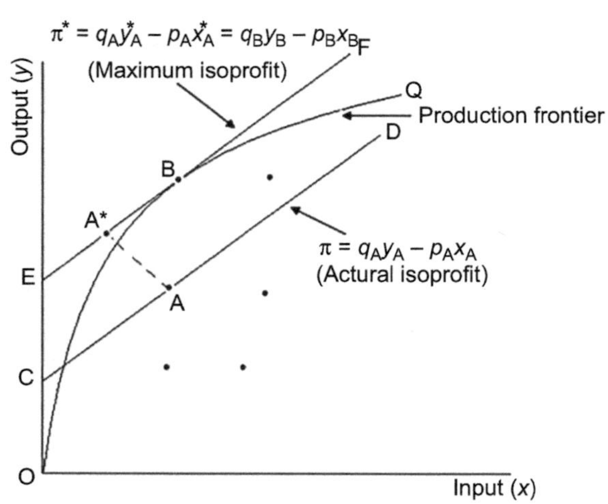

Figure 3.4 Profit efficiency. *(Kumar, S., Gulati, R., 2013. Regulation and Efficiency of Indian Banks. Springer, India.)*

3.3 THE MEASUREMENT OF EFFICIENCY

The methods used to measure efficiency can be mainly divided into two streams: one is called the parametric approach and the other one is called the non-parametric approach. The former can be more specifically divided into three analyses which include stochastic frontier analysis (SFA), distribution free approach (DFA) and think frontier approach (TFA). The non-parametric approach can be further divided into two analyses, which are data envelopment analysis (DEA) and free disposal hull (FDH) analysis. With regards to the parametric approach, a pre-specified functional form for the best-practice frontier is required. The efficiency of a firm is compared to the benchmark firm (firm with best practice). A firm is inefficient if the cost is higher than the best practice from, or the profit is lower than, the benchmark firm. The non-parametric approach is a mathematical programming technique to estimate efficiency and Stephard's distance function methodology is implemented.

The main argument for the DEA over a parametric technique, such as SFA, lies to the fact that it works particularly well with small samples. Furthermore, it is able to handle multiple inputs and outputs stated in different measurement units, and does not necessitate knowledge of any functional form of the frontier (see Charnes et al., 1995). Most empirical papers show that using DEA to estimate the efficiency frontier can yield robust results (see Seiford and Thrall, 1990). DEA has a number of drawbacks: first, the efficiency scores derived from DEA are sensitive to the selection of inputs and outputs. Secondly, the number of efficiency firms on the frontier tends to increase with the number of input and output variables. Thirdly, DEA assumes that it has no statistical noise and it is sensitive to extreme observations and measurement errors.

This section will be arranged as follows: Section 3.3.1 will discuss the parametric approach. As outlined previously, three specific analyses are focussed upon, which include SFA, DFA as well as TFA. In Section 3.3.2, two non-parametric approaches will be explained which are DEA and FDH.

3.3.1 Parametric Approach

3.3.1.1 Stochastic Frontier Approach

One of the most widely used parametric technique to measure bank efficiency is SFA, which was proposed by Aigner et al. (1997), Battese and Corra (1997) and Meeusen and Van Den Broeck (1997). The assumption of this method is that the decision-making unit (DMU) does not totally control the deviation from the frontier. Random errors, which are linked together with the choice of the functional form are allowed by SFA. The SFA model is also called the composed error model in which two terms are included and considered, the statistical noise term follows a symmetric distribution, whereas another term, which represents inefficiency, follows a one-sided distribution.

To make clearer with regards to the formation of the SFA, the following stochastic cost function model is used:

$$\ln C_i = \ln C(y_i, w_i) + \varepsilon_i = \ln C(y_i, w_i) + v_i + \mu_i$$

In the above function, C represents the total cost, i represents the specific bank, y stands for a vector of output and w is the input price. In the banking operation, normally three input prices are considered which are price of funds, price of labour and price of capital; v represents the statistical noise and u stands for the non-negative disturbance term. μ_i measures the distance of a specific individual firm from the efficient cost frontier and this term represents the technical and allocative efficiency of the firm. The deterministic cost frontier is represented by $C(y_i, w_i)$.

Aigner et al. (1977) and Mester (1993) argue that v_i follows the normal distribution and μ_i follows the half-normal or exponential distribution. Berger (1993) argues that the half-normal or exponential distribution term on inefficiency assumes that most firms nearly reach the full efficiency and are clustered together. The possibility of higher inefficiency is relatively low. However, this is not always the case due to the fact that some specific DMU would experience a higher degree of inefficiency. Rather than using the half-normal distribution for U_i, Stevenson (1980) and Berger and DeYoung (1997) suggested that alternative distribution for inefficiency such as a truncated normal distribution is more appropriate. Besides the truncated normal distribution, the normal-gamma distribution is considered by Greene (1990).

One of the obvious disadvantages of the truncated normal distribution as well as normal-gamma distribution lies in the fact that the inefficiency is difficult to separate from random error. Berger and Humphrey (1997) argue that random error of these two distributions is close to a symmetric normal distribution.

There are mainly two methods being used to estimate the parameters of the frontier model and the error terms which are the maximum likelihood estimation or the corrected ordinary least square (OLS) (see Battese and Coelli, 1995; Coelli, 1995; Fried et al., 1993). In comparison, the maximum likelihood estimation is preferred to the corrected OLS estimator due to the fact the maximum likelihood estimation produces more accurate results in large samples (Coelli, 1995; Olesen et al., 1980). Jondrow et al. (1982) argue that the distribution of the inefficiency term conditional on the estimate of the two error terms will be used to obtain estimates of inefficiency.

3.3.1.2 Distribution Free Approach

DFA, another parametric method, was proposed by Schmidt and Sickles (1984) and Berger (1993). It is a panel estimation method. The distributional assumptions on the error component were not imposed by this parametric method. The similarity between DFA and SFA lies in the fact that the former specifies a functional form for the efficiency frontier. The main difference between these two parametric methods is that the inefficiencies from the residual are separated in a different way. DFA assumes that inefficiencies are relatively stable and should persist over time which disentangles them from random errors. The random errors in DFA have the following characteristics: (1) they are momentary and (2) the random errors tend to cancel one another through averaging. DFA estimates the cost or profit function for each period of a panel data set. There are two parts included in the residual which are inefficiency terms and random error term. Due to the assumption that the error term tends to average out over time, the inefficiency of the bank can be estimated by the average of a bank's residuals.

Due to the fact that the distribution of inefficiency or error terms do not have any restrictive assumptions, so, compared to the SFA, the DFA is easier to implement. The reason lies in the fact that the maximum likelihood methods are not required by DFA to estimate the cost or profit function. There are mainly two methods used to estimate the cost or profit function which is generalized least square (GLS), reflected by the work of Schmidt and Sickles (1984). The second method is OLS which is represented by the work of Berger (1993). The difference between average residual and average residual of the firm on the frontier gives the estimate of inefficiency.

There are some disadvantages to DFA. Misleading results can be obtained if the period under examination is too long; the results will also be biased if the inefficiency component of the error term is not constant. The accuracy of the results will also be affected if the random error term is averaged out by an insufficient number of available data years. The appropriate number of years enough to address all the above issues is six, as argued by DeYoung (1997).

3.3.1.3 Thick Frontier Approach

The last parametric method used to measure efficiency is the TFA, which was developed by Berger and Humphrey (1991, 1992). Similar to other parametric frontier approaches, a functional form is specified for the frontier cost function in TFA. The main difference between this method and other parametric methods lies to the fact that a thick frontier is estimated by this approach whereas with regards to other parametric techniques, a frontier edge is used to measure the efficiency. Furthermore, the distributional assumption for cross-sectional data is also avoided by this method. This method is implemented by estimating the cost function. Both the lowest average-cost quartile and the Highest average cost quartile of the firm are estimated. Two groups of efficiencies are represented by firms in these two different quartiles. More specifically, the assumption is that firms in the lowest average-cost quartile have efficiency greater than the average level and they form the thick frontier. On the other hand, firms in the highest average-cost quartile have efficiency lower than the average level. The difference between the two groups of firms with higher than average efficiency and lower than average efficiency represent the inefficiency as well as the exogenous difference in the regression. Random error and luck are assumed to be represented by the error term within each of the frontiers. The difference in the parameters between the upper cost frontier and lower cost frontier is used by TFA to measure cost efficiency, whereas with regards to the exogenous factors, they are estimated by calculating the difference between the lowest cost unction and highest cost function. One disadvantage of TFA lies in the fact that the overall level of efficiency rather than the efficiency of the individual DMU is estimated. TFA may not generate a robust estimate of the overall level of efficiency because the assumption made by this approach does not usually hold.

3.3.2 Non-Parametric Approach

3.3.2.1 Data Envelopment Analysis

The idea of the non-parametric efficiency approach was first originated by Farrell (1957) in his seminal paper. One of the disadvantages of his work lies to the fact that single-output case is considered, whereas it cannot applied to large dataset with multiple inputs and outputs. His work has been significantly extended by Charnes et al. (1978), in which a mathematical programming algorithm was proposed, namely DEA. This method was used to measure the efficiency of a set of DMUs, from which a significant improvement of their work compared to Farrell (1957) lies in the fact that this method can be applied to multiple inputs and outputs and, until now, many research studies use this method to measure efficiency, in particular, in the banking sector.

Two different DEA models are available with regards to the input or output orientation. Input-oriented DEA aims to minimize the amount of input to produce a certain level of output. On the other hand, output-oriented DEA focusses on keeping the same amount of input to maximize the output production. With regards to the choice of orientation, it depends over which aspect the managers have more control. More specifically, Coelli (1998) argued that input-oriented is more appropriate if producers can freely adjust the input usage and are required to meet the market demand, whereas if only a certain amount of resources is available for the firm to maximize the output production, the output-oriented model would be more appropriate. Coelli and Perelman (1999) suggest that there is very minor impact of the choice of input- or output-oriented model on the estimation of the efficiency score.

3.3.2.2 Free Disposal Hull

One non-parametric technique used to measure efficiency is called FDH analysis. The FDH model was firstly proposed by Deprins (1984) and then the model was extended by Tulkens (1993). The FDH analysis relaxes the convexity assumption of basic DEA models. Both DEA and FDH are consistent estimators if the true production set is convex. However, due to the fact that FDH requires fewer assumptions, thus a lower rate of convergency is shown by FDH compared to DEA. On the other hand, if the true production set is not convex, FDH has the ability to estimate the efficiency in a more precise way in comparison to DEA.

Because Both DEA and FDH are non-parametric methods, compared to the parametric method such as SFA; no particular functional form for the boundary is assumed and the measurement error is ignored by the non-parametric method. The boundary of a reconstructed production possibility subset is regarded as the best-practice technology which can be represented by enveloping a set of observations. Berger and Humphrey (1997) argue that the set of production possibilities comprises only the DEA vertices and the FDH points interior to these vertices. One of the assumptions made by the DEA is that linear substitution between observed input combinations on an isoquant is possible, while the observations in piecewise linear form generate the isoquant. In comparison, one of the assumptions made by the FDH is that linear substitution between observed input combinations is impossible. Therefore, the isoquant is more like a step function formed by the intersection of lines drawn from observed Leontief-type input combinations. Thus, compared to DEA frontier, the data are enveloped more tightly in the FDH which has a staircase shape. The relationship between DEA and FDH frontiers can be described as two possible situations: first, the FDH frontier could be congruent with the DEA frontier. The second situation is that the FDH frontier could be interior to the DEA frontier. Tulkens (1993) argues that larger estimates of average efficiency are typically generated by FDH compared to DEA.

3.4 THEORY OF BANK COMPETITION

Similar to other industries, the types of competition in the banking sector can be mainly classified into the following categories: perfect competition, monopolistic competition, oligopoly and monopoly.

The perfect competitive environment in the banking sector has the following characteristics (see Mankiw and Taylor, 2006): (1) there are a large number of banks in the market; (2) banks offer a homogenous product with regards to the cost and attribute of the product; (3) the cost for new banks to enter the market is very low. In a perfectly competitive environment, banks are price-takers rather than price-makers. The price of a product offered by banks will be determined by the industry supply or demand, whereas they have no ability to influence the volumes of demand and supply in the market. Another type of competition is called monopolistic competition. Under this competitive environment, lots of banks are in the market, but unlike perfectly competitive markets, these banks offer differentiated products to customers. The cost of entry to and exit from the banking market is low. Banks have a degree of control over the price of the product offered. In other words, they are price makers rather than price takers to some extent. The third type of competition is called oligopoly. Under this competitive environment, there are a small number of banks in the markets, whereas all of them provide either homogenous or heterogeneous products in the market; the entry or exit to the market is quite expensive. The banks operating in the oligopoly market have power to set the price in the market. The degree of price control by banks in oligopoly is higher than in monopolistic competition. One special characteristic of oligopoly over monopolistic competition and perfect competition is the interdependence among banking firms. The market in the condition of oligopoly is made up of a few large banks; because the size of the banks is very large, their actions will affect the market conditions due to the fact that, in the oligopoly market, few banks are operating and each bank is large enough that its actions will affect market conditions. Thus, other banks will be aware of one bank's action and respond appropriately to keep their competitive position in the market. Finally, the market in the condition of monopoly has only one bank, because this bank is the only firm that provides financial services to the market, there is no competition and this bank has absolute power in setting the price in the market. Furthermore, other potential banks are unable to enter the market. They also have the ability to charge a different price to different markets, ie, they may charge a lower price in a very elastic market to increase the quantity sold, whereas a higher price would be charged to the consumers in a relatively inelastic market to maximize the profit.

3.4.1 Structure–Conduct–Performance (SCP) Theory

The SCP paradigm states that market structure would determine firm conduct which would determine performance. Market structure can be measured by a number of factors, such as the number of competitors in an industry, the heterogeneity of product and the cost of entry and exit. Conduct refers to a number of specific actions taken by a firm, which include price taking, product differentiation, tacit collusion and exploitation of market power. The performance of the firm can be measured from a number of indicators such as productive efficiency, allocative efficiency and profitability.

The range of options and constraints facing a firm is defined by the attributes of the industry within which a firm operates. In some industries with higher competition, very few options are available to the firms and the firms have lots of constraints. Firms in these industries generate maximized social welfare and in the long run, the returns earned by the firms can only cover the cost of capital. In summary, the industry structure determines the firm's conduct and long-run firm performance. On the other hand, the firms operating in a lower competitive industry environment have a greater range of conduct options and the number of constraints faced by the firms is limited. Firms can make use of the available options to obtain the competitive advantage. For instance, the firms in these industries can use market power to set prices that generate significant economic value.

Figure 3.5 The structure–conduct–performance (SCP) model. *(Own illustration.)*

However, the sustainability of their advantages is determined by one of the attributes of industry—structure barriers to entry. If there are no barriers to entry, the competitive advantages of the firms in the industry will disappear when new competitors enter the market. Therefore, industry structure has an important effect on firm conduct and performance even though firms in these industries can sometimes have competitive advantages (Barney and Clark, 2007). The SCP model is summarized in Fig. 3.5.

3.4.2 Lerner Index

The Lerner index was developed in 1934 by the American economist, Abba Lerner. The Lerner index is defined as the difference between price and marginal cost, divided by price and it can be specified as $LI_{it} = (P_{it} - MC_{it})/P_{it}$, in which P is the price of banking outputs, MC represents the margin cost, whereas i and t represent the specific bank at specific year. The value of Lerner index ranges from a minimum of zero to a maximum of one. When $P = MC$, the Lerner index is zero, which indicates that the firm has no pricing power. As the value of Lerner index increases, the difference between price and marginal cost becomes bigger which indicates that banks have higher market power (Ariss, 2010). In other words, $LI = 0$ indicates that there is perfect competition, whereas $LI = 1$ means the market is in a condition of monopoly.

Casu and Girardone (2009) argue that the Lerner index of monopoly power measures the degree of market power very well and is a good and widely used indicator in measuring competition in banking literature. It represents the extent to which banks have the market power to set their price above the marginal cost (Berger et al., 2009). A similar opinion is held by Demirguc-Kunt and Peria (2010) who suggest that computing direct measures of market power is an alternative way to examine the competitive condition in the banking industry and the Lerner index, defined as the difference between price and marginal cost (relative to price), is frequently used in the banking sector. Lerner (1934) argues that market power is determined by demand elasticity, and the Lerner index provides a number which links with the demand–price elasticity (inverse relationship). Rojas (2011) suggests that the Lerner index is popular due to the fact that it shows the firm's market power location between perfect competition and monopoly; it also reflects the role that demand elasticity plays in determining a firm's mark-up. Compared to the traditional concentration ratio, the Lerner index provides a more accurate measurement of bank market power. The advantage of the Lerner index over the Panzar–Rosse H-statistic (which will be discussed later) lies in the fact that the former is not a long-run equilibrium measure of competition and can be calculated at each point in time (Demirguc-Kunt and Peria, 2010).

There are also some arguments relating to the disadvantages of the Lerner index. Fernandez de Guevara et al. (2005) argue that there are several problems with regards to the estimation of the Lerner index. First, the value of the Lerner index changes according to different revenues used by the study. Frequently, only interest revenue and costs are considered, whereas other non-interest revenues and expenses are omitted. The consideration of traditional loan–deposit services as the revenue ignores the banking activities of providing other services which have grown substantially during recent years. This will lead to an inaccurate result regarding the competitive condition in the banking sector. Second, the cost of risk, which is very important in the profit and loss account of a banking system, is not considered in general practice. The ignorance of the cost of risk can be attributed to reasons such as insufficient data and calculation difficulties. If the cost of risk in not included in the estimation of cost function, it will lead to a wrong interpretation of the Lerner index because the margin is overestimated. Third, Bikker et al. (2007) argue that the weakness of the Lerner index is attributed to the fact that the prices and costs required to calculate the index are not clearly identified by the available bank balance-sheet data, so that prices and costs can be proxied by many debatable choices.

3.4.3 Panzar and Rosse (1987) H-Statistic

An empirical test is developed by John C. Panzar and James N. Rosse to discriminate between monopoly, oligopolistic, monopolistically competitive and perfectly competitive markets. They have provided a concise indicator (the so-called H-statistic), which is based on the static properties of reduced-form revenue equation. The H-statistic can be interpreted as a continuous and increasing measure of the overall level of competition in a specific market. This method makes the assumption that different pricing strategies will be employed in reaction to changes in input costs. In other words, market power is measured by the extent to which changes in factor prices (unit price of funds, capital and labour) are reflected in revenue.

The H-statistic ranges from minus infinity to unity (see Table 3.1). A negative H arises when the competitive structure is a monopoly, a perfect colluding oligopoly or a conjectural variation of short-run oligopoly. In all the cases, an increase in input prices will translate into higher marginal costs, a reduction of equilibrium output and, subsequently, a fall in total revenue (Vesala, 1995). If H lies between zero and unity, the market structure is characterized by monopolistic competition. Under monopolistic competition, potential entry leads to contestable market equilibrium and revenue increases less than proportionally to the changes in input prices, as the demand facing individual banks for banking products is inelastic (Triole, 1987). Under perfect competition, the H-statistic equals unity. In this particular situation, a proportional increase in factor input prices raises both marginal and average costs and induces an equi-proportional change in revenues without distorting the optimal output of any firm. The H-statistic would also equal to one if a contestable market exists. Baumol et al. (1982), who put forward the contestability theory, argue that under very restrictive circumstances, such as free entry to and exit from the market and higher price elastic demand for industry's output, the competition in a highly concentrated market still exists. Due to the existence of these features, larger firms in the market need to take competitive measures to price their outputs.

One assumption of PR H-statistic is that the test can only be applied to firms which produce a single output. Therefore, banks are regarded as providers of traditional loan–deposit services as well as non-traditional

Table 3.1 Discriminatory power of H-statistic

Estimated value of H	Competitive environment	Market equilibrium
$H \leq 0$	• Monopolistic market behaviour • Conjectural variation short-run oligopoly	$H = 0$: Equilibrium $H \neq 0$: Disequilibrium
$0 \leq H < 1$	• Monopolistic competition	
$H = 1$	• Natural monopoly in a perfectly contestable market • Perfect competition	

activities using factor inputs, such as labour, funds and capital. In other words, all the activities should be considered to estimate the competitive condition of the specific market. Nevertheless, supposing the above assumption is omitted, the competitive conditions of separate segments cannot be analysed due to the fact that there are no detailed data available for the estimation of the reduced-form revenue equations.

The advantages of using PR H-statistic to measure the competition are: (1) It works well with firm-specific data on revenues and factor prices; (2) it does not require information about equilibrium output prices and quantities for the firm and/or industry; (3) this method can generate concise competitive condition if the sample size is small (Matthews et al., 2007). Due to the fact that H-statistic was developed on the basis of a static model, there are no predictions on the H-value which is one of the weaknesses of this test. In addition, the overall market equilibrium required by the test cannot be fulfilled because of market entry and exit, which leads to further limits on the interpretation of such analysis.

Due to the fact that the H-statistic is a static approach, one characteristic of the implementation is that the test needs to be undertaken on observations that are in long-run equilibrium. In other words, in the equilibrium test, the dependent variable will be replaced by the profitability measure, such as return on assets (ROA) or return on equity (ROE) rather than the revenues. In equilibrium, the resulting H-statistic will be significantly equal to zero. However, the significant and negative H-statistic indicates that the test is not in long-run equilibrium. The purpose of the test is to justify on the ground that competitive markets will equalize risk-adjusted return across firms such that, in equilibrium, rate of return should not be correlated with factor input prices.

3.4.4 Boone Indicator

Nowadays, a growing number of studies in the literature use the Boone (2008) indicator to measure banking-sector competition. This indicator is based on the efficiency hypothesis which was proposed by Demsetz (1973). The efficiency hypothesis argues that the growth of efficient firms leads to improvement in industry performance. In other words, the hypothesis emphasizes the relationship between efficiency and performance. This indicator is based on the assumption that efficiency leads to improvement in performance. This hypothesis mainly argues that banks with higher efficiency have higher levels of performance in the form of higher profit and then have higher ability to attract a larger number of market shares. The theory/assumption of the Boone indicator is in line with the studies by Stiorh (2000) and Stiroh and Straham (2003) who suggest that a large proportion of assets will be transformed from banks with lower profit to the ones with higher profit due to the increase in competition.

The basic idea under the Boone indicator argues that stronger competition leads to the reallocation of assets. A number of reasons explain the increase in competition such as increase in the number of banks providing banking services or a higher degree of aggressive interaction between banks under the condition that individual banks have a certain level of efficiency. The industry with a higher degree of competition will make the profit of the higher-efficiency bank increase at the expense of banks with lower levels of efficiency. Schaeck and Cihak (2010) argue that there are a number of advantages of the Boone indicator compared to other competition indicators such as Panzar and Rosse (1987) H-Statistic and the Lerner index. More specifically, compared to the PR H-statistic which requires one to identify a situation from the statistic, the Boone indicator is monotonically related to competition. Xu et al. (2013) argue that the Boone indicator will provide robust results under binding interest-rate regulations. Finally, the Boone indicator has an additional advantage for studies on developing countries. This indicator only requires information on profit and cost, and the computation of the Boone indicator does not require information on prices (Leon, 2014). A number of studies use the Boone indicator to measure competition in banking markets (van Leuvensteijn et al., 2007; Maslovych, 2009; Schaeck and Cihak, 2010; among others). However, Leon (2015) argues that the Boone indicator is still a young tool and, therefore, has not been thoroughly scrutinized by the literature.

3.5 SUMMARY AND CONCLUSION

Efficiency, as one important measure of performance, has received greater attention from government, companies as well as academic researchers. Both the government and company management try to use different ways to improve efficiency and further promote performance. Efficiency can be measured from different perspectives. More specifically, technical efficiency mainly focusses on volume of production investment and output. In other words, technical efficiency mainly concentrates on using a certain amount of input to maximize output production or producing a certain volume of output using fewer numbers of inputs. In firm operation in daily life, not only does the volume of investment and output concern the managers, but more importantly, is how efficiently the firm controls the cost. In other words, how to use a certain amount of inputs to minimize cost is the goal which needs to be achieved within the firm. It is well known that controlling cost as efficiently as possible is not the final step for the company; the company must aim to maximize the revenue and more importantly the profit. Thus, how efficiently a company uses input resources to generate profit attracts the greatest attention from the public. This chapter explains the theories from technical, cost, revenue and profit perspectives, thus systematically discussing the theories of technical, cost, revenueand profit efficiencies.

Not only the theories of efficiency being discussed, this chapter also explains two mainly streams of methods used to measure efficiency which are parametric method as well as non-parametric method. To be more specific, three parametric approaches are discussed in the chapter which include SFA, DFA as well as TFA, on the other hand, there are mainly two non-parametric approaches being discussed in the chapter, which are DEA and FDH. Not only are specific methods explained in this chapter, but also the different methods are compared.

After the discussion about the theory and measures of efficiency, this chapter systematically explains the theories of bank competition. Starting from the traditional structure—conduct—performance hypothesis, which mainly uses the concentration ratio or Herfindal—Hirschman index as a competition indicator. After the discussion of the concentration ratio, the chapter further discusses the Lerner index competition indicator. The advantages of this indicator lie in the fact that it not only measures competitive conditions, but, more importantly, it reflects the market power of banks. Then the chapter discusses the Panzar-Rosse H statistic. Finally, the chapter discusses the Boone competition indicator. One characteristic of Boone compared to the other competition indicators lies in the fact that this indicator can measure the competition of different banking markets, ie, loan market, deposit market and non-interest income market. This indicator is the newest competition indicator used in academic research today.

Through the systematic explanation and discussion of the theories of efficiency and competition, not only can we have a clear and better understanding of efficiency and competition, but provide a basis for our analysis and discussion in future chapters.

REFERENCES

Aigner, D., Lovell, C.A.K., Schmidt, P., 1977. Formation and estimation of stochastic frontier production function models. Journal of Econometrics 6 (1), 21–37.

Ariss, R.T., 2010. On the implications of market power in banking: evidence from developing countries. Journal of Banking and Finance 34, 765–775.

Barney, J.B., Clark, D.N., 2007. Resource-Based Theory: Creating and Sustaining Competitive Advantage. Oxford University Press, Oxford.

Battese, G.E., Coelli, T.J., 1995. A model for technical inefficiency effects in a stochastic frontiers production function for panel data. Empirical Economics 20 (2), 325–332.

Battese, G.E., Corra, G.S., 1977. Estimation of a production frontier model: with applications to the pastoral zone of eastern Australia. Australian Journal of Agricultural Economics 21 (3), 169–179.

Baumol, W.J., Panzar, J.C., Willig, R.D., 1982. Contestable Markets and the Theory of Industry Structure. Harcourt Brace Jovanovich, San Diego, CA.

Berger, A.N., DeYoung, R., 1977. Problem loans and cost efficiency in commercial banks. Journal of Banking and Finance 21 (6), 849–870.

Berger, A.N., Humphrey, D.B., 1991. The dominance of inefficiencies over scale and product mix economies in banking. Journal of Monetary Economics 28 (1), 117–148.

Berger, A.N., Humphrey, D.B., 1992. Measurement and efficiency issues in commercial banking. In: Griliches, Z. (Ed.), Output Measurement in the Service Sectors. University of Chicago Press, Chicago and London, pp. 245–279.

Berger, A.N., Humphrey, D.B., 1997. Efficiency of financial institutions: international survey and directions for future research. European Journal of Operational Research 98, 175–212.

Berger, A.N., Klapper, L.F., Turk-Ariss, R., 2009. Bank competition and financial stability. Journal of Financial Services Research 35, 99–118.

Berger, A.N., Mester, L.J., 1997. Inside the black box: what explains differences in the efficiencies of financial institutions. Journal of Banking and Finance, 21, 895–947.

Berger, A.N., 1993. Distribution free estimates of efficiency of the US banking industry and tests of the standard distributional assumptions. Journal of Productivity Analysis 4 (3), 261–292.

Bikker, J.A., Spierdijk, L., Finnie, P., 2007. The Impact of Market Structure, Contestability and Institutional Environment on Bank Competition. DNB working paper No. 156.

Boone, J., 2008. A new way to measure competition. Economic Journal 118, 1245–1261.

Casu, B., Girardone, C., 2009. Testing the relationship between competition and efficiency in banking: a panel data analysis. Economics Letters 105, 134–137.

Charnes, A., Cooper, W.W., Rhodes, E., 1978. Measuring the efficiency of decision making units. European Journal of Operational Research 2 (6), 429–444.

Charnes, A., Cooper, W.W., Lewin, A.Y., Seiford, L.M., 1995. Data Envelopment Analysis: Theory, Methodology and Applications. Kluwer, Boston.

Coelli, T., Perelman, S., 1999. A comparison of parametric and non-parametric distance functions: with application to European Railways. European Journal of Operational Research 117 (2), 326–339.

Coelli, T.J., 1995. Estimators and hypothesis tests for a stochastic frontier function: a Monte Carlo analysis. Journal of Productivity Analysis 6 (3), 247–268.

Coelli, T., 1996. A Guide to DEAP Version 2.1: A Data Envelopment Analysis (Computer) Program. CEPA working paper, 1996/08.

Coelli, T., 1998. A multi-stage methodology for the solution of oriented DEA models. Operations Research Letters 23 (3–5), 143–149.

Debreu, G., 1951. The coefficient of resource utilization. Econometrica 19, 273–292.

Demirguc-Kunt, A., Peria, M.S.M., 2010. A Framework for Analysing Competition in the Banking Sector: An Application to the Case of Jordan. Policy Research working paper No. 5499, 1–24.
Demsetz, H., 1973. Industry structure, market rivalry and public policy. Journal of Law and Economics 16, 1–9.
Deprins, D., Simar, L., Tulkens, H., 1984. Measuring labour efficiency in post offices. In: Marchand, M., Pestieau, P., Tulkens, H. (Eds.), The Performance of Public Enterprises: Concepts and Measurement. North-Holland, Amsterdam.
DeYoung, R., 1997. A diagnostic test for the distribution fee efficiency estimator: an example using US commercial bank data. European Journal of Operational Research 98 (2), 243–249.
Farrell, M.J., 1957. The measurement of productive efficiency. Journal of the Royal Statistical Society 120, 253–290.
Fernandez de Guevara, J., Maudos, J., Perez, F., 2005. Market power in European banking. Journal of Financial Services Research 27, 109–137.
Fried, H.O., Lovell, C.A.K., Schmidt, S.S., 1993. The Measurement of Productive Efficiency: Techniques and Application. Oxford University Press, New York.
Greene, W.H., 1990. A gamma-distributional stochastic frontier model. Journal of Econometrics 46 (1–2), 141–163.
Jondrow, J., Knox Lovell, C.A., Materor, I.S., Schmidt, P., 1982. On the estimation of technical inefficiency in the stochastic frontier production function model. Journal of Econometrics 19 (2–3), 233–238.
Koopmans, T.C., 1951. An analysis of production as an efficient combination of activities. In: Koopmans, T.C. (Ed.), Activity Analysis of Production and Allocation. Wiley, New York.
Kumar, S., Gulati, R., 2013. Regulation and Efficiency of Indian Banks. Springer, India.
Leon, F., 2014. Measuring competition in banking: a critical review of methods. Series etudes et documents du CERDI, 12, 1–14.
Leon, F., 2015. Measuring Competition in Banking: A Critical Review of Methods. Working paper, Halshs No. 01015794.
Lerner, A.P., 1934. The concept of monopoly and the measurement of monopoly power. The Review of Economic Studies 1, 157–175.
Mankiw, N.G., Taylor, M., 2006. Economics. Cengage Learning EMEA, London.
Maslovych, M., 2009. The Boone Indicator as a Measure of Competition in the Banking Sector: The Case of Ukraine. Kier School of Economics (MA thesis).
Matthews, K., Murinde, V., Zhao, T., 2007. Competitive conditions among the major British Banks. Journal of Banking and Finance 31, 2025–2042.
Meeusen, W., Van Den Broeck, J., 1977. Efficiency estimation from Cobb-Douglas production functions with composed error. International Economic Review 18 (2), 435–444.
Mester, L.J., 1993. Efficiency in the savings and loan industry. Journal of Banking and Finance 17 (2–3), 267–286.
Olesen, J.A., Schmidt, P., Waldman, D.M., 1980. A monte carlo study of estimators of stochastic frontier production function. Journal of Econometrics 13 (1), 67–82.
Panzar, J.C., Rosse, J.N., 1987. Testing for monopoly equilibrium. Journal of Industrial Economics 35, 443–456.
Rojas, C., 2011. Market power and the lerner index: a classroom experiment. Journal of Industrial Organization Education 5, 1–19.
Schaeck, K., Cihak, M., 2010. Competition, Efficiency and Soundness in Banking: An Industrial Organization Perspective. European Banking Center discussion paper No. 2010–20.
Schimidt, P., Sickles, R.C., 1984. Production frontiers and panel data. Journal of Business and Economic Statistics 2 (4), 367–374.

Seiford, L.M., Thrall, R.M., 1990. Recent development in DEA: the mathematical programming approach to frontier analysis. Journal of Econometrics 46, 7–38.
Stevenson, R.E., 1980. Likelihood functions for generalised stochastic frontier estimation. Journal of Econometrics 13 (1), 57–66.
Stiroh, K.J., Strahan, P.E., 2003. Competitive dynamics of deregulation: evidence from US banking. Journal of Money, Credit and Banking 35, 801–828.
Stiroh, K.J., 2000. Compositional Dynamics and the Performance of the US Banking Industry. Federal Reserve Bank of New York staff report, No. 98.
Triole, J., 1987. The Theory of Industrial Organization. MIT press, Cambridge.
Tulkens, H., 1993. On FDH efficiency analsysis: some methodological issues and applications to retail banking: courts and urban transit. Journal of Productivity Analysis 4, 183–210.
Van Leuvensteijn, M., Bikker, J.A., van Rixtel, A.A.R.J.M., Kok Sorensen, C., 2007. A New Approach to Measuring Competition in the Loan Markets of the Euro Area. European Central Bank working paper No. 768.
Vesala, J., 1995. Testing for Competition in Banking: Behavioural Evidence From Finland. Bank of Finland Studies, p. E1.
Xu, B., van Rixtel, A., van Leuvensteijn, M., 2013. Measuring Bank Competition in China: A Comparison of New Versus Conventional Approaches Applied to Loan Markets. BIS working paper, 422, pp. 1–68.

CHAPTER 4

Literature Review on Bank Efficiency and Bank Competition

4.1 INTRODUCTION

As one of several important performance indicators, a number of industries including the banking sector have focused on efficiency. In particular, a growing number of studies in the empirical literature have investigated the efficiency of banking sectors in the United States, Europe, as well as emerging-market economies. In the Chinese banking industry, most empirical studies show that the efficiency of state-owned commercial banks is quite low. Relatively few articles evaluate the competitive condition in the Chinese banking industry, as their results show that Chinese banking industry is operated under conditions of perfect competition, monopolistic competition, or oligopoly.

In this chapter, comprehensive studies investigating the efficiency of banking sectors are reviewed including efficiency estimation in international studies, single-country studies, as well as studies investigating efficiency in the Chinese banking sector. The second part of this chapter focuses on reviewing the empirical literature on banking sector competition. This part will first discuss relevant theories and measurement of bank competition followed by empirical literature on evaluating the competitive condition in the Chinese banking industry and internationally. This chapter not only reviews the empirical literature on bank efficiency and competition but also discussed, the theory regarding the impact of competition on efficiency, including the competition-efficiency and competition-inefficiency hypotheses which are followed by reviewing relevant studies investigating this relationship in the banking sector. Finally, the summary and conclusion is provided for this whole chapter.

4.2 LITERATURE REVIEW ON BANK EFFICIENCY

4.2.1 International Studies on Bank Efficiency

Using a sample of 2095 commercial banks in 105 countries over the period 1998–2003, Lensink et al. (2008) investigated the relationship between

ISBN 978-0-08-100074-8

bank efficiency and foreign ownership. The efficiency was derived from a stochastic translog function. The results show that foreign ownership negatively affects bank efficiency. The findings further report that the negative impact of foreign ownership on bank efficiency is less pronounced in countries with good governance and higher quality of home-country institutions and higher similarity between home- and host-country institutional quality reduces foreign bank inefficiency.

Lozano-Vivas and Pasiouras (2010) used a sample of 752 publicly quoted commercial banks from 87 countries to test the effect of nontraditional activities on the estimation of bank efficiency. Both cost and profit efficiencies were estimated by using a traditional function which considered loans and other earning assets as the only outputs, as well as a nontraditional function that accounts for nontraditional activities (off-balance-sheet item or noninterest income as an additional output). The results show that cost efficiency increases when nontraditional activities are considered, whereas regulation that restricts bank activities and enhances monitoring and supervision provisions improves both cost and profit efficiency.

Using eight emerging Asian countries over the period 1998—2008, Sun and Chang (2011) tested the impact of risk on efficiency in the banking sector. Three types of risk were measured, credit risk, operational risk, and market risk, whereas the efficiency was derived from the translog form of a cost function. Both the overall effect and the marginal effect of risk on efficiency were investigated; the findings suggest that risk has a significant effect on the level of variability of bank efficiency.

Using a panel data set covering the period 1985—2010 for banks from Argentina, Brazil, Chile, and Mexico, Goddard et al. (2014) examined the cost efficiency for banking sectors in Latin America; the recently developed random-parameter models for stochastic frontier analysis were applied. Their findings suggest that incorrectly parameterized cost functions affect the accuracy of inefficiencies, whereas compared to fixed or random effects, the random-parameter stochastic frontier models yield higher mean cost efficiencies. Finally, they conclude that in Latin America banking industries, efficiency improves in the 2000s before modestly reversing after the 2007 crisis.

Using data of 3886 commercial banks from 78 countries over the period from 2000 to 2006, Gaganis and Pasiouras (2013) investigated the impacts of the central bank's involvement in financial supervision, the unification of financial authorities, and the independence of the central bank on bank profit efficiency. A multiproduct translog specification was used to derive the profit efficiency. The empirical results show that efficiency decreases as the number of financial sectors that are supervised by the central bank increases. Furthermore, it is found that banks operating in countries with greater unification of supervisory authorities are less profit efficient. Finally, bank profit efficiency is significantly and negatively affected by central bank independence.

Chortareas et al. (2012) used the Data Envelopment Analysis (DEA) technique to estimate the efficiency for a sample of banks from 22 EU countries over 2000–08. In the second stage, they further examined the impact of key regulatory and supervisory policies on bank efficiency. Under truncated regression as well as a fractional logit estimator, the results show that strengthening capital restrictions and official supervisory powers can improve the bank efficiency, whereas the levels of bank efficiency can also be improved by enhancing private sector monitoring and restricting bank activities.

Using a large sample of commercial banks operating in 27 EU member states over the 2000s, Chortareas et al. (2013) investigated the link between the financial freedom and bank efficiency levels. Bank-specific efficiency scores were estimated using DEA, whereas a truncated regression model combined with bootstrapped confidence intervals was developed to test the relationship. The empirical findings suggest that the higher the degree of an economy's financial freedom, the higher the benefits for banks in terms of cost advantages and overall efficiency. The results also show that the effects of financial freedom on bank efficiency tend to be more pronounced in countries with freer political systems in which governments formulate and implement sound policies and higher-quality governance.

Using an unbalanced panel data set of 4050 banks, with observations in 72 countries over the period 1999–2007, Barth et al. (2013) examined the impacts of bank regulation, supervision, and monitoring on bank operating efficiency using DEA to derive the efficiency. The empirical results find that tighter restrictions on bank activities are negatively associated with bank efficiency, whereas greater capital regulation stringency is marginally and positively associated with bank efficiency. In addition, the results show that strengthening official supervisory power is positively associated with bank efficiency only in countries with independent supervisory authorities, whereas independence coupled with a more experienced supervisory authority tends to improve bank efficiency. Finally, it is found that bank efficiency is significantly and positively affected by financial transparency.

Using 510 banks across 22 countries over the period 1995–2009, Beck et al. (2013a) compared the business model, efficiency, asset quality, and stability between Islamic and conventional banks. The business model was measured by fee income, nondeposit funding, and loan/deposit ratio; efficiency was measured by cost/income ratio, overheads, and loss reserve; asset quality was measured by loan loss provisions, nonperforming loans, and maturity match, whereas *Z*-score, return on assets, as well as equity/assets ratio were used to measure stability. The findings show that Islamic banks are less cost-effective but they have higher intermediation ratio, better asset quality, and higher levels of capitalization. The results report that stock performance of listed Islamic banks during the recent crisis is due to higher levels of capitalization and better asset quality.

4.2.2 Bank Efficiency Studies on Single Countries

Rossi et al. (2009) tested the impact of diversification of banks across size and industry on risk, cost, and profit efficiencies and bank capitalization. The efficiency estimates were obtained by employing a stochastic frontier approach, whereas the robustness of the results was cross-checked by a thick frontier approach as well as a distribution-free approach. The findings show that diversification has a negative impact on cost efficiency, whereas this impact is significant and positive for profit efficiency; it is further found that diversification reduces banks' risk and increases the banks' levels of capitalization.

Interesting research was undertaken by Kauko (2009). The author used a sample of 309 Finnish saving and cooperative banks over the period 1999–2004 to test the impact of managers on efficiency. The efficiency was derived from a stochastic frontier approach. The findings show that manager age and education have strong effects on efficiency. More specifically, the results show that the impact of age on efficiency depends on education; educational background is less important for young managers than for mature ones. Retirement causes an efficiency improvement and mature managers outperform their younger colleagues.

Hsiao et al. (2010) investigated the impact of a first financial restructuring on the operating efficiency for a sample of 40 Taiwanese commercial banks over the period 2000–05. The efficiency was estimated by DEA. The findings show that banks have lower operating efficiency on average during the reform period (2002–03) compared to the prereform period (2000–01); improved operating efficiency is reflected in the postreform period (2004–05). The results are robust when controlling for nonperforming loan ratio, capital adequacy ratio, bank ownership, size, and gross domestic product growth rate. The results suggest that the improved efficiency in the postreform period is attributed to enhanced banking- and risk-management practices and compliance with the first financial restructuring.

Using an innovative methodological approach introduced by Barros et al. (2012), namely the weighted Russell directional distance model, Fujii et al. (2014) examined the technical efficiency and productivity growth in the Indian banking sector over the period 2004–11. Their findings show that the inefficiency levels are significantly different among different types of bank ownership in India. It is further suggested that foreign banks have strong market position, and they pull the production frontier in a more efficient direction. Furthermore, the findings suggest that state public banks and domestic private banks have higher inefficiency.

Using the Greek banking industry over the period 2007–11, Halkos and Tzeremes (2013) employed a bootstrapped data envelopment analysis to investigate the degree of operating efficiency gains of 45 possible bank mergers and acquisitions. The results show that a year before and a year after the initiation of the Greek fiscal crisis, the majority of the potential bank mergers and acquisitions under examination were unable to generate short-run efficiency gains. Furthermore, the findings show that the majority of bank mergers and acquisitions led to short-run operating efficiency gains in 2011. Finally, it is found that the efficiency is not significantly improved when the mergers and acquisitions are conducted between efficient banks.

4.2.2.1 Literature Review on Bank Efficiency in China

Few empirical studies have investigated efficiency in the Chinese banking sector. Ariff and Can (2008) used the nonparametric approach to examine the cost and profit efficiencies of 28 Chinese commercial banks over the period 1995–2004. The results show that joint-stock commercial banks (JSCBs) are more efficient than state-owned commercial banks (SOCBs). The findings also suggest that the efficiency of Chinese commercial banks can be improved by speedier reform to open the banking market and improving risk management.

Fu and Heffernan (2008) used a stochastic frontier approach to investigate the cost X-efficiency of Chinese commercial banks during the period 1985–2002. The findings suggest that JSCBs are more X-efficient than SOCBs, whereas increased privatization, greater foreign bank participation, and liberalized interest rate are helpful in improving the efficiency of Chinese commercial banks.

Berger et al. (2009) used a stochastic frontier approach to test the cost and profit efficiencies for a sample of Chinese commercial banks with different ownership over the period 1994–2003. The empirical results show that the efficiency of Chinese commercial banks can be improved by reducing state-ownership and increasing foreign participation, whereas they further suggest that the big four SOCBs have the lowest efficiency because of the large volumes of nonperforming loans, whereas foreign banks have higher efficiency.

Yao and Jiang (2010) employed a one-stop stochastic frontier approach to evaluate the cost and profit efficiencies of Chinese commercial banks over the period 1995–2008. The findings show that both profit and cost efficiencies have improved over the examined period, whereas the efficiency of SOCBs is lower than JSCBs and city commercial banks. They finally argue that foreign ownership participation negatively affect the profit efficiency in the long run, whereas the profit efficiency in the short run can be improved by initial public offerings.

Lin et al. (2009) used a stochastic frontier approach to investigate the technical efficiency of a sample of Chinese commercial banks during 1997–2006. The results show that compared to SOCBs and JSCBs, Chinese city commercial banks have the highest efficiency. The findings further show that after China entered the WTO, the technical efficiency of Chinese commercial banks improved significantly.

Sufian and Habibullah (2011) assessed the impact of economic globalization on technical efficiency of Chinese banking sector over the period 2000–07. The findings suggest that scale efficiency contributes more than does pure technical efficiency to the overall efficiency of Chinese commercial banks. They further argue that the efficiency of Chinese commercial banks is significantly and positively affected by trade flows, culture proximity, and political globalization; however, more liberalized restrictions of capital accounts leads to a decline in efficiency of Chinese commercial banks.

Sufian and Majid (2009) used a DEA windows analysis to examine the technical efficiency of Chinese commercial banks over the period 1997–2006. Their study focused on the investigation of the relationship between efficiency and share-price performance. The empirical results suggest that large Chinese commercial banks have higher technical and pure technical efficiencies than medium and small banks, whereas medium banks have higher scale efficiency. Their results indicate that a significant and positive relationship exists between share-price performance and Chinese bank efficiency scores.

Using a nonparametric DEA method, Sufian (2009) tested the impact of nontraditional activities on technical, pure technical, and scale efficiencies for a sample of Chinese SOCBs and JSCBs over the period 2000–05. The empirical findings suggest that the improvement in scale efficiency contributes to the overall technical efficiency enhancement of SOCBs when nontraditional activities are considered, whereas higher technical efficiency of JSCBs is attributed to the improvement in pure technical efficiency.

Laurenceson and Zhao (2008) used a DEA to investigate the efficiency levels of 11 Chinese commercial banks over the period 2003–07. The empirical findings suggest that the differences in efficiency levels are quite small among the banks examined, whereas few of China's major banks have lower efficiency, and the efficiency levels certainly do lag in China's less-prominent banks.

Kumbhakar and Wang (2007) used an input distance function to examine the effect of banking reforms on technical efficiency and total factor productivity change in Chinese banking industry over the period 1993–2002. The findings show that JSCBs have higher efficiency than SOCBs, and the productivity growth of SOCBs is lower than JSCBs.

Yao et al. (2008) used DEA approach and Malmquist productivity index to examine the technical efficiency and productivity for a sample of Chinese commercial banks during 1998–2005. The empirical results suggest that two SOCBs, namely, China Construction Bank and Bank of China, are more technically efficient than other SOCBs and JSCBs. They further report that over the examined period Chinese banking sector experienced 6.5% productivity growth per year. The findings suggest that the efficiency improvement contributes to the productivity growth of SOCBs, whereas the productivity growth of JSCBs is attributed to technological progress.

Hu et al. (2009) employed a four-stage DEA to test the operational environmental-adjusted efficiency of 11 Chinese national banks during 1995–2004. The empirical findings suggest that ownership reform is helpful in increasing SOCBs' efficiency.

Jiang et al. (2009) employed a stochastic distance function to test the bank technical efficiency, and the static selection and dynamic governance effects on bank efficiency were differentiated during 1995–2005. The empirical findings suggest that foreign acquisition leads to efficiency gains of domestic commercial banks, whereas public listing has a significant and positive influence on the efficiency of Chinese commercial banks in the short term.

Using a three-stage least square estimator, Tan and Floros (2013a) investigated technical efficiency/productivity for a sample of Chinese commercial banks over the period 2003–09. Their study focused on examining the interrelationships between technical efficiency/productivity, risk, and capitalization of Chinese commercial banks. Their findings suggest that a significant and negative relationship exists between risk and capitalization, whereas a significant and positive relationship exists between risk and technical efficiency of Chinese commercial banks. In addition, their results show that banks with larger total assets have higher technical efficiency; however, higher bank liquidity leads to lower technical efficiency of Chinese commercial banks. They further argue that technical efficiency of Chinese commercial banks is lower in a higher concentrated banking market. Finally, their findings suggest that Chinese commercial banks have higher productivity growth during the periods of economic boom.

Sufian and Habibullah (2011) investigated the impact of economic freedom on bank efficiency using a sample of Chinese commercial banks under a DEA. The empirical results suggest that the inefficiency of Chinese commercial banks is attributed to scale rather than pure technical inefficiency. They further argued that the impact of business freedom on bank efficiency is significant and positive, indicating that more freedom provided to entrepreneurs to start businesses improves the efficiency of Chinese commercial banks. The efficiency of Chinese commercial banks is significantly and positively affected by monetary freedom, suggesting that a stable and reliable monetary policy for the business environment is very important. Finally, the findings report that financial freedom negatively and significantly affects the efficiency of Chinese commercial banks, implying that more financial freedom improves Chinese bank efficiency.

Luo and Yao (2010) examined the impact of initial public offerings on efficiency for 14 listed Chinese banks over the period 1999–2008 under a DEA. The empirical findings suggest that, on average, the efficiency of Chinese commercial banks increases by almost 5% after listing. Over the examined period, although JSCBs have better performance than SOCBs, the latter manages to catch up and reduce the efficiency gap with the former over a few years.

Zhang et al. (2012) studied the total factor productivity and the impact of market development on profit efficiency for 150 Chinese commercial banks over the period 1999–2008. Under an output-oriented stochastic distance function approach, the empirical findings show that the improvements in technical efficiency and technical change contribute to the productivity growth of Chinese commercial banks. Furthermore, a number of market development variables such as the proportion of nonstate business, level of government intervention in the market, competition in the financial industry, and competition in credit allocation significantly affect the efficiency of Chinese commercial banks.

Matthews and Zhang (2010) examined the productivity growth of nationwide banks of China and a sample of city commercial banks over the period 1997–2007. The total factor productivity growth was estimated under a bootstrap method and the productivity growth of SOCBs is compared with JSCBs and city commercial banks. The empirical findings suggest that total factor productivity growth for the SOCBs and JSCBs has been neutral over the examined period, whereas it is positive for the city commercial banks for the second part of the period (2003–07). The results report that cost reductions lead to efficiency gains, whereas technical innovation is closely linked with greater diversification of revenue away from interest earnings. Finally, the findings show that the opening up of the banking market did not lead to improvement in bank productivity growth.

Using a stochastic frontier analysis, Yin et al. (2013) investigated the efficiency for a sample of Chinese commercial banks over the period 1999–2010. The empirical findings show that Chinese commercial banks are about 18% more efficient in generating lending assets than profits. The results further report that an upward trend of bank efficiency has occurred since China entered the WTO in 2001. They argue that significant improvement in bank efficiency is found for the largest banks with substantial state ownership, whereas the majority of state-owned banks have the lowest efficiency. Higher efficiency of Chinese commercial banks is found for the ones with higher levels of capitalization, whereas bank efficiency decreases as the size of the bank becomes smaller; however, efficiency is gained through economies of scale when a bank increases its size. Finally, it is reported that efficiency is negatively and significantly affected by the fee-generating business, and Chinese banks with better management have higher efficiency.

Sun et al. (2013) used 72 Chinese city commercial banks over the period 2002–09 to investigate the effect of strategic investors on bank efficiency. "The profit efficiency was estimated using translog function form for the profit function". Their results show that strategic investors significantly increase the efficiency of Chinese city commercial banks, whereas the effect of strategic investors on the efficiency of Chinese city commercial banks is negatively correlated to the level of regional economic development.

Pessarossi and Weill (2015) used both SFA and DEA to derive the cost efficiency for a sample of Chinese commercial banks over the period 2004–08, and then they further tested the impact of capital requirement on bank efficiency in the second stage. The findings show that higher capital requirement improves the levels of efficiency of Chinese commercial banks, whereas the size of this impact is closely linked to the bank ownership type.

Using a sample of Chinese commercial banks over the period 1995–2010, Jiang et al. (2013) tested the static effect of ownership and dynamic effect of privatization on bank efficiency. Four types of efficiency were estimated including cost, profit, interest income, and noninterest income efficiencies derived from stochastic frontier functions. The findings show that JSCBs and city commercial banks have better performance compared to SOCBs. The results further report that publicly traded banks have better performance. Finally, they found that Chinese commercial banks are more efficient in generating interest income than earning noninterest revenue.

4.3 LITERATURE REVIEW ON BANK COMPETITION

4.3.1 Literature Review on the Theory of Bank Competition and Its Measurement

The empirical literature uses a number of methods to estimate competition in the banking sector through analyzing market power and efficiency. Bresnahan (1982) and Lau (1982) developed a method to estimate bank competition by measuring market power. This method has been recently used by Bikker (2003), Uchida and Tsutsui (2005), and Qin and Shaffer (2014). The aggregate level of bank behavior was analyzed and average conjectural variation of banks was estimated through this method. This model is based on two structural equations, namely an inverse demand equation and a supply equation, both of which are derived from the first-order condition of profit maximization. This model estimates the mark-up of price over marginal cost as a measure of market power. Thus, this method is also called mark-up test. If the output price equals marginal cost, as reflected by a zero value of conjectural variation, perfect competition exists in the market, whereas if the value equals one, this indicates that a monopoly exists in the market.

The second approach that measures bank competition was developed by Panzar and Rosse (1987). The model measures the extent to which a change in a vector of input prices is reflected in gross revenue. Thus, this method is also called the revenue test. The H-statistic is used in the method to estimate bank competition. The H-statistic is defined as the sum of the elasticities of the reduced-form revenues with respect to the input prices. A value equal to or smaller than zero indicates that the market is operated under a monopoly, whereas a value of the H-statistic between zero and one suggests that the market is in a condition of monopolistic competition. If the value of the H-statistic equals 1, it shows that the market is perfectly competitive. This approach has been widely used in the empirical literature to measure banking sector competition (see Bikker and Haaf, 2002; Matthews et al., 2007; Goddard and Wilson, 2009; Moch, 2013; Barbosa et al., 2015, among others).

The third type of indicator to measure bank competition is through the analysis of market power. Two indicators, the Hirschman—Herfindahl index (HHI) and the concentration ratio, measure the degree of market concentration. These two indicators are used based on the structure—conduct—performance (SCP) hypothesis, which assumes that the banks' behavior is affected by market power, whereas market structure plays a decisive role in bank performance. The idea of this hypothesis lies to the fact that in a more concentrated market in which significant shares are occupied by a few banks, the competitive condition is lower, whereas higher concentration leads to greater market power, and the resultant increase in the collusive behavior leads to higher profits. These indicators were recently used by Al-Muharrami et al. (2006) and Fu et al. (2014) to measure competition in the banking industry.

Market power can also be reflected by profitability because higher profits achieved by the bank may indicate a lower level of competition. The price—cost margin is an indicator used to measure competition. The profit—cost margin can be estimated by the difference between output price and marginal cost, then it is divided by the output price. The so-called Lerner index is widely used in the empirical literature to measure competition. The Lerner index ranges from zero to one. The Lerner index equals zero under a condition of perfect competition; the degree of competition decreases as the Lerner index increases its value. The market is operated under a monopoly if the value of the Lerner index equals one. Empirical literature using the Lerner index to measure competition includes Cipollini and Fiordelisi (2012) and Fungacova et al. (2014), among others.

The SCP hypothesis, discussed previously, suggests that market structure affects competitive behavior which further influences bank performance. In other words, this hypothesis argues that bank profitability is derived from market structure. However, Demsetz (1973) developed the efficient-structure hypothesis, which argues that differing profitability achieved by the bank is derived from efficiency. Thus, this hypothesis suggests that banks with higher efficiency have a higher ability to increase their market shares and bank size, which further leads to excess profit. A new indicator was developed by Boone (2008) to measure bank competition. The so-called Boone indicator considers the impact of efficiency on performance with regard to profitability and market share. It also considers that competition improves the performance of efficient firms and weakens the performance of inefficient ones. The Boone indicator can be positive as well as negative. A more negative Boone indicator indicates a higher level of competition, whereas a larger positive value indicates the competition is lower. Considerable literature has recently used this measurement of competition in the banking sector, including Delis (2012) and Tabak et al. (2012), among others.

4.3.2 Literature Review on Bank Competition in China

A few studies have examined competitive conditions in the Chinese banking industry. Yuan (2006) analyzed the competitive conditions in the industry over the period 1996–2000. The competition was measured by the Panzar–Rosse H-statistic. The results suggest that China's banking sector is already near a state of perfect competition (that is, before foreign banks began to enter China's financial markets).

The competitive conditions facing 16 Chinese banks during the period 2004–07 were evaluated by Masood and Sergi (2011). The Panzar–Rosse H-statistic was used to derive the competitive condition. The results show that the Chinese banking sector is monopolistically competitive over the period examined.

Fu (2009) examined the competitive conditions for a panel of 76 Chinese banks over the period 1997–2007 under a Panzar–Rosse H-statistic. The results indicate also monopolistic competition in the Chinese banking sector. She suggests that, after China's accession to the WTO, competition in the core market for bank lending increases, whereas the off-balance-sheet market seems to become less competitive.

Market concentration and competition in the Chinese banking industry over the period 1992–2008 was examined by Park (2013). Both the Panzar–Rosse H-statistic and the Boone indicator were used to measure the competition. The study indicates that the Chinese banking industry is still highly concentrated and its level of competition is closer to oligopoly.

Using the Lerner index as the competition indicator, Tan and Floros (2013b) investigated the competitive conditions of Chinese SOCBs, JSCBs, and city commercial banks (CCBs) over the period 2003–11. The empirical findings suggest that competition among CCBs is the lowest over the examined period, followed by SOCBs, whereas competition among JSCBs is the highest.

Tan (2014) used both the Panzar–Rosse H-statistic and the Lerner index to investigate competitive conditions in the Chinese banking sector over the period 2003–11. The empirical results suggest that the industry operates under monopolistic competition, whereas competition among CCBs is the lowest, and competition among JSCBs is the highest. He further examined the impact of competition on risk-taking behavior (credit risk and insolvency risk). The findings show that in a more competitive environment, Chinese commercial banks tend to undertake higher credit risk.

The Bresnahan–Lau model (1982) was applied by Qin and Shaffer (2014) to test the degree of competition of China's banking industry over the period 1986–2011. Their results strongly reject the monopoly power and the findings show that perfect competition exists in the Chinese banking industry and China's entry into the WTO does not cause any measurable shift in bank competition.

4.3.3 Literature Review on Bank Competition in Other Countries

Using a sample of banks in all EU countries during the 2000s, Weill (2013) employed both the Lerner index and the Panzar–Rosse H-statistic to investigate the evolution of bank competition. The empirical results show no general improvement in bank competition occurred in the EU over the examined period. In addition, their findings show a convergence in bank competition in EU countries.

Extending the Panzar and Rosse (1987) model to the case of a multi-product baking firm, Barbosa et al. (2014) used a new data set on the Brazilian banking industry to investigate the competitive aspects of multi-product banking operations. The results show that higher economies of scope in multiproduct banking are associated with lower Panzar–Rosse measures of competition in the banking sector. In addition, they find that banks that offer classic banking products (ie, loans and credit cards) and other banking products (ie, brokerage services, insurance, and capitalization bonds) have substantially higher market power than banks that offer only classic products.

Using five different measures, namely net interest margin, the Lerner index, Return on Assets, the Panzar–Rosse H-statistic, and HHI market concentration, Carbó et al. (2009) investigated the banking market competition for 14 countries using a balanced panel of 1912 banks over the period 1995–2011. The empirical results show that for analyzing competition within a single country, net interest margins are the preferred measure when the focus is on traditional loan and deposit services, whereas the Lerner index and ROA better reflect competition in broader banking activity.

Using a sample of Italian banks over the period 1997–2009, Coccorese and Pellecchia (2013) assessed the impact of multimarket contact of banks on their market power by means of a simultaneous-equations model. The empirical results suggest that multimarket contact is positively and significantly related to the market power index and supports the idea that firms which have a greater amount of contact are more likely to collude.

Using a sample of banks for 146 countries over the period 1999–2011, Mirzaei and Moore (2014) employed both the Lerner index and the Boone indicator to investigate the determinants of bank competition. The empirical results reveal that characteristics of the competition drivers across different income groups of countries are distinctive. The findings further show that a concentrated banking system jeopardizes competitiveness in developing economies, whereas this impact is absent for advanced and emerging economies. Finally, it is found that contestability and institutional development boost competition in less-developed banking systems, whereas interindustry competition and financial freedom are beneficial to advanced banking systems.

Using a unique data set covering the Spanish banking system, Jimenez et al. (2013) explicitly examined the relationship between bank competition and risk. Using the nonperforming loan ratio as the risk indicator and market concentration as the competition indicator, the findings show clear support of a nonlinear relationship between competition and risk in both loan and deposit markets. When using a direct measure of market power, such as the Lerner index, the empirical results are more supportive of the original franchise-value hypothesis[1], but only in the loan market. Finally, the number of banks is found to have little effect on nonperforming loan ratios.

[1] As the number of banks and competition increases, the level of bank risk would decline.

The degree of market power at the bank level for 84 banking systems worldwide was estimated by Delis (2012) and then the source of bank competition was analyzed with an emphasis on the impacts of financial reform and the quality of institutions. The competition was measured by the Boone indicator and the results were cross-checked by the Lerner index and a three-bank concentration ratio. The empirical results suggest that financial liberalization policies reduce the market power of banks in developed countries with advanced institutions. On the other hand, bank competition does not improve at the same pace in countries with weaker institutions and a lower level of institutional development. The research concludes that a certain level of institutional development is a precondition for the success of reforms aimed at enhancing the competition and efficiency of the banking market.

Not just the determinants of bank competition have been investigated; Fu et al. (2014) examined the trade-off between competition and financial stability for a sample of banks in 14 Asia Pacific economies over the period 2003–10. Various competition indicators were used including three-bank concentration ratio, the Lerner index, as well as an efficiency-adjusted Lerner index. The empirical findings suggest that greater concentration fosters financial fragility and that lower pricing power induces bank risk exposure. With regard to regulations and institutions, the findings show that tougher entry restrictions may benefit bank stability, whereas stronger deposit insurance schemes are associated with greater bank fragility.

Using a sample of Korean commercial banks and mutual saving banks over the period 1999–2011, Jeon and Lim (2013) investigated the relationship between bank competition and financial stability. The Boone indicator and concentration ratio, as well as the Herfindahl–Hirschman index were used as the competition indicators. The results of multiple regressions show that bank competition has a significant and positive effect on the stability of mutual saving banks with weak corporate governance. On the other hand, competition pressure significantly reduces the stability of commercial banks, but this relationship turns out nonlinear. Finally, the results show that the positive effects of competition on the stability of mutual saving banks become even greater after deregulations by the Korean government and after the global financial crisis.

The dynamic relationship between competition and bank soundness among European cooperative banks between 1998 and 2009 was assessed by Fiordelisi and Mare (2014). The Lerner index as well as a fund-adjusted Lerner index were used as the competition indicators. The empirical results suggest that bank market power Granger-causes bank soundness, indicating a positive relationship between competition and stability. In addition, it was found that this relationship did not change during the 2007–09 financial crises. Finally, it was shown that increased homogeneity in the cooperative banking sector positively affects bank soundness.

Using the Boone indicator as a competition indicator and stability inefficiency as a risk indicator, Tabak et al. (2012) addressed the effects of bank competition on the risk-taking behaviors of banks in 10 Latin American countries between 2003 and 2008. The empirical findings suggest that competition affects risk-taking behavior in a nonlinear way as both high and low competition levels enhance financial stability, whereas they find the opposite effect for average competition. In addition, the empirical results show that the larger a bank is, the more it benefits from competition, whereas a greater capital ratio is advantageous for banks that operate in collusive markets, and capitalization only enhances the stability of larger banks under high and average competition.

Soedarmono et al. (2011) used the Lerner index as the competition (market power) indicator and *Z*-score as the stability (risk) indicator to investigate the impact of competition on the risk-taking behavior of a sample of commercial banks from 12 Asian countries during the 2001–07 period. Their findings show that greater market power (lower competition) leads to higher instability. The results further report that in a less-competitive banking market, banks are better capitalized, but their default risk is higher. Finally, they find that higher economic growth contributes to neutralize greater risk taking and higher instability in less-competitive markets.

Using four South Asian banking markets, namely Bangladesh, India, Pakistan, and Sri Lanka over the period 1998–2008, Nguyen et al. (2012) investigated the association between bank market power and revenue diversification, and the research further examined whether revenue diversification interacting with market power influences individual bank stability. Both the Lerner index as well as a fund-adjusted Lerner index were used as the competition indicators. Under the Generalized Methods of Moments (GMM) estimators, the findings suggest that South Asian banks with greater market power focus more on traditional interest income-generating activities, whereas it is found that these banks become more stable when they diversify across both interest and noninterest income activities.

Information on banks around the globe over the period 1994–2009 was collected by Beck et al. (2013b) to document large international variation in the relationship between bank competition and bank stability. The reasons for this variation were also explored focusing on several factors such as market feature, regulatory feature, as well as institutional feature. The Lerner index was used as the competition indicator. The empirical findings report that an increase in competition has a larger impact on banks' fragility in countries with stricter activity restrictions, lower system fragility, better-developed stock exchanges, more generous deposit insurance, and more effective systems of credit information sharing.

Anginer et al. (2014) used 1872 unique publicly traded banks in 63 countries from 1997 to 2009 to examine the impact of bank competition on systemic risk. The Lerner index was used as the competition indicator, whereas the competitive condition was cross-checked by alternative competition indicators such as the Panzar–Rosse H-statistic, the bank concentration ratio, as well as the Hirfindahl–Hirschman index. The empirical findings show that greater competition encourages banks to take on more diversified risks, making the banking system less fragile to shocks. With regard to the impact of the institutional and regulatory environment on bank systemic risk, the empirical results report that banking systems are more fragile in countries with weak supervision and private monitoring, greater government ownership of banks, and with public policies that restrict competition. Finally, it is argued that the negative effect of the lack of competition can be mitigated by a strong institutional environment that allows for efficient public and private monitoring of financial institutions.

Data from the Central and Eastern European banking sectors over the period 1998–2005 was used by Agoraki et al. (2011) to investigate whether regulations have an independent effect on bank risk taking or whether their effect is channeled through the market power possessed by banks. The Lerner index was used as the competition indicator. The empirical findings suggest that banks with market power tend to take on lower credit risk and have a lower probability of default. With regard to regulations, the empirical results show that capital requirements reduce risk in general, but for banks with market power, this effect significantly weakens or can even be reversed. Higher activity restrictions in combination with more market power reduce both credit risk and the risk of default, whereas the official supervisory power has a direct impact on bank risk.

A sample of US banks over the period 1984–2004 was used by Bos et al. (2013) to evaluate the relationship between competition and innovation in the financial sector. The new measure of overall innovation was introduced by estimating and enveloping annual minimum-cost frontiers to create a global frontier. The distance to the global frontier constitutes each bank's technology gap, which decreases if the bank manages to innovate. The Lerner index was used as the competition indicator. The empirical findings show an inverted-U relationship between competition and innovation. The results further indicate that interstate banking deregulation results in lower bank innovation.

Using a large panel of banks from 12 European-area countries for the period 2002–10, Fungacova et al. (2014) examined how competition influences the bank-lending channel. The Lerner index was used as the main competition indicator, and the results were cross-checked by the Panzar–Rosse H-statistic and banking sector concentration ratio. The empirical findings show that the effect of monetary policy on bank lending is dependent on bank competition. More specifically, it is found that the transmission of monetary policy via the bank-lending channel is less pronounced for banks with extensive market power. Furthermore, the empirical results report that banks with less market power are more sensitive to monetary policy only before the financial crisis. In conclusion, they argue that bank market power has a significant impact on the effectiveness of monetary policy.

Leroy (2014) used banking microdata from Eurozone countries over the period 1999–2011 to examine how banks respond to the monetary policy of European central banks according to their characteristics and, in particular, to their market power. The results show that banks with market power which is proxied by the Lerner index, have a credit supply that is less sensitive to monetary policy shock. Therefore, the findings suggest that increased competition enhances the effectiveness of monetary policy transmission through the bank-lending channel.

4.4 LITERATURE REVIEW ON THE IMPACT OF COMPETITION ON BANK EFFICIENCY

4.4.1 Competition-Inefficiency Hypothesis

The competition-inefficiency hypothesis suggests that competition leads to a decline in bank efficiency for the following reasons. First, as argued by Boot and Schmeits (2005), the relationships between customers and banks are less stable and shorter in a more competitive environment. Furthermore, higher bank competition increases customers' propensity to switch to other service providers. The information asymmetries will be amplified by this phenomenon and additional resources for screening and monitoring borrowers are required. Second, Chan et al. (1986) argued that a shorter duration of bank relationships can be expected in a competitive environment and the reduction of relationship-building activities inhibits the reusability and value of information. The negative impact of competition on efficiency is supported by the empirical studies of Evanoff and Ors (2002), DeYoung et al. (1998) and Kumbhakar et al. (2001).

4.4.2 Competition-Efficiency Hypothesis

The competition-efficiency hypothesis is derived from the "Efficient Structure hypothesis" and suggests a positive impact of competition on efficiency. This effect can be explained by Zarutskie (2013) who argued that higher competition induces banks to specialize and focus on certain types of loans or particular groups of borrowers. It will also induce bank managers to adjust their lending technologies. The costs of processing and originating loans can be lowered and the borrowers can be better monitored. This positive impact can also be explained by the "Quiet Life hypothesis," which argues that managers with monopoly power enjoy a share of monopoly rents, they are careless in expense management, and the working effort will be reduced which leads to a decline in efficiency. The positive impact of competition on efficiency was also supported by Chen (2007) and Dick and Lehnert (2010).

4.4.2.1 The Impact of Competition on Bank Efficiency

The relationship between competition and efficiency in the European banking sector over the period 1997–2003 was investigated by Casu and Girardone (2006). The efficiency was measured by DEA, whereas the competition was derived from the Panzar–Rosse H-statistic. The findings suggest that increased competition has forced banks to become more efficient, whereas increased efficiency does not seem to foster a more competitive European Union banking market.

The relationship between competition and efficiency in the banking sectors of five European Union countries (France, Germany, Italy, Spain, and the United Kingdom) over the period 2000–05 was investigated by Casu and Girardone (2009). Both SFA and DEA were used to measure the efficiency, whereas the Lerner index was used to derive the competition. A number of econometric techniques were employed including ordinary least square, fixed effects, random effect, difference GMM estimator, as well as a system GMM estimator. The findings suggest that banks with higher market power (lower competition) have higher levels of efficiency, whereas the impact of efficiency on competition is weak.

The impact of Schumpeterian competition on efficiency for a panel of United Kingdom commercial banks over the period 2001–12 was investigated by Duygun et al. (2013). The cost and alternative-profit frontiers were estimated to proxy the efficiency measures, whereas the intensity of competition through product innovation was measured by the trademark intensity. The results show that the trademark intensity in the commercial banking sector does negatively affect the mean cost and profit efficiencies in the sector. In addition, the findings suggest that trademark intensity increases in the sector, and commercial banks react by improving their cost and profit efficiencies.

The competitive conditions in the banking industries of 11 Latin American countries for the period 1993–2000 were examined by Yildirim and Philippatos (2007). The results show that the banks in the sample earn their revenues as if operating under monopolistic competition. The findings further report that market concentration is not significantly related to competitive conduct. With regard to the countries investigated, it is found that the competition in Brazil, Chile, and Venezuela decreased in the late 1990s which may be attributed to increased consolidation. In addition, it is observed that deregulation and opening up of the financial markets for foreign participation serve as an important catalyst to increase the competitiveness of banking markets. Higher degrees of competition lead to reduced bank margins and profitability but improved cost efficiency.

The efficiency was estimated by Williams (2012) for a sample of 419 Latin American commercial banks between 1985 and 2010 under a random-parameter stochastic frontier function model, whereas in the second stage, the author tested the quiet-life hypothesis[2] (the impact of market power on bank efficiency). The market power was derived from both the conventional Lerner index as well as the efficiency-adjusted Lerner index. The findings show that the quiet-life hypothesis is firmly rejected and the results further report that privatization has a more significant and positive impact on improving bank efficiency compared to foreign acquisition, whereas bank restructuring has promoted competition and yielded efficiency gains at banks under conditions of monopolistic competition.

[2] The quiet life hypothesis is firstly derived by Hics (1935) who argues that firms with higher market power put less effort in pursing cost efficiency. In other words, firms with market power has lower efficiency.

4.5 SUMMARY AND CONCLUSION

This chapter mainly reviews the empirical literature with regard to bank efficiency and competition. Regarding bank efficiency, this chapter divides the literature into two streams which are international bank efficiency studies and single-country studies. More specifically, this chapter comprehensively examines the efficiency studies in the Chinese banking industry.

The second part of this chapter mainly focuses on reviewing relevant literature with regard to banking sector competition. First, it reviews the literature regarding the relevant theories on banking sector competition and the measurement; this includes a brief explanation of different competition indicators such as Bresnahan (1982) and Lau (1982) mark-up method, Panzar–Rosse H-statistic, Hirfindahl–Hirschman, and banking sector concentration ratio, the Boone indicator, as well as the Lerner index. This section then focuses on reviewing relevant literature investigating the competitive conditions of both the Chinese banking industry and that of other countries.

Finally, this chapter reviews relevant theories and studies with regard to the impact of competition on efficiency in the banking sector by explaining the competition-efficiency and the competition-inefficiency hypotheses.

REFERENCES

Agoraki, M.K., Delis, M.D., Pasiouras, F., 2011. Regulation, competition and bank risk-taking in transition countries. Journal of Financial Stability 7, 38–48.

Al-Muharrami, S., Matthews, K., Khabari, Y., 2006. Market structure and competitive conditions in the Arab GCC banking system. Journal of Banking and Finance 30, 3487–3501.

Anginer, D., Demirguc-Kunt, A., Zhu, M., 2014. How does competition affect bank systemic risk? Journal of Financial Intermediation 23, 1–26.

Ariff, M., Can, L., 2008. Cost and profit efficiency of Chinese banks: a non-parametric analysis. China Economic Review 19, 260–273.

Barbosa, K., Rocha, B.D.P., Salazar, F., 2015. Assessing competition in the banking industry: A multi-product approach. Journal of Banking and Finance 50, 341–362.

Barros, C.P., Managi, S., Matousek, R., 2012. The technical efficiency of the Japanese banks: non-radial directional performance measurement with undesirabe output. Omega 40, 1–8.

Barth, J.R., Lin, C., Ma, Y., Seade, J., Song, F.M., 2013. Do bank regulation, supervision and monitoring enhance or impede bank efficiency. Journal of Banking and Finance 37, 2879–2892.

Beck, T., Demirguc-Kunt, A., Merrouche, O., 2013a. Islamic vs. conventional banking: business model, efficiency and stability. Journal of Banking and Finance 37, 433–447.

Beck, T., Jonghe, O.D., Schepens, G., 2013b. Bank competition and stability: cross-country heterogeneity. Journal of Financial Intermediation 22, 218–244.

Berger, A.N., Hasan, I., Zhou, M., 2009. Bank ownership and efficiency in China: what will happen in the world's largest nation? Journal of Banking and Finance 33, 113–130.

Bikker, J.A., 2003. Testing for imperfect competition on the EU deposit and loan markets with Bresnaha's market power model. Kredit and Kapital 36, 167–212.

Bikker, J.A., Haaf, K., 2002. Competition, concentration and their relationship: an empirical analysis of the banking industry. Journal of Banking and Finance 26, 2191–2214.

Boone, J., 2008. A new way to measure competition. Economic Journal 118, 1245–1261.

Boot, A.W.A., Schmeits, A., 2005. The Competitive Challenge in Banking. Amsterdam Center for Law and Economics. Working Paper No. 2005–08.

Bos, J.W.B., Kolari, J.W., Lamoen, R.C.R.V., 2013. Competition and innovation: evidence from financial services. Journal of Banking and Finance 37, 1590–1601.

Bresnahan, T.F., 1982. The oligopoly solution concept is identified. Economics Letters 10, 87–92.

Carbo, S., Humphrey, D., Maudos, J., Molyneux, P., 2009. Cross-country comparisons of competition and pricing power in European banking. Journal of International Money and Finance 28, 115–134.

Casu, B., Girardone, C., 2006. Bank competition, concentration and efficiency in the single European market. The Manchester School 74, 441–468.

Casu, B., Girardone, C., 2009. Testing the relationship between competition and efficiency in banking: a panel data analysis. Economics Letters 105, 134–137.

Chortareas, G.E., Girardone, C., Ventouri, A., 2012. Bank supervision, regulation, and efficiency: evidence from the European Union. Journal of Financial Stability 8, 292–302.

Chortareas, G.E., Girardone, C., Ventouri, A., 2013. Financial freedom and bank efficiency: evidence from the European Union. Journal of Banking and Finance 37, 1223–1231.

Chan, Y., Greenbaum, S.I., Thakor, A.V., 1986. Information reusability, competition and bank asset quality. Journal of Banking and Finance 10, 255–276.

Chen, X., 2007. Banking deregulation and credit risk: evidence from the EU. Journal of Financial Stability 2, 356–390.

Cipollini, A., Fiordelisi, F., 2012. Economic value, competition and financial distress in the European banking system. Journal of Banking and Finance 36, 3101–3109.

Coccorese, P., Pellecchia, A., 2013. Multimarket contact, competition and pricing in banking. Journal of International Money and Finance 37, 187–214.

Delis, M.D., 2012. Bank competition, financial reform, and institutions: the importance of being developed. Journal of Development Economics 97, 450–465.

Demsetz, H., 1973. Industry structure, market rivalry, and public policy. Journal of Law and Economics 16, 1–9.

DeYoung, R., Hasan, I., Kirchhoff, B., 1998. The impact of out-of-state entry on the cost efficiency of local commercial banks. Journal of Economics and Business 50, 191–203.

Dick, A.A., Lehnert, A., 2010. Personal bankruptcy and credit market competition. Journal of Finance 65, 655–686.

Duygun, M., Sena, V., Shaban, M., 2013. Schumpeterian competition and efficiency among commercial banks. Journal of Banking and Finance 37, 5176–5185.

Evanoff, D.D., Ors, E., 2002. Local Market Consolidation and Bank Productive Efficiency. Federal Reserve Bank of Chicago. Working Paper No. 2002–25.

Fiordelisi, F., Mare, D.S., 2014. Competition and financial stability in European cooperative banks. Journal of International Money and Finance 45, 1–16.

Fu, X., Heffernan, S., 2008. Economies of scale and scope in China's banking sector. Applied Financial Economics 18, 345–356.

Fu, M., 2009. Competition in Chinese commercial banking. Banking and Finance Review 1 (1), 1–16.

Fu, X., Lin, Y., Molyneux, P., 2014. Bank competition and financial stability in Asia Pacific. Journal of Banking and Finance 38, 64–77.
Fujii, H., Managi, S., Matousek, R., 2014. Indian bank efficiency and productivity changes with undesirable outputs: a disaggregated approach. Journal of Banking and Finance 38, 41–50.
Fungacova, Z., Solanko, L., Weill, L., 2014. Does competition influence the bank lending channel in the euro area? Journal of Banking and Finance 49, 356–366.
Gaganis, C., Pasiouras, F., 2013. Financial supervision regimes and bank efficiency: international evidence. Journal of Banking and Finance 37, 5463–5475.
Goddard, J., Wilson, J.O.S., 2009. Competition in banking: a disequilibrium approach. Journal of Banking and Finance 33, 2282–2292.
Goddard, J., Molyneux, P., Willians, J., 2014. Dealing with cross-firm heterogeneity in bank efficiency estimates: some evidence from Latin America. Journal of Banking and Finance 40, 130–142.
Halkos, G.E., Tzeremes, N.G., 2013. Estimating the degree of operating efficiency gains from potential merger and acquisition: a DEA bootstrapped approach. Journal of Banking and Finance 37, 1658–1668.
Hicks, J., 1935. Annual survey of economic theory: the theory of monopoly. Econometrica 3, 256–263.
Hsiao, H., Chang, H., Cianci, A., Huang, C., 2010. First financial restructuring and operating efficiency evidence from Taiwanese commercial banks. Journal of Banking and Finance 34, 1461–1471.
Hu, J., Chu, W., HU, X., Lee, C., 2009. Operational environment-adjusted nationwide bank efficiency in China. Journal of Management Research 9, 142–158.
Jeon, J.,Q., Lim, K.K., 2013. Bank competition and financial stability: a comparison of commercial banks and mutual saving banks in Korea. Pacifica-Basin Finance Journal 25, 253–272.
Jiang, C., Yao, S., Zhang, Z., 2009. The effects of governance changes on bank efficiency in China: a stochastic distance function approach. China Economic Review 20, 717–731.
Jiang, C., Yao, S., Feng, G., 2013. Bank ownership, privatization and performance: evidence from a transition country. Journal of Banking and Finance 37, 3364–3372.
Jimenez, G., Lopez, J.A., Saurina, J., 2013. How does competition affect bank risk-taking. Journal of Financial Stability 9, 185–195.
Kauko, K., 2009. Managers and efficiency in banking. Journal of Banking and Finance 33, 546–556.
Kumbhakar, S.C., Lozano-Vivas, A., Knox Lovell, C.A., Hasan, I., 2001. The effects of deregulation on the performance of financial institutions: the case of Spanish saving banks. Journal of Money, Credit and Banking 33, 101–120.
Kumbhakar, S.C., Wang, D., 2007. Economic reforms, efficiency and productivity in Chinese banking. Journal of Regulatory Economics 32, 105–129.
Lau, L., 1982. On identifying the degree of competitiveness from industry price and output data. Economics Letters 10, 93–99.
Laurenceson, J.S., Zhao, Y., 2008. Efficiency among China's banks: a DEA analysis five years after WTO entry. China Economic Journal 1, 275–285.
Lensink, R., Meesters, A., Naaborg, I., 2008. Bank efficiency and foreign ownership: do good institutions matter? Journal of Banking and Finance 32, 834–844.
Leroy, A., 2014. Competition and the bank lending channel in Eurozone. Journal of International Financial Markets, Institutions and Money 31, 296–314.
Lin, H., Tsao, C., Yang, C., 2009. Bank reforms, competition and efficiency in China's banking system: are small city bank entrants more efficient? China and World Economy 17, 69–87.

Lozano-Vivas, A., Pasiouras, F., 2010. The impact of non-traditional activities on the estimation of bank efficiency: international evidence. Journal of Banking and Finance 34, 1436–1449.
Luo, D., Yao, S., 2010. World financial crisis and the rise of Chinese commercial banks: an efficiency analysis using DEA. Applied Financial Economics 20, 1515–1530.
Masood, O., Sergi, B.S., 2011. China's banking system, market structure and competitive conditions. Frontier of Economics in China 6 (1), 22–35.
Matthews, K., Murinde, V., Zhao, T., 2007. Competitive conditions among the major British banks. Journal of Banking and Finance 31, 2025–2042.
Matthews, K.G.P., Zhang, N., 2010. Bank productivity in China: 1997–2007: measurement and convergence. China Economic Review 21, 617–628.
Mirzaei, A., Moore, T., 2014. What are the driving forces of bank competition across different income groups of countries? Journal of International Financial Markets, Institutions and Money 32, 38–71.
Moch, N., 2013. Competition in fragmented markets: new evidence from the German banking industry in the light of the subprime crisis. Journal of Banking and Finance 37, 2908–2919.
Nguyen, M., Skully, M., Perera, S., 2012. Market power, revenue diversification and bank stability: evidence from selected South Asian countries. Journal of International Financial Markets, Institutions and Money 22, 897–912.
Panzar, J.C., Rosse, J.N., 1987. Testing for "monopoly" equilibrium. Journal of Industrial Economics 35, 443–456.
Pessarossi, P., Weill, L., 2015. Do capital requirements affect cost efficiency? Evidence from China. Journal of Financial Stability 19, 119–127.
Park, K.H., 2013. Testing for competition in the south korean and Chinese commercial banking markets. Asia-Pacific Journal of Financial Studies 42 (1), 56–75.
Qin, B., Shaffer, S., 2014. A test of competition in Chinese banking. Applied Economics Letters 21 (9), 602–604.
Rossi, S.P.S., Schwaiger, M.S., Winkler, G., 2009. How loan portfolio diversification affects risk, efficiency and capitalization: a managerial behavior model for Austrian banks. Journal of Banking and Finance 33, 2218–2226.
Soedarmono, W., Machrouh, F., Tarazi, A., 2011. Bank market power, economic growth and financial stability: evidence from Asian banks. Journal of Asian Economics 22, 460–470.
Sufian, F., Majid, M.Z.A., 2009. Bank efficiency and share prices in China: empirical evidence from a three-stage model. International Journal of Computational Economics and Econometrics 1, 23–45.
Sufian, F., Habibullah, M.S., 2011. Opening the black box on bank efficiency in China: does economic freedom matter? Global Economic Review: Perspectives on East Asian Economies and Industries 40, 269–298.
Sufian, F., 2009. Analysis of the relevance of non-traditional activities items upon the efficiency of Chinese banks: a non-stochastic frontier DEA approach. Review of Economics and Business Studies 4, 83–102.
Sun, L., Chang, T., 2011. A comprehensive analysis of the effects of risk measures on bank efficiency: evidence from emerging Asia countries. Journal of Banking and Finance 35, 1727–1735.
Sun, J., Harimaya, K., Yamori, N., 2013. Regional economic development, strategic investors and efficiency of China city commercial banks. Journal of Banking and Finance 37, 1602–1611.
Tabak, B.M., Fazio, D.M., Cajueiro, D.O., 2012. The relationship between banking market competition and risk-taking: do size and capitalization matter? Journal of Banking and Finance 36, 3361–3381.

Tan, Y., Floros, C., 2013a. Risk, capital and efficiency in Chinese banking. Journal of International Financial Markets, Institutions and Money 26, 378–393.
Tan, Y., Floros, C., 2013b. Market power, stability and performance in the Chinese banking industry. Economic Issues 18 (2), 65–89.
Tan, Y., 2014. Performance, Risk and Competition in the Chinese Banking Industry. Chandos Publishing, Oxford.
Uchida, H., Tsutsui, Y., 2005. Has competition in the Japanese banking sector improved? Journal of Banking and Finance 29, 419–429.
Weill, L., 2013. Bank competition in the EU: how has it evolved? Journal of International Financial Market, Institutions and Money 26, 100–112.
Williams, J., 2012. Efficiency and market power in Latin American banking. Journal of Financial Stability 8, 263–276.
Yao, S., Han, Z., Feng, G., 2008. Ownership reform, foreign competition and efficiency of Chinese commercial banks: a non-parametric approach. The World Economy 31, 1310–1326.
Yao, S., Jiang, C., 2010. Banking Reforms and Efficiency in China: 1995–2008. University of Nottingham. Research Paper Series No. 2010/11.
Yildirim, H.S., Philippatos, G.C., 2007. Restructuring, consolidation and competition in Latin American banking markets. Journal of Banking and Finance 31, 629–639.
Yin, H., Yang, I., Mehran, J., 2013. An empirical study of bank efficiency in China after WTO accession. Global Finance Journal 24, 153–170.
Yuan, Y., 2006. The state of competition of the Chinese banking industry. Journal of Asia Economics 17 (3), 519–534.
Zarutskie, R., 2013. Competition, financial innovation and commercial bank loan portfolio. Journal of Financial Intermediation 22, 373–396.
Zhang, J., Qu, B., Xu, Z., Wang, P., 2012. Market development and bank profit efficiency in China: application of the generalized Malmquist productivity index. Asia-Pacific Journal of Accounting and Economics 19, 181–197.

CHAPTER 5

The Measurement of Bank Efficiency and Bank Competition in China

5.1 INTRODUCTION

In terms of the estimation of efficiency in the banking industry, the empirical literature divides the methods into two streams which are parametric method and non-parametric method. The parametric methods include production, cost, profit and revenue functions as alternative methods of describing the production technology and estimating efficiency, whereas on the other hand, the non-parametric methodology involves mainly the use of linear programming techniques (Ajibefun, 2008). The current study makes use of both of these two types of methods to estimate the efficiency in the Chinese banking industry. More specifically, the technical, pure technical and scale efficiencies of Chinese commercial banks will be estimated by the non-parametric data envelopment analysis (DEA), whereas the cost, profit and revenue efficiencies of Chinese commercial banks will be estimated by the parametric method.

With regards to the estimation of competition in the banking industry, the empirical literature uses a number of different methods/indicators. The use of these different indicators/measurements is based on two different streams of literature, namely traditional industrial organization theory and the new industrial organization theory. The former mainly focuses on using structural indicators to measure bank competition such as the banking sector concentration ratio, whereas the latter concentrates on estimating competition using non-structural methods such as Panzar—Rosse H-statistic, the Lerner index and the Boone indicator. The current study uses all the above-mentioned methods to evaluate competition in the Chinese banking industry.

This chapter will be structured as follows: Section 5.2 explains the methodology to estimate bank efficiency in China, with Section 5.2.1

Efficiency and Competition in Chinese Banking
ISBN 978-0-08-100074-8

discussing the estimation of technical, pure technical and scale efficiencies in the Chinese banking industry. Section 5.2.2 demonstrates the estimation of cost, profit and revenue efficiencies in the Chinese banking industry. Section 5.3 discusses the estimation of competition in the Chinese banking industry. This section is further divided into four subsections with Section 5.3.1 explaining the first method to estimate bank competition which is the Boone indicator. Section 5.3.2 concentrates on the second method which is the Panzar–Rosse H-statistic; Section 5.3.3 discusses the Lerner index, whereas the last indicator, which is the banking sector concentration ratio, will be explained in Section 5.3.4. Section 5.4 will discuss the models used to test the impact of competition on efficiency in the Chinese banking industry which is followed by Section 5.5 describing the data used in the current study. Finally, Section 5.6 provides a summary and conclusion for the whole chapter.

5.2 THE MEASUREMENT OF EFFICIENCY IN THE CHINESE BANKING INDUSTRY

5.2.1 Estimation of Technical, Pure Technical, and Scale Efficiencies of Chinese Commercial Banks

The efficiency estimates in our study have been obtained using DEA. DEA, which was originated by Charnes et al. (1978), is a linear programming technique (Charnes, Cooper, and Rhodes [CCR] model). The CCR model measures the efficiency of each decision-making unit (DMU) that is obtained as the maximum of a ratio of weighted outputs to weighted inputs. This denotes that the fewer inputs invested in producing the given outputs, the more efficient the production[1]. The CCR model presupposes that no significant relationship exists between the scale of operation and that of efficiency by assuming constant return to scale (CRS). The CRS assumption is only suitable when all DMUs are operating at optimal scale.

Banker et al. (1984) extended the CCR model by relaxing the CRS assumption. The resulting Banker, Charnes, and Cooper (1984) (BCC) model is used to assess the efficiency of DMUs characterized by variable return to scale (VRS). The VRS assumption provides the measurement of

[1] Technical efficiency is estimated using four outputs (total loans, securities, total deposits, and non-interest income) and three inputs (total cost which includes interest expenses and non-interest expenses, price of funds, and price of capital).

purely technical efficiency (PTE), which is the measurement of technical efficiency devoid of the scale efficiency effect. The CCR model can be expressed as follows:

$$\begin{aligned} &\min_{\theta,\lambda}\theta, \\ &\text{subject to} \\ &-y_i + Y\lambda \geq 0, \\ &\theta x_i - X\lambda \geq 0, \\ &\lambda \geq 0 \end{aligned} \qquad [5.1]$$

in which θ is a scalar and λ is an $N \times 1$ vector of constants, Y represents all input and output data for N firms, x_i are individual inputs and y_i the outputs for the ith firm. The efficiency score for each DMU is given by θ; it takes a value between 0 and 1, which indicates the efficiency level.

The CRS linear programming problem can be easily modified to account for VRS by adding the convexity constraint, $N1'\lambda = 1$, to provide:

$$\begin{aligned} &\min_{\theta,\lambda}\theta, \\ &\text{subject to} \\ &-y_i + Y\lambda \geq 0, \\ &\theta x_i - X\lambda \geq 0, \\ &N1'\lambda = 1 \\ &\lambda \geq 0 \end{aligned} \qquad [5.2]$$

in which $N1$ is an $N \times 1$ vector of ones. This approach forms a convex hull of intersecting plans which envelop the data points more tightly than the CRS conical hull; this provides pure technical efficiency scores which are greater than or equal to those obtained using the CRS model. If the efficiency scores obtained from CRS model and VRS model are different, this indicates that the DMU has scale inefficiency, and that the scale inefficiency can be calculated from the difference between the VRS technical efficiency score and the CRS technical efficiency score. The relationship between CRS and VRS is given as:

$$\mathrm{TE_{CRS}} = \mathrm{TE_{VRS}} \times \mathrm{SE} \qquad [5.3]$$

The main argument for the DEA over the parametric techniques, such as stochastic frontier approach (SFA), lies in the fact that it works particularly well with small samples. Furthermore, it is able to handle multiple inputs and outputs stated in different measurement units and does not

Table 5.1 Summary statistics of inputs and outputs used to estimate the efficiency scores

Variables	Observations	Mean	SD	Min	Max
Inputs					
Total cost (interest expenses and non-interest expenses)	777	3.35	0.97	−0.79	6.86
Price of funds (the ratio of interest expenses over total deposits)	777	1.27	0.18	0.74	1.96
Price of capital (the ratio of non-interest expenses over fixed assets)	776	1.92	0.26	0.68	2.83
Outputs					
Total loans	784	4.59	0.99	0.34	7.95
Securities	782	4.21	1.04	−0.405	7.87
Non-interest income	767	2.34	1.1	−2.4	5.81
Total deposits	784	4.85	0.98	0.66	8.26

necessitate knowledge of any functional form of the frontier (see Charnes et al., 1995). Most empirical papers show that using DEA to estimate the efficient frontier can yield robust results (see Seiford and Thrall, 1990). In addition, DEA is used in the current study to compare to the findings of Garcia-Herrero et al. (2009) who used the parametric techniques in estimating efficiency in the Chinese banking industry.

The intermediation approach is taken for the selection of inputs and outputs rather than the production approach, with the latter suited to branch evaluation. Banks are viewed as financial intermediaries which accumulate deposits and purchase funds and then intermediate these funds (Sealey and Lindley, 1977). In selecting the input and output variables, our study follows the suggestions made by Berger and Humphrey (1997); they argue that deposits have the dual role and should be regarded as both input (which is used to fund loans) and output (through which it provides services to depositors). The inputs and outputs used in this study and their statistics are shown in Table 5.1. More specifically, we use three inputs which include total cost (interest expenses and non-interest expenses[2]), price of funds (measured by the ratio of interest paid on deposits over total deposits) and the price of capital (measured by the ratio of interest expenses over

[2] The non-interest expenses include the price of labour.

fixed assets). The choice of input follows the study of Chen et al. (2005). On the other hand, four outputs are selected in the current study which are total loans, securities, non-interest income and total deposits. This selection follows the study of Fu and Heffernan (2007). From the input variables perspective, the table shows that Chinese banks are substantially different in total cost. The total cost mainly includes the interest expenses and non-interest expenses. The large difference is mainly attributed to the fact that large banks, such as state-owned commercial banks (SOCBs), have larger volumes of deposits which incur higher volumes of interest expenses. In addition, bigger commercial banks have larger volumes of non-interest expenses as well (ie, larger volumes of salaries for bigger banks with higher number of staff). It is clearly reflected in the table that Chinese banks have different abilities to engage in non-interest generating activities and security business as shown by the larger standard deviation of these two variables.

5.2.2 The measurement of cost, profit and revenue efficiencies in the Chinese Banking Industry

As discussed previously, DEA has a few advantages compared to SFA with regards to the efficiency estimation; however, it also suffers from a number of disadvantages. First and foremost, DEA does not assume statistical noise, which means that the error term in the estimation is attributed to inefficiency (Sun and Chang, 2011). Therefore, the influence of a number of factors such as bad data, luck and extreme observations is accounted as inefficiency in DEA. Secondly, Sun and Chang (2011) further argue that measuring DEA in small samples is sensitive to the difference between the number of firms and the sum of inputs and outputs used.

The SFA was proposed by Aigner et al. (1977) and Meeusen and van den Broeck (1977). The traditional assumption of a deterministic production frontier is modified by this approach, whereas a composed error with two components is specified by both of these two studies: a one-sided error and random error. The former measures the non-negative inefficiency effects, whereas the latter considers the factors that are not controlled by the DMU.

Cost, profit and revenue efficiency measure how well a bank is predicted to perform relative to a "best-practice bank" producing the same outputs under the same environmental conditions (Berger et al., 2009). More specifically, the cost efficiency measures the distance of a specific bank to the benchmark bank with regards to the difference in the ability to minimize cost in producing the same volume of output. On the other hand, the profit efficiency measures the difference between the specific bank and the benchmark bank in the ability to generate profit using the same level of inputs. Finally, the revenue efficiency measures the different ability of a specific bank and the best-practice bank in using the same levels of inputs to generate revenue. Higher degrees of the difference indicate higher levels of inefficiency, thus, lower levels of inefficiency. The efficiency levels can be estimated by specifying the commonly used translog functional form for the cost, profit and revenue functions; the cost function can be specified as follows:

$$\begin{aligned}\text{LNCOST}_{it} = {} & \alpha_0 + \alpha_1 \text{LNASSETS}_{it} + \frac{1}{2}\alpha_2(\text{LNASSETS}_{it})^2 \\ & + \sum_{j=1}^{3} \beta_{itj}\text{LNINPUT}_{itj} \\ & + \sum_{j=1}^{3}\sum_{k=1}^{3} \beta_{itjk}\text{LNINPUT}_{itj}\text{LNINPUT}_{itk} \\ & + \sum_{j=1}^{3} \gamma_{itj}\text{LNASSETS}_{it}\text{LNINPUT}_{itj} + \varepsilon_{it}\end{aligned} \quad [5.4]$$

$$\varepsilon_{it} = v_{it} + u_{it} \quad [5.5]$$

LN denotes the natural logarithm, COST denotes total cost, i and t indicate the specific bank operating at the specific year; ASSETS represents the total assets, INPUT represents the three input prices used in the current study and different input prices are represented by the subscripts j and k: INPUT1 is the price of funds (ratio of interest expenses to total funding), INPUT2 indicates the price of capital (ratio of other non-interest expenses to fixed assets), INPUT3 stands for the price of labour (ratio of personnel expenses to total assets). α_0 and ε stand for the constant and error terms, respectively. With regards to the estimation of profit and revenue efficiencies, we use the same specification and just replace the dependent variable to profit and gross revenue. The profit indicator used is return on assets (ROA).

The error term is also called the composed error term which includes two components: v_{it} is a two-sided normal disturbance term with zero mean and variance σ_v^2 and represents the effect of statistical noise, and u_{it} is a non-negative random disturbance term capturing the effects of inefficiency. Table 5.2 defines the variables used to measure the cost, profit and revenue efficiency, whereas Table 5.3 provides the summary statistics of the variables.

Table 5.2 The definition of variables used to estimate the efficiency

Variable	Notation	Measurement
Total cost	COST	Interest expenses plus non-interest expenses
Revenue	Gross revenue	
Profit	Return on assets (ROA)	Net income/total assets
Total assets	ASSETS	
Input prices	INPUT	Input price 1: Price of fund – ratio of interest expenses to total funding Input price 2: Price of capital – ratio of other non-interest expenses to fixed assets Input price 3: Price of labour – ratio of personnel expenses to total assets

Table 5.3 Summary statistics of the variables used to measure cost, profit, and revenue efficiencies

Variables	Observation	Mean	SD	Min	Max
Total cost	777	3.35	0.97	−0.79	6.86
Gross revenue	778	216.63	689.53	0.001	5777.95
Profit	745	0.009	0.007	−0.04	0.106
Total assets	811	4.89	0.97	0.71	8.32
Price of funds	777	1.27	0.18	0.74	1.96
Price of capital	776	1.92	0.26	0.68	2.83
Price of labour	432	1.7	0.87	−2.93	4.77

5.3 THE MEASUREMENT OF COMPETITION IN THE CHINESE BANKING INDUSTRY

5.3.1 Boone Indicator

The Boone indicator Boone (2008) holds the idea that the performance of efficient firms is improved and the performance of inefficient firms is weakened by competition. The basic logic of the Boone indicator is in line with the argument of efficiency structure hypothesis as developed by Demsetz (1973) which links the efficiency to performance. The performance can be measured by profit and market share. The stronger effect will lead to more negative Boone indicator. The Boone indicator for bank *I* can be defined by the simplest equation as follows:

$$\mathrm{LN}(\mathrm{MS}_{ki}) = \alpha + \beta \mathrm{LN}(\mathrm{MC}_{ki}) \quad [5.6]$$

in which *i* represents the specific bank, *k* stands from a specific bank output, MS is the market share whereas marginal cost (MC) measures the marginal cost. β denotes the Boone indicator. In this book, *I* focus on the analysis of competition in different markets reflecting interest income activities as well as non-interest generating business; this significantly contributes to the empirical banking literature which just focus on the examination of the loan market. Thus, $K=$ loans, deposits, and non-interest income.

Compared to other competition indicators, the Boone indicator has the advantages of measuring competition for several specific product markets and different categories of banks. This advantage provides more insight for future research and more valuable information for relevant government and banking regulatory authorities to make relevant policies because it does not only know from this indicator on which banking output is subject to more or less competitive pressures but also different types of banks in terms of competition are compared (Tabak et al., 2012). A study undertaken by Leuvensteijin et al. (2011) used the Boone indicator to investigate the competition across different types of banks for a sample of European countries. The results show that in Germany and the United States, there is a higher competitive condition amongst commercial banks than cooperative and saving banks.

The Boone indicator assumes that the banks' efficiency gains are partly passed on to their clients. More specifically, it is assumed that this passing behaviour does not diverge strongly amongst banks, whereas another assumption made by the Boone indicator is that the level of quality product provided by banks are more or less similar amongst each other over time. In addition, it is assumed that banks will follow the level of innovation of their counterparts (peers). Therefore, as argues by Bikker and Bos (2005), the Boone indicator focuses on the relationship between efficiency and market share, affected by competition, whereas other aspects are disregarded. Leuvensteijin et al. (2011) argue that these distortions of ignoring other aspects will be more likely to impair the annual estimation of beta rather than the estimates covering the full sample. With regards to the disadvantage of the Boone indicator, it is surrounded by a degree of uncertainty due to the fact that it is an estimate. Some other indicators such as the Panzar–Rosse H-statistic, suffers from the same disadvantage.

The Boone indicator is time dependent. In other words, it reflects the changes in competition over time, thus the Boone indicator, beta, will be estimated on a year-by-year basis. No benchmark exists for the value of beta; it is only known that, the more negative the value, the stronger the competition is.

Because the MC cannot be obtained directly from a database, a number of studies use the ratio of average variable cost and revenues as the approximation of marginal cost (see Centraal Planbureau CPB, 2000; Boone et al., 2004; amongst others). More specifically, the relative values of profit are used by CPB (2000) as the dependent variable and the ratio of variable cost and revenues as the independent variable, whereas the absolute rather than relative values of profits are considered by Boone et al. (2004).

With regards to the calculation of MC, rather than using the average variable cost, *I* use the translog cost function to estimate it which not only provides more robust results, but is also in accordance with theory. The advantage of using translog cost function to estimate the MC lies to the fact that it allows focusing on segments of the market, such as loan market, deposit market, as well as non-interest income market, in which no direct observations of individual cost items are available. Furthermore, rather than using profit as the dependent variable, *I* use the market shares. The theoretical framework mainly argues the impact of efficiency on market share and its relation with competition; however, the impact of efficiency on profit margin is not strongly documented in the empirical literature. In other words, using market share as the dependent variable provides more accurate results. The second advantage of using market share rather than profit as the dependent variable is that the market shares are always positive, whereas the profit values can be either positive or negative. If the log linear specification is used, the negative profits would be excluded. In other words, the biased estimation results will be obtained due to the fact that banks with higher inefficiency and higher levels of losses would have to be ignored.

The MC is estimated on the basis of a translog cost function with one output (total assets) and three input prices (price of labour, price of capital and price of funds). Symmetry and linear homogeneity restrictions in input prices are imposed. The specification of translog cost function is the same as the one previously used to estimate efficiency, whereas the estimated coefficients of the cost function are then used to compute the MC.

$$MC_{it} = \frac{COST_{it}}{ASSETS_{it}}\left(\widehat{a}_1 + \widehat{a}_2 LNY + \sum_{j=1}^{3} \widehat{\gamma}_{itj} LNINPUT_{itj}\right) \qquad [5.7]$$

5.3.2 Panzar—Rosse H-Statistic

In the empirical analysis, the following reduced-form revenue equation (Eq. [5.8]) is selected to derive the Panzar—Rosse H-statistic:

$$\begin{aligned}\mathrm{LNTR}_{it} = {} & \alpha + \beta_1 \mathrm{LNP}_{1,it} + \beta_2 \mathrm{LNP}_{2,it} + \beta_3 \mathrm{LNP}_{3,it} + \gamma_1 \mathrm{LNQUAST}_{it} \\ & + \gamma_2 \mathrm{LNLATA}_{it} + \gamma_3 \mathrm{LNNIIGR}_{it} + \gamma_4 \mathrm{LNNPLGL}_{it} \\ & + \gamma_5 \mathrm{LNASSETS}_{it} + \varepsilon_{it} \end{aligned} \qquad [5.8]$$

For $t = 1,\ldots, T$, in which T is the number of periods observed, and $i = 1,\ldots, I$, in which I is the total number of banks. Subscripts i and t refer to bank i at time t. The dependent variable (TR) is the total revenue over total assets. The reason to use total revenue instead of interest revenue is to consider the fact that non-interest income from fee-based products and off-balance sheet activities have increased dramatically in recent years. As argued by De Bandt and Davis (2000), in a more competitive environment the distinction between interest and non-interest income becomes less relevant, as banks are competing on both fronts. Finally, the scaled variable is considered as the dependent variable to account for size difference.

Consistent with the intermediation approach[3], we assume that banks use three inputs, which are (1) deposits, (2) labour and (3) capital. LNP_1 is the average cost of funds (interest expenses/total funds), LNP_2 is the average cost of labour (personnel expenses/total assets), LNP_3 is the average cost of capital (other operating expenses/fixed assets).

The equation of our specification includes on the right-hand side a set of bank-specific variables that reflect differences in capitalization (EQAST), liquidity (LATA), product mix (NIIGR), bank risk (NPLTL) and bank size (ASSETS) to allow for bank heterogeneity. These variables are the ratio of equity to total assets, the ratio of liquid assets to total assets and the ratio of non-interest income over gross revenue. The ratio of non-interest income over gross revenue (NIIGR) is included as an explanatory variable to account for the influence of the generation of other income on the model's underlying marginal revenue (MR) and cost functions, the ratio of non-performing loans over gross loans and the natural logarithm of total assets. There is no a priori expectation with regard to the impact of capitalization on bank revenue. The coefficient of

[3] The intermediation approach takes deposits as inputs and defines loans and investments as output.

capitalization is expected to be negative due to the fact that lower capital ratios should lead to higher bank revenue (Molyneux et al., 1994). However, a higher capital ratio may suggest a higher risky loan portfolio, which results in higher bank revenue. This positive effect is supported by Coccorese (2004). The ratio of liquid assets to total assets is used to control for bank liquidity. The coefficient is expected to be positive because higher proportions of loans in bank's total assets normally lead to higher bank revenue. The ratio of non-interest income to gross revenue is used to control for the differences in business mix. A positive coefficient is expected because higher volume of non-interest income contributes to greater bank revenue. Because the larger volume of non-performing loans reduces the bank revenue, it is expected that the variable will have a negative coefficient. Large bank size such as SOCBs have higher ability to engage in a number of different activities, a larger variety of business engaged in by banks increases the bank revenue; therefore, it is expected that this variable will have a positive sign. An important feature of Panzar—Rosse H-statistic is that the test must be undertaken on data that represent the market in long-run equilibrium. This suggests that competitive capital markets will equalize risk-adjusted rate of return across banks such that, in equilibrium, rates of return should be uncorrelated with input prices (Molyneux et al., 1994). In addition, the long-run equilibrium test will be carried out using H-statistic, in which case it measures the sum of elasticity of ROA with respect to input prices, as shown in the equation that follows (Eq. [5.9]). The resulting H-statistic is expected to be significantly equal to zero in equilibrium and significantly negative in case of disequilibrium (see Shaffer, 1982; Molyneux et al., 1994; Claessens and Laeven, 2004).

$$\begin{aligned} \mathrm{LNROA}_{it} = {} & \alpha + \beta_1 \mathrm{LNP}_{1,it} + \beta_2 \mathrm{LNP}_{2,it} + \beta_3 \mathrm{LNP}_{3,it} \\ & + \gamma_1 \mathrm{LNQUAST}_{it} + \gamma_2 \mathrm{LNLATA}_{it} + \gamma_3 \mathrm{LNNIIGR}_{it} \\ & + \gamma_4 \mathrm{LNNPLGL}_{it} + \gamma_5 \mathrm{LNASSETS}_{it} + \varepsilon_{it} \end{aligned} \quad [5.9]$$

Taking into consideration the fact that small negative values of ROA arise for some banks in a specific year, the measurement of ROA in the previous equation is given by LN(1 + ROA). The equilibrium statistics resulting from the above equation is tested using the *F*-test. Table 5.4 defines the variables used to measure the Panzar—Rosse H-statistic, whereas Table 5.5 provides the descriptive statistics.

Table 5.4 Definition of variables used to measure the Panzar–Rosse H-statistic

Variables	Notation	Measurement
Dependent variable	TR	The ratio of total revenue to total assets
Input prices	P	P1: Price of fund–ratio of interest expenses to total funding P2: Price of capital–ratio of other non-interest expenses to fixed assets P3: Price of labour–ratio of personnel expenses to total assets
Bank capitalization	QUAST	The ratio of shareholder's equity to total assets
Bank liquidity	LATA	The ratio of liquid assets to total assets
Bank diversification	NIIGR	The ratio of non-interest income to gross revenue
Bank risk	NPLGL	The ratio of non-performing loans to gross loans
Bank size	ASSETS	natural logarithm of total assets

Table 5.5 Summary statistics of the variables used to measure the Panzar–Rosse H-statistic

Variable	Observations	Mean	SD	Min	Max
TR	764	0.00029	0.00014	0.00022	0.023
P1	777	1.27	0.18	0.74	1.96
P2	776	1.92	0.26	0.68	2.83
P3	432	1.7	0.87	−2.93	4.77
QUAST	843	5.75	2.83	−14	31
LATA	777	0.27	0.11	0.02	0.67
NIIGR	828	13.98	13.31	−12.94	79.4
NPLGL	632	2.78	4.48	0.01	41.86
ASSETS	843	4.9	0.992	0.71	8.51

5.3.3 Lerner Index

During recent years, a number of research articles have used different methods to investigate the competitive condition in the banking industry (see Al-Muharrami et al., 2006; Matthews et al., 2007; Jeon et al., 2011; Olivero et al., 2011; Tabak et al., 2012; Cipollini and Fiordelisi, 2012; Fungacova et al., 2014; Fu et al., 2014; Tan, 2016). More specifically, the competition in the Gulf Cooperation Council (GCC) banking system over the period 1993–2002 was estimated by Al-Muharrami et al. (2006) using three different indicators, namely K-bank concentration ratio, Herfindahl–Hirschman index as well as the Panzar–Rosse H-statistic; whereas the Panzar–Rosse H-statistic was used by Matthew et al. (2007) to investigate the competitive condition of British banks over the period 1980–2004. The Panzar–Rosse H-statistic was used by Jeon et al. (2011) to evaluate the competitive condition of the Asia and Latin America banking sector over the period 1997–2008. Olivero et al. (2011) assessed the competitive condition of the Asian and Latin American banking sector over the period 1996–2006 under the Panzar–Rosse H-statistic; the Boone indicator was used by Tabak et al. (2012) to investigate the competition of the Latin American banking industry during 2003 and 2008. Cipollini and Fiordelisi (2012) used Lerner index as well as the Herfindahl–Hirschman index to examine to the competitive condition of a sample of European banks over the period 1996–2009. Fungacova et al. (2014) used the Lerner index to examine the competitive condition for a sample of banks from 12 European area countries over the period 2002–10, whereas both the three-bank concentration ratio as well as the Lerner index were used by Fu et al. (2014) to evaluate the competition in the Asian Pacific banking industry over the period 2003–10. Using a sample of Chinese commercial banks over the period 2003–11, Tan (2016) investigated the joint impacts of risk and competition on bank profitability in China. The Lerner index was used to measure the competitive condition in the Chinese banking industry.

Although a number of researchers are using the Panzar–Rosse H-statistic to investigate the competition in the banking sector, it mainly suffers from two drawbacks. First, as argued by Leuvensteijin et al. (2011), the H-statistic was developed on the basis of a static model, and there are no predictions on the H-statistic which is one of the weaknesses of this test. In other words, the estimate is surrounded by a degree of uncertainty. Furthermore, as argued by Claessens and Laeven (2004), the overall market equilibrium required by the test cannot be fulfilled because of market entry and exit, which leads to further limits on the interpretation of such analysis.

Furthermore, the Boone indicator also suffers from two disadvantages. First, as argued by Tabak et al. (2012), it makes the assumption that part of the efficiency gains achieved by the banks will be passed onto consumers. In addition, this indicator also suffers from idiosyncratic variation, ie, uncertainty.

The Lerner index is used in this study mainly because of the following reasons: (1) it can be easily estimated by each bank at each year; and also it matches with its determinants, which are bank-level variables at each year; (2) we can estimate the competitive conditions (market power) for three different ownership types of Chinese banks.

The Lerner index is defined as the difference between a bank's price and the MC, divided by the price. The index value ranges from a maximum of one to a minimum of zero, with higher numbers indicating greater market power and hence less competition. The Lerner index represents the extent to which a particular bank has market power to set its price above the MC.

The price is computed by estimating the average price of bank production (proxied by total assets) as the ratio of total revenue over total assets following Fernandez de Guevara et al. (2005) and Carbo et al. (2009a,b). The cost function is specified as the same used to measure the efficiency and the estimation of MC follows the specification used to evaluate the Boone indicator.

Once the MC is estimated and the price of output computed, we calculate the Lerner index for each bank and obtain a direct measure of bank competition. We use the same three input prices to calculate the MC, which are the price of funds, price of capital and price of labour. $\widehat{a}_1, \widehat{a}_2\ \widehat{\gamma}_{itj}$ are the coefficients estimated from the Eq. [5.4]. The variables used to estimate the Lerner index are defined in Table 5.3.

5.3.4 Bank Concentration Ratio

The concentration ratios measure the competition from the perspectives of the number and size distribution of firms in the industry. In other words, the concentration measurement emphasizes the evaluation of competition on the number of firms and their size distribution.

Traditional industrial organization theory indicates that the cost of collusion is lower in a more concentrated industry, whereas the lower cost of collusion leads to anti-competitive behaviour and higher profitability. This theory is in line with the Structure—Conduct—Performance (SCP) paradigm. Early empirical literature tests whether the SCP paradigm or the efficiency hypothesis holds (Smirlock, 1985; Evanoff and Fortier, 1988). The efficiency hypothesis is in direct contrast with the SCP hypothesis arguing that the higher profitability is not derived from higher concentration (lower competitive condition/anti-competitive behaviour), but it is the result of higher operating efficiency of large banks. Early literature such as Berger (1995) found that the efficiency hypothesis holds in the US banking industry, whereas the findings do not show any results which are in accordance with the SCP paradigm. In summary, some of the early empirical literature found evidence that higher efficiency rather than lower competitive condition explains the better performance in the US banking industry, although there are a couple of studies in favour of the efficiency hypothesis rather than the SCP paradigm (Gibert, 1984; Berger et al., 2004). The three-bank concentration is used in this book and it can be expressed as follows:

Three-bank concentration ratio = the total assets of the three largest banks/the total assets of the whole banking industry.

5.4 MODELLING THE IMPACT OF COMPETITION ON BANK EFFICIENCY

Our study follows the estimation method proposed by Simar and Wilson (2007) who investigated the determinants of bank efficiency using the bootstrap technique. Before illustrating the estimation procedure, the following model is given:

$$\widehat{\delta}_i = Z_i\beta + \varepsilon_i \qquad [5.10]$$

in which Z_i is a vector of explanatory variables which are supposed to have impacts on bank efficiency, β refers to a vector of parameters with some statistical noise ε_i. Simar and Wilson (2007) argued that estimating the determinants of bank efficiency using ordinary least square (OLS) might lead to estimation problems due to the correlation and dependency problems of the efficiency scores which violate the regression assumption that ε_i are independent of Z_i. The advantages of the Simar and Wilson (2007) bootstrapped truncated regression lies in the fact that it produces, with bias-corrected estimates of $\widehat{\delta}$, valid estimates for the parameters in the regression model.

The bootstrap algorithm is described in the following steps:

1. Calculate the efficiency score $\widehat{\delta}$ for each bank at each year, using both the non-parametric and parametric methods described earlier.
2. Use the maximum likelihood method to estimate the truncated regression of $\widehat{\delta}$ on Z_i to provide estimate $\widehat{\beta}$ of β and an estimate of $\widehat{\sigma}_\varepsilon$ of σ_ε.
3. For each bank $i = 1\ldots, I$, repeat the next four steps (1−4) L times to yield a set of bootstrap estimates as $\text{A} = \left\{\left(\widehat{\beta}^*, \widehat{\sigma}_\varepsilon^*\right)_b\right\}_{b=1}^{L}$.
   a. Draw ε_i from the $N\left(0, \widehat{\sigma}_\varepsilon^2\right)$ distribution with left truncation at $\left(1 - \widehat{\beta} Z_i\right)$.

b. Compute $\widehat{\delta}_i^* = \widehat{\beta} Z_i + \varepsilon_i$.

c. The maximum likelihood method is used to estimate the truncated regression of $\widehat{\delta}_i^*$ on Z_i, yielding estimates $\left(\widehat{\beta}^*, \widehat{\sigma}_\varepsilon^*\right)$.

4. Use the bootstrap results to construct confidence intervals.

Besides the bootstrap truncated regression, some researchers show that other econometric methods can be used to investigate the determinants of bank efficiency. McDonald (2009) and Estelle et al. (2010) argue that using OLS in the second stage regression analysis can yield robust results when DEA is used in the first stage, whereas Garza-Garcia (2012) argues that Tobit regression is useful when the dependent variable is set between certain limits which is the case of efficiency scores. In this book, we use both of these two methods to check the robustness of our results.

5.5 DATA

The banking data is composed of annual figures of 100 Chinese commercial banks over the period 2003–13. The ownership types of banks considered mainly include SOCBs, JSCBs, city commercial banks, the number of which are 5, 12 and 83, respectively. Because not all banks have information available for every year, an unbalanced-panel data set is chosen not to lose a degree of freedom. Besides investigating the impact of competition on efficiency in the Chinese banking industry, the current study also controls a number of other bank-specific, industry-specific as well as macroeconomic variables. The bank-specific variables considered in the current study include bank size, credit risk, bank capitalization, bank profitability as well as bank diversification, whereas three industry-specific variables are considered which included banking sector development and stock market development and banking sector competition. With regards to the macroeconomic variables, both inflation and annual GDP growth rate are considered. The data for bank specific variables are obtained from the Bankscope database maintained by Fitch/Intervest Bankshare Corp. (International Bank Credit Analysis Ltd.) Bureau Van Dijk. The information for industry-specific variables and macroeconomic variables is collected from the websites of China Banking Regulatory Commission and the world bank database (http://data.worldbank.org).

Bank size is measured by the natural logarithm of total assets. This measurement is widely used in the empirical literature (see Goddard et al., 2004; Athanasoglou et al., 2008; Dietrich and Wanzenried, 2011). Banks with larger size are able to reduce costs from economies of scale and scope, the cost reduction precedes an improvement in efficiency; hence, it is expected that size is significantly and positively related to the efficiency of Chinese banks. Bank diversification is measured by the ratio of non-interest income to gross revenue (see Tan and Floros, 2012a,b,c). An increase in the variety of business engaged in by banks can decrease the operational cost from the economies of scope; the resultant reduction in cost precedes an increase in bank efficiency; thus, it is expected that this variable has a significant and positive sign. According to the bad luck hypothesis, increases in risk result in additional costs and managerial effort which further precede declines in bank efficiency (Berger and DeYoung, 1997). So, it is expected that risk has a significant and negative impact on bank efficiency. Profitability is measured by the traditional accounting indicator—ROA; ROA is chosen as the profitability indicator because it has emerged as the key ratio for the evaluation of bank profitability and has become the most common measure of bank profitability in the literature (Golin, 2001; Athanasoglou et al., 2008; Garcia-Herrero et al., 2009). It is expected that ROA affects bank efficiency positively. The profitable banks are more able to control all aspects of costs which leads to higher efficiency (Girardone et al., 2004). There are a number of studies investigating the impact of bank capitalization on bank efficiency (see Williams, 2004; Altunbas et al., 2007; Fiordelisi et al., 2011; Tan and Floros, 2013; amongst others). They have different findings with regards to the effect, thus, there is no a priori expectation on the impact of bank capitalization on bank efficiency.

Bank competition is measured by different competition indicators including three-bank concentration ratio, Panzar-Rosse H statistic, Lerner index and Boone indicator. Following the competition-efficiency and competition-inefficiency hypotheses discussed in the literature review, there is no prior expectation on this variable. Further, banking sector development is measured by the ratio of banking sector assets to GDP (see Tan and Floros, 2012a,b,c). A higher-developed banking market indicates that the demand for banking services is large, because it is quite difficult for new banks to enter the market; hence, the relatively short supply and increase in the demand lifts up the prices for banking services. The resulted improvement in bank profitability induces bank managers to be less careful in controlling the costs which precede a decline in bank efficiency. Therefore, it is expected that this variable has a significant and negative impact on bank efficiency. Stock market development is measured by the ratio of stock market capitalization to GDP (see Tan and Floros, 2012a,b,c). It is expected to be significantly and positively related to bank efficiency. A more highly developed stock market provides valuable information to the banks in terms of credit conditions of different companies, and hence, the resulting reduction in monitoring cost leads to an improvement in bank efficiency.

Inflation is expected to affect bank efficiency negatively due to the fact that under inflationary conditions, banks might feel less pressure to control their inputs, and therefore become less efficient (Lozano-Vivas and Pasiouras, 2010). Higher GDP growth stimulates investment; the resulting increase in the volumes of banking business in terms of traditional loan-deposit services and non-interest generating activities reduces bank costs and leads to an improvement in bank efficiency. Therefore, it is expected that GDP growth rate affects efficiency positively. Table 5.6 presents the variables used in the paper.

Table 5.7 shows the summary statistics of the independent variables used in the current study. The table shows Chinese commercial banks have relatively larger differences in the levels of credit risk undertaken, whereas the higher levels of credit risk undertaken by Chinese commercial banks are attributed to the fact that during 2003–06, large volumes of non-performing loans exist in SOCBs, especially in the Agricultural Bank of China. Further, the large difference in bank capitalization is attributed to the opening of one joint-stock commercial bank; namely, the China Bohai Bank in 2006 which had a total regulatory capital ratio of over 60%. The data indicate that Chinese banks have big differences in the degree of diversified activities engaged in, whereas the difference in the profitability amongst Chinese banks is relatively smaller. The difference in the bank size is attributed to the fact that SOCBs are bigger than JSCBs, whereas city commercial banks (CCBs) are the smallest. The statistics further show that stronger volatility attends to the stock market development than to banking sector development and the macroeconomic environment. The stronger volatility of stock market development can be attributed mainly to the segregation reform initiated by the Chinese government in 2005 which led to a substantial number of

Table 5.6 Description of the variables used in the bootstrap truncated regression model

Variable	Description	Hypothesized relationship with efficiency	Data source
Bank-specific variables			
Credit risk	The ratio of impaired loans to gross loans	−	Bankscope
Bank size	Natural logarithm of total assets	+	Bankscope
Bank capitalization	The ratio of shareholder's equity to total assets	+	Bankscope
Bank diversification	The ratio of non-interest income to gross revenue	+	Bankscope
Bank profitability	Return on assets	+	Bankscope
Industry-specific variables			
Banking sector competition	Panzar–Rosse H-statistic Lerner index Boone indicator Three-bank Concentration ratio	?	Bankscope
Banking sector development	Ratio of banking sector assets to GDP	−	China Banking Regulatory Commission
Stock market development	Capitalization of stock market to GDP	+	World Bank
Macroeconomic environment			
Inflation	Annual inflation rate	−	World Bank
GDP growth rate	Annual GDP growth rate	+	World Bank

companies being listed on the stock exchange. By the end of 2007, there were 1550 listed companies on the Shanghai and Hong Kong Stock Exchanges, the value of which reached RMB 32.71 billion, accounting for 132.6% of GDP at that year. On the other hand, the stock market development was in its early stage before 2005.

Table 5.7 Descriptive statistics of all variables considered in this study

Variables	Observations	Mean	SD	Min	Max
Bank-specific variables					
Credit risk	632	2.78	4.48	0.01	41.86
Bank capitalization	843	5.75	2.83	−14	31
Bank profitability	806	0.009	0.007	−0.04	0.106
Bank size	843	4.9	0.992	0.71	8.51
Bank diversification	828	13.98	13.31	−12.94	79.4
Industry-specific variables					
Banking sector development	1100	2.22	0.24	1.98	2.66
Stock market development	1027	71.2	43.49	31.9	184.1
Macroeconomic variables					
Inflation	1227	2.86	1.92	−0.77	5.86
GDP growth rate	1199	10.19	1.87	7.7	14.2

5.6 SUMMARY AND CONCLUSION

The types of methods used to estimate efficiency can be mainly classified into two groups which are parametric method and non-parametric method, whereas there is an ongoing debate on the choice of these two types of methods to measure the efficiency. Some of the scholars prefer the parametric method (eg, Berger, 1993), whereas other researchers prefer the non-parametric method (eg, Seiford and Thrall, 1990). The main disadvantage of the non-parametric method, such as the DEA, lies in the fact that it does not distinguish between technical inefficiency and statistical noise effects. However, it is able to yield reliable results if the sample size is relatively small. On the other hand, the main advantage of the parametric method lies to the fact that it allows the test of the hypothesis concerning the goodness of fit of the model. Although, it requires the definition of a specific functional form for the technology and for the inefficiency error terms. Both the specification and estimation problems are caused by this functional form requirement (Murillo-Zamorano and Vega-Cervera, 2000). The current study uses both of the methods, parametric and non-parametric, to estimate the efficiency in the Chinese banking industry. More specifically, the cost, profit and revenue functions are used to estimate the cost, profit and revenue efficiencies of Chinese commercial banks, whereas the non-parametric DEA is used to evaluate the technical, pure technical and scale efficiencies of Chinese commercial banks.

With regards to the measurement of banking sector competition, this book uses both the indicators from traditional industrial organization theory as well as the indicators from New industrial organization theory. More specifically, four different competition indicators are used namely, the three-bank concentration ratio, the Panzar–Rosse H-statistic, the Lerner index as well as the Boone indicator. In particular, the main contribution of the current study lies in the fact that it significantly extends the empirical literature in the banking industry, especially the Chinese banking industry, by estimating the competitive conditions of different market sectors in Chinese banking industry such as the deposit, loan, and the non-interest income markets. It is the first study in the banking industry examining the competition of different markets in the banking industry. The results not only fill the gap in the empirical literature but provide very important information to the Chinese government as well as banking regulatory authorities to make relevant policies. Various competition indicators used are supposed to provide more robust results not only to the general competitive conditions in the Chinese banking industry but, more importantly, provide more accurate results with regards to the impact of competition on bank efficiency in China. The robust and accurate results are not only guaranteed by different competition indicators, but the precise findings will be guaranteed by using different modern econometric techniques such as bootstrapped truncated regression, Tobit regression as well as ordinary least square estimator.

REFERENCES

Aigner, D.J., Lovell, C.A.K., Schmeidt, P., 1977. Formulation and estimation of stochastic frontier production function models. Journal of Econometrics 6, 21–37.

Ajibefun, I.A., 2008. An evaluation of parametric and non-parametric methods of technical efficiency measurement: application to small scale crop production in Nigeria. Journal of Agriculture and Social Sciences 4, 95–100.

Al-Muharrami, S., Matthews, K., Khabari, Y., 2006. Market structure and competitive conditions in the Arab GCC banking system. Journal of Banking and Finance 30, 3487–3501.

Altunbas, Y., Carobo, S., Gardener, E.P.M., Molyneux, P., 2007. Examining the relationship between capital, risk and efficiency in European banking. European Financial Management 13, 49–70.

Athanasoglou, P.P., Brissmis, S.N., Delis, M.D., 2008. Bank-specific, industry-specific and macroeconomic determinants of bank profitability. Journal of International Financial Markets, Institutions and Money 18, 121–136.

Banker, R.D., Charnes, A., Cooper, W.W., 1984. Some models for estimating technical and scale inefficiencies in data envelopment analysis. Management Science 30, 1078–1092.

Berger, A.N., 1993. Distribution-free estimates of efficiency in the U.S banking industry and tests of the standard distributional assumptions. Journal of Productivity Analysis 4, 261–292.

Berger, A.N., 1995. The profit-structure relationship in banking-tests of market-power and efficient-structure hypotheses. Journal of Money, Credit and Banking 27, 404–415.

Berger, A.N., DeYoung, R., 1997. Problem loans and cost efficiency in commercial banks. Journal of Banking and Finance 21, 849–870.

Berger, A.N., Humphrey, D.B., 1997. Efficiency of financial institutions: international survey and directions for future research. European Journal of Operational Research 98, 175–212.

Berger, A.N., Demerguc-Kunt, A., Levine, R., Haubrich, J.C., 2004. Bank concentration and competition. Journal of Money, Credit and Banking 36, 433–451.

Berger, A.N., Hasan, I., Zhou, M., 2009. Bank ownership and efficiency in China: what will happen in the world's largest nation? Journal of Banking and Finance 33, 113–130.

Bikker, J.A., Bos, J.W.B., 2005. Trends in Competition and Profitability in the Banking Industry: A Basic Framework. SUREF studies, No. 2005/2.

Boone, J., 2008. A new way to measure competition. Economic Journal 118, 1245–1261.

Boone, J., Griffith, R., Harrison, R., 2004. Measuring competition, Presented at the Eucore Metting, 2004. Measuring competition.

Carbo, S., Rodriguez-Fernandez, F., Udell, G., 2009a. Bank market power and SME financial constraints. Review of Finance 13, 309–340.

Carbo, S., Humphrey, D., Maudos, J., Molyneux, P., 2009b. Cross-country comparisons of competition and pricing power in European banking. Journal of International Money and Finance 28, 115–134.

Centraal Planbureau, 2000. Measuring Competition: How Are Cost Differentials Mapped into Profit Differentials. CPB working document, no. 131.

Charnes, A., Cooper, W.W., Rhodes, E., 1978. Measuring the efficiency of decision making units. European Journal of Operational Research 2, 429–444.

Charnes, A., Cooper, W.W., Lewin, A.Y., Seiford, L.M., 1995. Data Envelopment Analysis: Theory Methodology and Applications. Kluwer, Boston.

Chen, X., Skully, M., Brown, K., 2005. Bank efficiency in China: application of DEA to pre- and post- deregulation eras: 1993–2000. China Economic Review 16, 229–245.

Cipollini, A., Fiordelisi, F., 2012. Economic value, competition and financial distress in the European banking system. Journal of Banking and Finance 36, 3101–3109.

Claessens, S., Laeven, L., 2004. What drives banking competition? some international evidence. Journal of Money. Credit and Banking 36, 563–583.

Coccorese, P., 2004. Banking competition and macroeconomic conditions: a disaggregate analysis. International Journal of Financial Markets, Institutions and Money 14, 203–219.

De Bandt, O., Davis, E.P., 2000. Competition, contestability and market structure in European banking sectors on the eve of EMU. Journal of Banking and Finance 24, 1045–1066.

Demsetz, H., 1973. Industry structure, market entry and public policy. Journal of Law and Economics 16, 1–9.

Dietrich, A., Wanzenried, G., 2011. Determinants of bank profitability before and during the crisis: evidence from Switzerland. Journal of International Financial Markets, Institutions and Money 21, 307–327.

Estelle, S.M., Johnson, A.C., Ruggiero, J., 2010. Three-stage DEA models for incorporating exogenous inputs. Computers and Operations Research 37, 1087–1090.

Evanoff, D.D., Fortier, D.L., 1988. Re-evaluation of the structure-conduct-performance paradigm in banking. Journal of Financial Services Research 1, 277–294.

Fernandez de Guevara, J., Maudos, J., Perez, F., 2005. Market power in European Banking. Journal of Financial Services Research 27, 109–137.
Fiordelisi, F., Marques-Ibanez, D., Molyneux, P., 2011. Efficiency and risk in European banking. Journal of Banking and Finance 35, 1315–1326.
Fu, X., Heffernan, S., 2007. Cost X-efficiency in China's banking sector. China Economic Review 18, 35–53.
Fu, X., Lin, Y., Molyneux, P., 2014. Bank competition and financial stability in Asia Pacific. Journal of Banking and Finance 38, 64–77.
Fungacova, Z., Solanko, L., Weill, L., 2014. Does competition influence the bank lending channel in the Euro area? Journal of Banking and Finance 49, 356–366.
Garcia-Herrero, A., Gavila, S., Santabarbara, D., 2009. What explains the low profitability of Chinese banks? Journal of Banking and Finance 33, 2080–2092.
Garza-Garcia, J.G., 2012. Determinants if bank efficiency in Mexico: a two-stage analysis. Applied Economics Letters 19, 1679–1682.
Gibert, R.A., 1984. Bank market structure and competition: a survey. Journal of Money, Credit and Banking 16, 617–645.
Girardone, C., Molyneux, P., Gardener, E., 2004. Analysing the determinants of bank efficiency: the case of Italian banks. Applied Economics 36, 215–227.
Goddard, J., Molyneux, P., Wilson, J.O.S., 2004. Dynamic of growth and profitability in banking. Journal of Money, Credit and Banking 36, 1069–1090.
Golin, J., 2001. The Bank Credit Analysis Handbook: A Guide for Analyst, Bankers and Investors. John Wiley and Sons, Asia.
Jeon, B.N., Olivero, M.P., Wu, J., 2011. Do foreign bank increase competition? Evidence from emerging Asian and Latin American banking markets. Journal of Banking and Finance 35, 856–875.
Leuvensteijin, M.V., Bikker, J., Rixel, X.V., Sorensen, C.K., 2011. A new approach to measuring competition in the loan markets of the Euro area. Applied Economics 43, 3155–3167.
Lozano-Vivas, A., Pasiouras, F., 2010. The impact of non-traditional activities on the estimation of bank efficiency: international evidence. Journal of Banking and Finance 34, 1436–1449.
Matthews, K., Murinde, V., Zhao, T., 2007. Competitive conditions among the major British banks. Journal of Banking and Finance 31, 2025–2042.
Meeusen, W., van den Broeck, J., 1977. Technical efficiency and dimension of the firm: some results on the use of frontier production functions. Empirical Economics 2, 109–122.
McDonald, J., 2009. Using least square and Tobit in second stage DEA efficiency analyses. European Journal of Operational Research 197, 792–798.
Molyneux, P., Lloyd-Williams, D.M., Thornton, J., 1994. Competitive conditions in European banking. Journal of Banking and Finance 18, 445–459.
Murillo-Zamorano, L.R., Vega-Cervera, J., 2000. The use of parametric and non-parametric frontier methods to measure the productive efficiency in the industrial sector: a comparative study. In: Discussion Papers in Economics. The University of York.
Olivero, M.P., Li, Y., Jeon, B.N., 2011. Competition in banking and the lending channel: evidence from bank-level data in Asia and Latin America. Journal of Banking and Finance 35, 560–571.
Seiford, L.M., Thrall, R.M., 1990. Recent development in DEA: the mathematical programming approach to frontier analysis. Journal of Econometrics 46, 7–38.
Sealey, C.E., Lindley, J.T., 1977. Inputs, outputs and a theory of production and cost at depository financial institutions. Journal of Finance 32, 1251–1266.

Shaffer, S., 1982. A non-structural test for competition in financial markets. Proceedings of a conference on bank structure and competition. Federal Reserve Bank of Chicago 225–243.

Smirlock, M., 1985. Evidence of the (non) relationship between concentration and profitability in banking. Journal of Money, Credit and Banking 17, 69–83.

Simar, L., Wilson, P.W., 2007. Estimation and inference in two-stage, semi-parametric models of production processes. Journal of Econometrics 136, 31–64.

Sun, L., Chang, T., 2011. A comprehensive analysis of the effects of risk measures on bank efficiency: evidence from emerging Asian countries. Journal of Banking and Finance 35, 1727–1735.

Tabak, B.M., Fazio, D.M., Cajueiro, D.O., 2012. The relationship between banking market competition and risk-taking: do bank size and capitalization matter? Journal of Banking and Finance 36, 3366–3381.

Tan, Y., Floros, C., 2012a. Bank profitability and inflation: the case of China. Journal of Economic Studies 39, 675–696.

Tan, Y., Floros, C., 2012b. Bank profitability and GDP growth in China: a Note. Journal of Chinese Economic and Business Studies 10, 267–273.

Tan, Y., Floros, C., 2012c. Stock market volatility and bank performance in China. Studies in Economics and Finance 29, 211–228.

Tan, Y., Floros, C., 2013. Risk, capital and efficiency in Chinese banking. Journal of International Financial Markets, Institutions and Money 26, 378–393.

Tan, Y., 2016. The impacts of risk and competition on bank profitability in China. Journal of International Financial Markets. Institutions and Money 40, 85–110.

Williams, J., 2004. Determining manager behaviour in European banking. Journal of Banking and Finance 28, 2427–2460.

CHAPTER 6

The Impact of Competition on Efficiency in the Chinese Banking Industry

6.1 INTRODUCTION

This chapter reports the results with regard to the impact of competitive condition on efficiency in the Chinese banking industry. More specifically, this chapter is structured as follows: Section 6.2 mainly focuses on the efficiency estimates of Chinese commercial banks with Subsection 6.2.1 presenting the results of technical, pure technical, and scale efficiencies of Chinese commercial banks. Subsection 6.2.2 focuses on the explanation of cost, profit, and revenue efficiencies in the Chinese banking industry. This subsection will be further divided into three parts discussing the findings of cost, revenue, and profit efficiencies on a one-by-one basis. Section 6.2.3 reports the findings with regard to the competitive condition of the Chinese banking industry, and is divided into four subsections: Subsection 6.2.3.1 talks about the competitive condition of the Chinese banking industry using the Lerner index. Subsection 6.2.3.2 addresses the results of competitive condition of the Chinese banking sector under the three-bank concentration ratio, which will be followed by Subsection 6.2.3.3 discussing the competitive condition of the Chinese banking industry using Panzar–Rosse H-statistic. Finally, and in particular, Subsection 6.2.3.4 will focus on the competitive condition in different banking segments in China such as the loan, the deposit, as well as the non-interest income markets under the Boone indicator. The final part of this chapter will focus on discussing the impact of competition on bank efficiency under different modern econometric techniques, such as Bootstrapped truncated regression, Tobit regression, as well as ordinary least square estimator.

Efficiency and Competition in Chinese Banking
ISBN 978-0-08-100074-8

6.2 EFFICIENCY IN THE CHINESE BANKING INDUSTRY

6.2.1 Technical efficiency in the Chinese Banking Industry

Table 6.1 and Fig. 6.1 show the technical efficiency, pure technical efficiency, and scale efficiency scores of Chinese state-owned commercial banks (SOCBs), joint-stock commercial banks (JSCBs), and city commercial banks (CCBs) derived from the nonparametric data envelopment analysis (DEA) Charnes, Cooper, and Rhodes (CCR), and Banker, Charnes, and Cooper (BCC) models. The results show that the SOCBs have the highest technical efficiency over the examined period, which is then followed by the CCBs. The JSCBs are found to be least technically efficient. The highest technical efficiency of the SOCBs can be attributed to the fact that all of them finished their initial public offerings over the

Table 6.1 Mean values of technical, pure technical, and scale efficiencies for all Chinese commercial banks: 2003–2013

Banks/efficiency scores	Technical efficiency	Pure technical efficiency	Scale efficiency
State-owned commercial banks	0.97	0.975	0.995
Joint-stock commercial banks	0.913	0.928	0.977
City commercial banks	0.915	0.926	0.974

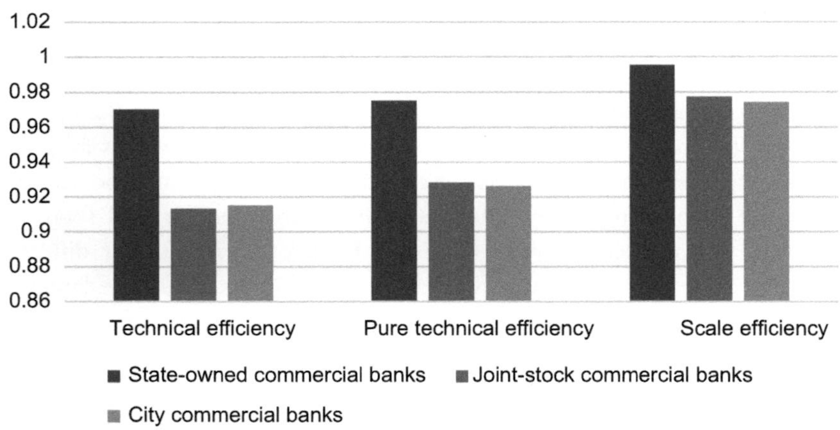

Figure 6.1 Mean values of technical, pure technical, and scale efficiencies of all Chinese commercial banks: 2003–2013.

examined period. The initial public offerings improve bank management and precede further improvements in bank efficiency, whereas the lowest technical efficiency of JSCBs can be explained by the fact that they mainly service small- and medium-size enterprises all over the country, easily outnumbering the large state-owned enterprises. The resulting higher competition leads to a decline in efficiency.

Based on the decomposition of technical efficiency into pure technical and scale efficiencies, the results suggest that SOCBs have the highest pure technical efficiency which is followed by JSCBs, whereas CCBs have the lowest pure technical efficiency. It is further noticed that scale efficiency is higher than pure technical efficiency which indicates that scale efficiency contributes more than pure technical efficiency to the overall technical efficiency in the Chinese banking sector. In other words, the inefficiency of Chinese commercial banks is attributed to pure technical inefficiency rather than scale inefficiency. The results also suggest that Chinese commercial banks are pure technical inefficient and face misallocation of inputs and outputs in banking operation.

In addition, the current study not only reports the results with regard to different technical, pure technical, and scale efficiencies of different types of ownership of Chinese commercial banks over the examined period, but also reports the findings and compares the technical, pure technical, and scale efficiencies of different ownership types on a year-by-year basis, as shown in Fig. 6.2(a–c), respectively.

Starting from the technical efficiency which is reflected in Fig. 6.2(a), notice that, compared to JSCBs and city commercial banks, SOCBs have the highest technical efficiency over the examined period. Because the input-oriented criteria are used to measure technical efficiency, this finding indicates that SOCBs have the ability to generate the same amount of output using level volumes of input. This result can be mainly attributed to the fact that the SOCBs can benefit from lower cost derived from economies of scale as well as economies of scope. Furthermore, notice that in terms of the pure technical efficiency, as well as scale efficiency, JSCBs, and city commercial banks have a similar level over the examined period. With regard to the pure technical efficiency of different ownership types of Chinese commercial banks, Fig. 6.2(b) shows that the pattern follows the one for technical efficiency, which reports that SOCBs have the highest pure technical efficiency, followed by JSCBs and city commercial banks. This is because pure technical efficiency mainly reflects a banks' ability to manage and allocate resources in the production process. This finding

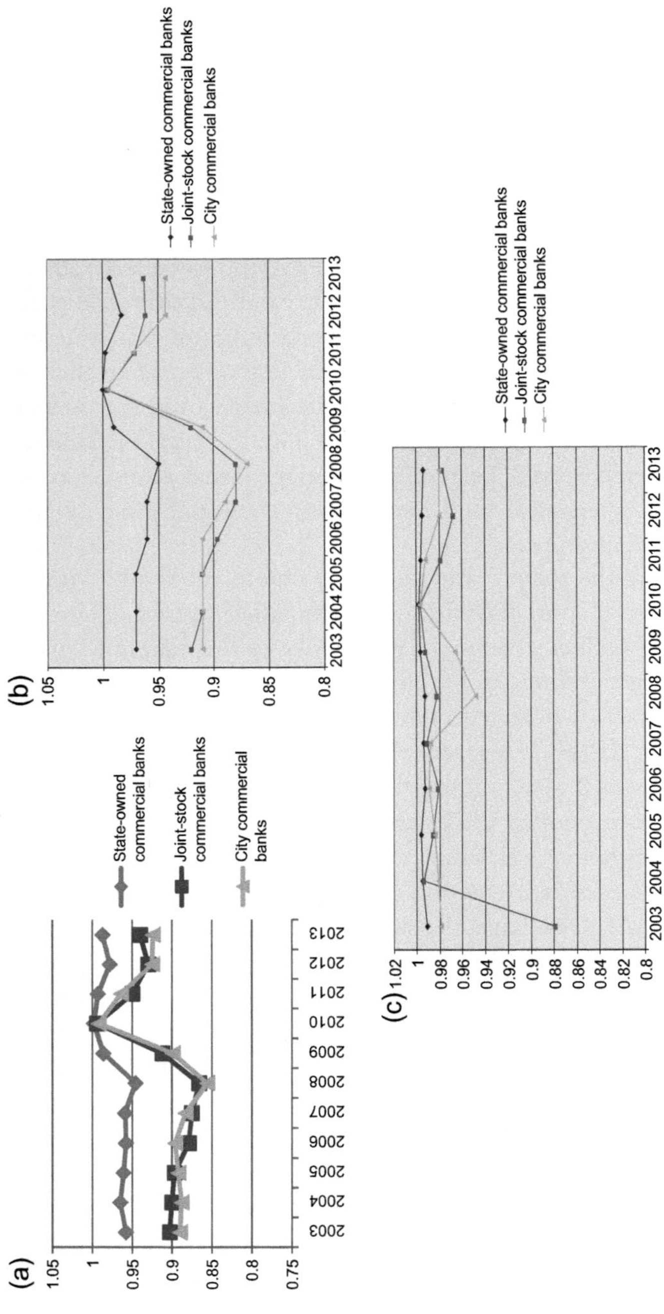

Figure 6.2 Efficiency in the Chinese banking industry. (a) Technical efficiency. (b) Pure technical efficiency. (c) Scale efficiency.

shows that SOCBs have a higher ability to allocate resources in banking production, and they can manage the resources in a better way compared to the JSCBs and city commercial banks. Finally, with regard to the scale efficiency of different ownership types of Chinese commercial banks over the examined period, it is found that the pattern does not follow the ones for technical and pure technical efficiencies; however, Fig. 6.2(c) shows that over the examined period, SOCBs have the highest scale efficiency compared to the JSCBs and city commercial banks. One special characteristic noticed for scale efficiency compared to technical and pure technical efficiencies is that the former is quite stable for SOCBs over the examined period, whereas there is a much stronger volatility for JSCBs and city commercial banks. This finding reflects the fact that compared to SOCBs, JSCBs, and city commercial banks do not manage the scale of their operation very well in the production process. This can mainly be attributed to the fact that JSCBs and city commercial banks normally focus on the provision of their banking products and services to medium and small enterprises in China, thus it is quite difficult to enlarge their size or scale of operation. In comparison, SOCBs provide financial product to large-scale enterprises and have greater flexibility to control the scale of their operations.

6.2.2 Cost, Profit, and Revenue Efficiencies of Chinese Commercial Banks over 2003–2013

This subsection mainly reports the findings with regard to the cost, profit, and the revenue efficiencies of Chinese commercial banks under the estimation of parametric stochastic frontier approach. The subsection begins with the description and explanation of cost efficiency of Chinese commercial banks, followed by revenue efficiency and profit efficiency. The cost, revenue, as well as profit efficiencies will be analyzed from different perspectives. More specifically, different efficiencies will first be analyzed and compared between different ownership types over the examined period and then each efficiency type will be discussed by comparison with the efficiency scores of different ownership types on a year-by-year basis.

6.2.2.1 Cost Efficiency of Chinese Commercial Banks

Fig. 6.3 reports the results with regard to the efficiency of three different ownership types of Chinese commercial banks over the examined period. It is noticed from the figure that city commercial banks have the highest cost efficiency, which is followed by SOCBs, whereas the JSCBs have the

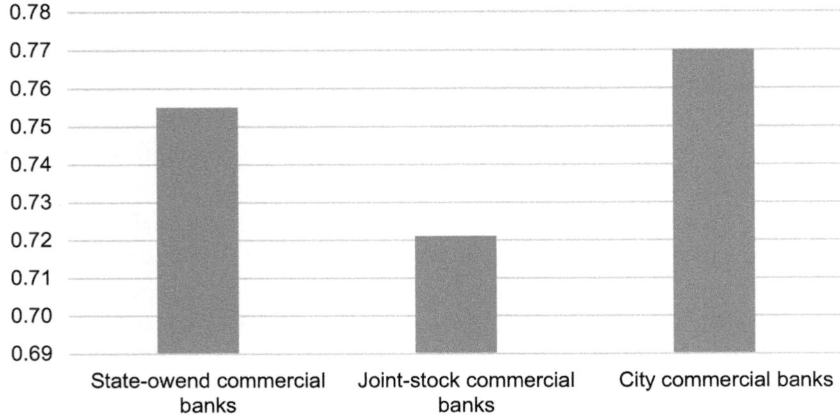

Figure 6.3 Cost efficiency of different ownership types of Chinese commercial banks over the period 2003–2013.

lowest cost efficiency over the examined period. The results show that the cost efficiencies for SOCBs, JSCBs, and city commercial banks are 0.755, 0.721, and 0.77, respectively. This indicates that generating the same volume of outputs under the same input prices, the SOCBs, JSCBs, and city commercial banks waste about 24.6%, 27.9, and 23%, respectively, of their costs relative to the best-price banks. This result is in line with the findings by Ding et al. (2015) regarding cost efficiency in the Chinese banking industry. However, this result is not in accordance with the findings of Du and Girma (2011), which show that JSCBs have higher cost efficiency compared to SOCBs. The different findings reported are mainly attributed to the fact that the current study examines the period of 2003–2013, whereas Du and Girma (2011) evaluate the period between 1995 and 2011.

Fig. 6.4 compares the cost efficiency of different types of Chinese commercial banks over the examined period on a year-by-year basis. It is noticed from the figure that SOCBs, JSCBs, and city commercial banks do not have big differences in cost efficiency over the period, whereas, in comparison, SOCBs have relatively higher volatility in cost efficiency. This finding is in contrast with the results reported by Zhao and Kang (2015) who find that the cost efficiencies of SOCBs and JSCBs have an upward trend over the period 2006–2010. Furthermore, they report that rather than experiencing volatility, the cost efficiency of SOCBs has improved significantly over the examined period. The different findings between this

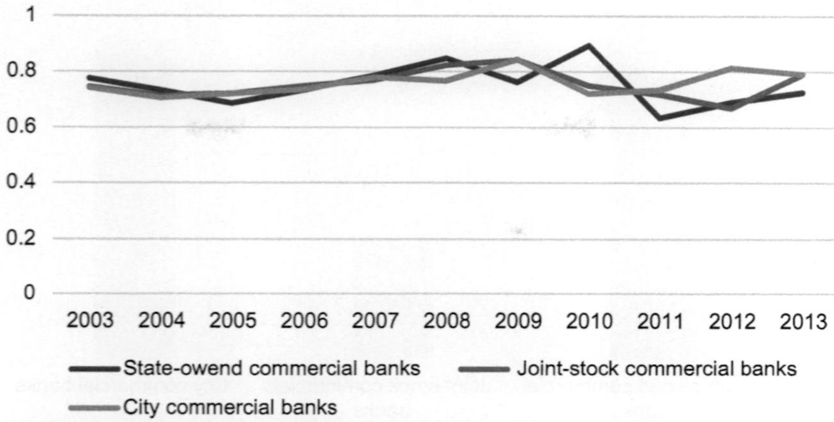

Figure 6.4 Cost efficiency of different ownerships of Chinese commercial banks on a year-by-year basis.

study and Zhao and Kang (2015) can be explained by the fact that different specification of cost function is used and also different number of commercial banks being examined whereas the current study including 100 Chinese commercial banks and 18 commercial banks being considered by Zhao and Kang (2015).

6.2.2.2 Revenue Efficiency of Chinese Commercial Banks

As far as I am concerned, there is no study so far investigating the revenue efficiency in the Chinese banking industry. Fig. 6.5 reports the findings and compared the revenue efficiency of Chinese SOCBs, JSCBs, and city commercial banks over the period 2003–2013. The figure shows that city commercial banks have the highest revenue efficiency, followed by SOCBs, whereas the revenue efficiency of JSCBs is the lowest over the examined period. More specifically, the revenue efficiency of SOCBs, JSCBs, and city commercial banks over the period are 0.678, 0.612, and 0.726, respectively, which generated the same level of output under the same input prices, Chinese SOCBs, JSCBs, and city commercial banks waste 67.8%, 61.2%, and 72.6%, respectively, of revenue compared to the best-practice bank.

Similar to the findings of cost efficiency just discussed, with regard to the revenue efficiency of different ownerships of Chinese commercial banks on a year-by-year basis, Fig. 6.6 shows the pattern that, rather than experiencing a constant trend, the revenue efficiency of Chinese

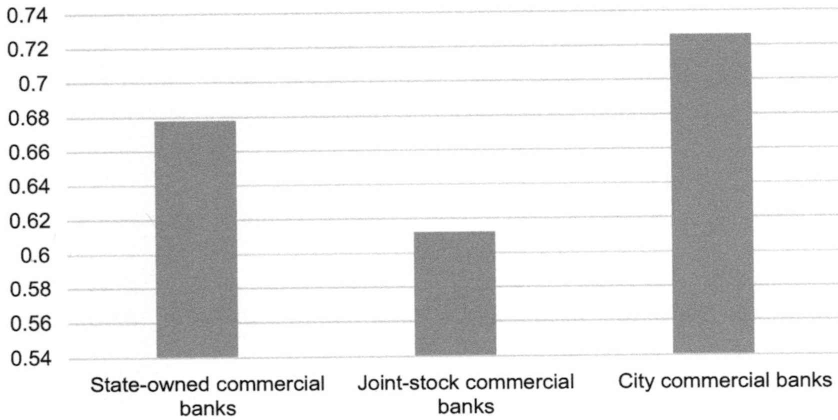

Figure 6.5 Revenue efficiency of different ownership types of Chinese commercial banks over the period 2003–2013.

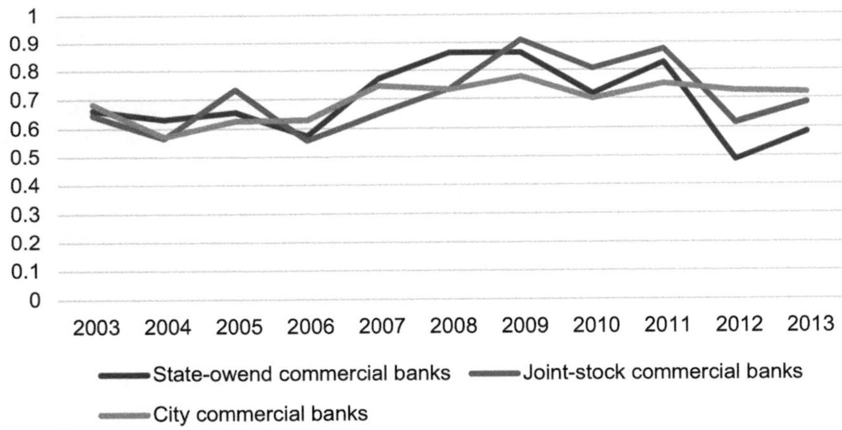

Figure 6.6 Revenue efficiency of different ownerships of Chinese commercial banks on a year-by-year basis.

commercial banks had undergone relative volatility over the examined period. In particular, it is noticed that compared to the city commercial banks, JSCBs, and SOCBs have strong volatility in revenue efficiency.

6.2.2.3 Profit Efficiency of Chinese Commercial Banks

Fig. 6.7 reports the results with regard to the profit efficiency of three different ownership types of Chinese commercial banks over the examined period. Similar to the findings of cost and revenue efficiencies, the figure of

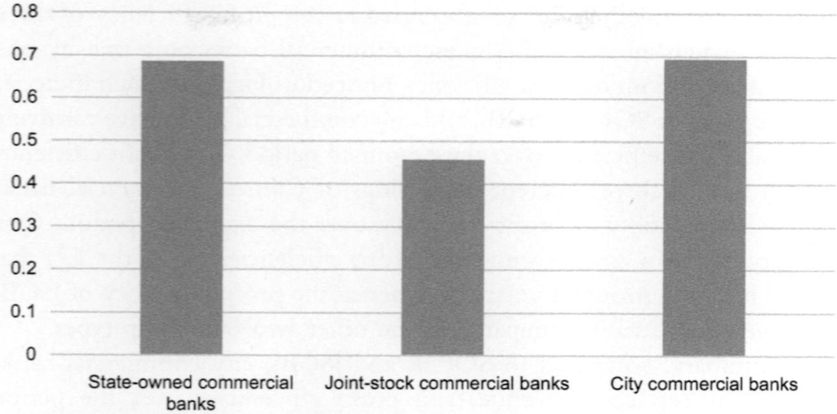

Figure 6.7 Profit efficiency of different ownership types of Chinese commercial banks over the period 2003–2013.

profit efficiency shows that over the examined period, the city commercial banks have the highest profit efficiency, which is followed by SOCBs, whereas the profit efficiency of JSCBs is the lowest. However, compared to the cost and revenue efficiencies discussed previously, the differences in profit efficiencies between SOCBs and city commercial banks are smaller. More specifically, the profit efficiency achieved by SOCBs, JSCBs, and city commercial banks over the period are 0.686, 0.456, and 0.693, respectively, which indicates that generating the same levels of outputs under the same input prices, these three types of banks produce 68.6%, 45.6%, and 69.3% of profit compared to the best-practice bank. The current results are different from the findings by Ariff and Can (2008) which suggest that JSCBs and city commercial banks have higher profit efficiency than SOCBs. The different results can be explained by (1) different periods examined, with the current study evaluating 2003–2013 and Ariff and Can (2008) assessed 1995–2004; (2) different methods used with the current study using the parametric stochastic frontier approach, whereas Ariff and Can (2008) used the nonparametric DEA to estimate the efficiency. The current finding is also different from the results reported by Berger et al. (2009) who argue that SOCBs are the least profit-efficient banking group. The differing results are attributed to the different period being examined with Berger et al. (2009) investigating the period between 1994 and 2003 and also the different results are attributed from a different specification of cost function.

Fig. 6.8 reports the results with regard to the profit efficiency of three different ownership types of Chinese commercial banks on a one-by-one basis. Different from the cost efficiency noticed in Fig. 6.4 which indicates that compared to SOCBs, JSCBs, and city commercial banks have relatively more stable cost efficiency over the examined period. The profit efficiency suggests that all three different ownerships of Chinese commercial banks have strong volatility of profit efficiency over the examined period. One similarity between cost, revenue and profit efficiencies lies in the fact that SOCBs have the strongest volatility, whereas the profit efficiency of JSCBs is relatively more stable compared to the other two ownership types.

In summary, compared to SOCBs and JSCBs, city commercial banks have the highest cost, revenue, and profit efficiencies over the period 2003–2013. In addition, the level of cost efficiency of Chinese commercial banks is generally higher than the ones for revenue and profit efficiencies, whereas the difference in the level of revenue and profit efficiencies is relatively small. With regard to the trend of different efficiencies among different ownership types, it is suggested that all ownership types of Chinese commercial banks have undergone volatility in all the efficiencies, whereas city commercial banks have relatively more stable cost and revenue efficiencies. On the other hand, JSCBs have relatively more stable profit efficiency, whereas SOCBs have stronger volatility in cost, revenue, and profit efficiencies compared to JSCBs and city commercial banks over the examined period.

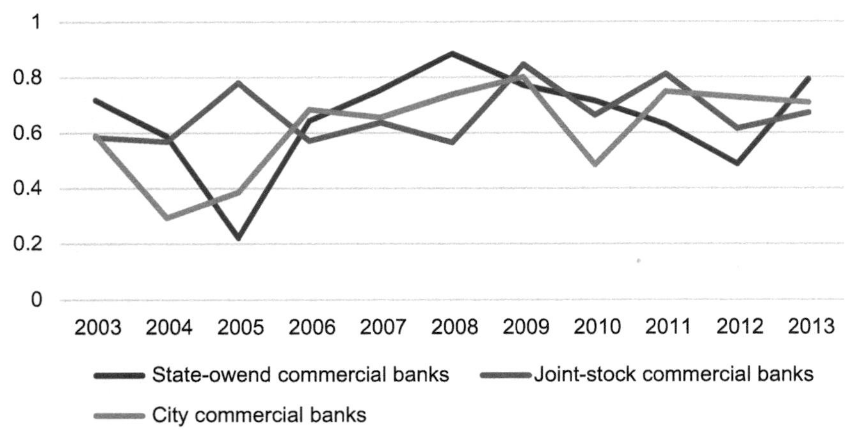

Figure 6.8 Revenue efficiency of different ownerships of Chinese commercial banks on a year-by-year basis.

6.2.3 The Competitive Condition in the Chinese Banking Industry

This subsection mainly focuses on evaluating the competitive condition in the Chinese banking industry. More specifically, this subsection will be mainly divided into the following parts, the first part will investigate the Lerner index to assess the competitive condition of the industry, which will provide a general picture of the competitive condition of different ownership types of Chinese commercial banks over the examined period. The second part of this subsection will focus on analyzing the competitive condition under the three-bank concentration ratio. The use of this indicator will examine the competitive condition in the Chinese banking industry on a year-by-year basis and relevant discussion and explanation will also be provided. Thirdly, this subsection will report the results of competitive condition of Chinese banking industry under the Panzar—Rosse H-statistic, similar to the concentration ratio; however, it further improves the ratio. This indicator is supposed to provide a picture of competitive condition in the Chinese banking industry on an annual basis. Finally, the last part of this subsection will discuss the findings with regard to the competitive condition of Chinese banking industry using Boone indicator. On an annual basis, this indicator will provide the competitive conditions for different banking markets in China such as loan, deposit, and the non-interest income markets.

6.2.3.1 The Competitive Condition in the Chinese Banking Industry—Lerner Index

Fig. 6.9 shows the competitive conditions in the Chinese banking industry over the period examined. The Lerner index suggests that over the period 2003—2013, SOCBs had the greatest market power. In other words, the competition among SOCBs in China is lower than for JSCBs and CCBs. This finding can be attributed mainly to the following factors: (1) the

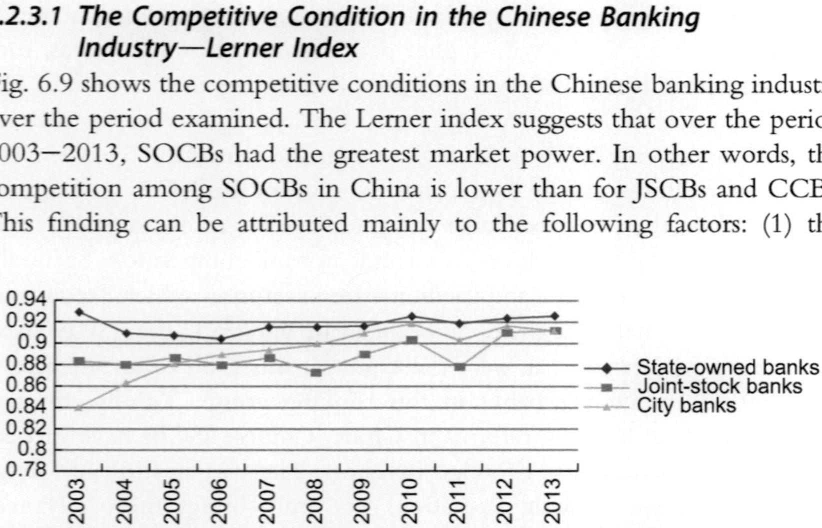

Figure 6.9 Competitive conditions of Chinese banks over the period 2003—2013 (Lerner index).

number of SOCBs is very low ie, there are only five SOCBs (the low number of banks in this bank ownership type limits the competition between them); (2) government support to these banks significantly reduces the competitive conditions among the banks in this banking ownership type. Due to the "too big to fail" issue, the government provided different kinds of support to these banks, such as nonperforming loan write-offs and capital injections. This support significantly reduced the banks' incentives to improve efficiency and further decreased competition among them; (3) although there have been several rounds of banking reforms in China, each of the SOCBs has not limited their business to the specific economic sector, they established long-run relationships with specific large-scale enterprises. In other words, each of the SOCBs conducts its business with specific enterprises and the link between the enterprises and the specific SOCB reduces competition.

Fig. 6.9 shows that, after 2005, CCBs had greater market power than JSCBs. In other words, there was less competition among CCBs compared to JSCBs. The lower competition among this banking ownership type can be explained as follows: (1) most of the CCBs had not yet offered their initial public offerings, whereas the lower pressure of obtaining funds from the general public further reduced the competition between them. Furthermore, one of the characteristics of this banking ownership type is that most of the CCBs are still operating within the city where they were established (although the geographical limitation for operation has already been removed for CCBs with higher performance). In other words, each city commercial bank just serves the enterprises within their own city. This results in a decline in bank competition. Finally, Fig. 6.9 shows that the competition among JSCBs is the highest over the period 2005–2013. The finding is attributed mainly to the fact that most of the JSCBs have already been listed on the stock exchange and the incentive to obtain more funds from the general public induces an increase in bank competition. Secondly, JSCBs mainly serve small- and medium-size enterprises which account for over 90% of total enterprises in China. In addition, the JSCBs have comprehensive branches all over the country; this leads to an increase in competition among the banks in this banking group. Thirdly, through several rounds of banking reforms in China, Chinese JSCBs have successfully attracted a number of foreign investors. The participation of foreign banks in Chinese banking operations not only brings more advanced technology and experience in risk management, but it also induces bank managers to further improve bank performance which then leads to an increase in competition among the banks in this banking group.

6.2.3.2 The Competitive Condition in the Chinese Banking Industry—Three-bank Concentration Ratio

Fig. 6.10 shows the competitive condition in the Chinese banking industry measured by the three-bank concentration ratio. The figure shows that the three-bank concentration ratio is the highest in 2003. In other words, the total assets of three largest Chinese commercial banks hold more than 50% of total assets in the whole banking industry. The largest Chinese commercial banks mainly mean the SOCBs in China especially the big four banks in China including the Agricultural Bank of China, Industrial and Commercial bank of China, Bank of China, as well as China Construction Bank. It is further noticed that the three-bank concentration ratio kept declining over the examined period and the lowest point was achieved in 2012, the percentage of which was less than 30. In other words, the total assets of the three largest Chinese commercial banks in China account for less than 30% of total assets of the whole banking industry. This consistent declining of three-bank concentration ratio was mainly attributed to the Chinese banking sector reform. In particular, in 2006 the foreign banks were to be treated exactly the same as the domestic banks, this significantly improved the competitive condition in the Chinese banking industry. Furthermore, the attraction of foreign strategic investors in Chinese banking industry play another significant role in improve the competitive condition in the Chinese banking industry. Finally, it is noticed that in 2013, compared to the previous year, the three-bank concentration ratio in the Chinese banking industry slightly increased. In other words, the largest three Chinese commercial banks held nearly 40% of the total banking sector assets. The slightly decline in the level of competitive condition of Chinese banking industry is attributed to the fact that in July 2013, the Chinese government and central bank decided to remove the limit of loan interest rate. In other words, the loan interest rate started to be determined

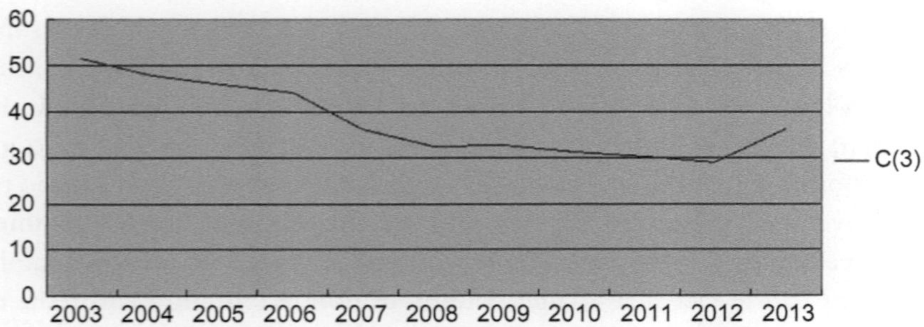

Figure 6.10 Competitive conditions of Chinese commercial banks over the period 2003–2013 (three-bank concentration ratio).

by market force rather than guided by the central bank or government intervention. The freedom in setting the loan interest rate gave the large SOCBs more opportunity to engage in higher volumes of loan business, and furthermore set the stage for an improvement in the volumes of assets held by these banks.

6.2.3.3 The Competitive Condition in the Chinese Banking Industry—Panzar–Rosse H-statistic

The reduced-form equation is estimated to obtain the Panzar–Rosse H-statistic. Before proceeding to the econometric estimation, one issue confronted is whether individual effects are fixed or random. As indicated by the Hausman test, the difference between fixed and random model is zero, providing evidence in favor of a random effect model. Table 6.2 reports the results with regard to the estimation of the reduced form equation under the random effect model. Two hypotheses of monopolistic market structure ($H = 0$) and perfectly competitive market structure ($H = 1$) have been tested by the Wald test. The results show that hypothesis of perfectly market structure is rejected at the 1% level and the hypothesis of monopolistic market structure has not been rejected. In other words, the findings show that over the examined period, the Chinese banking industry was operated under the monopolistic competition.

With regard to the independent variables in the reduced form equation, the table shows that the input prices including the prices of funds, capital, and labor are significantly and positively related to the revenue of Chinese commercial banks, indicating that higher input prices led to an improvement in bank revenue in the Chinese banking industry. This finding is in accordance with the results reported by Park (2013). It is further suggested from the finding that bank size is significantly and positively related to revenue of Chinese commercial banks. This can be explained by the fact that large commercial banks in China such as SOCBs, normally make loans to large state-owned enterprises, the demand volume of which is substantially higher than the ones of medium- and small-size enterprises, the large volumes of loan demand leads to higher revenue generated. In addition, the table shows that bank risk, as measured by the ratio of nonperforming loans to gross loans, is significantly and negatively related to bank revenue, indicating Chinese commercial banks with higher volumes of nonperforming loans have lower volumes of revenue. This is mainly attributed to the fact that a large volume of nonperforming loans reduces the amount of money paid back to banks by different companies and

Table 6.2 Test of competitive condition

	Coefficient	T-statistic
Constant	−0.632	−1.515
LnW1	0.383***	3.57
LnW2	0.175***	3.39
LnW3	0.262**	2.64
LnAssets	1.005***	10.642
LnEQUAST	0.013	1.513
LnNPLTL	0.005***	5.386
LNNIIGR	−0.383	−1.574
LNLATA	0.13**	2.88
Adjust R square	0.77	
H-statistic	0.82	
Wald test: $H = 0$	18.19	
P Value	0.113	
Wald test: $H = 1$	25.21***	
P Value	0.000	

*, **, *** denote significant at 10%, 5%, and 1% levels, respectively.
W1: input price 1 (price of fund) which is measured by the ratio of interest expenses to total funding; W2: input price 2 (price of capital) which is measured by the ratio of other non-interest expenses to fixed assets; W3: input price 3 (price of labour) which is measured by the ratio of personnel expenses to total assets; Assets: bank size which is measured by the natural logarithm of total assets; EQUAST: bank capitalization which is measured by the ratio of shareholder's euqity to total assets; NPLTL: bank risk which is measured by the ratio of non-performing loans to gross loans; NIIGR: bank diversification which is measured by the ratio of non-interest income to gross revenue; LATA: bank liquidity which is measured by the ratio of liquid assets to total assets.

further precedes a decline in bank revenue. Finally, bank liquidity, as measured by the ratio of liquid assets to total assets, is significantly and positively related to bank revenue, suggesting that banks with higher levels of liquidity have higher volumes of revenue. This can be explained by the fact that higher liquidity shows that banks can convert certain assets to cash in a quick way, in other words, higher liquidity makes banks more quickly get the cash when needed, and then the cash can be better used in activities which generate revenue.

Table 6.3 reports the results with regard to the equilibrium test using the natural logarithm of Return on Assets (ROA) as the dependent variable. Due to the fact that the return on assets for some banks over the examined period are negative, thus, the natural logarithm of 1 + ROA is used as the dependent variable in the equilibrium test. The hypothesis being tested is that the market is in equilibrium, which is $H = 0$, is not rejected. Therefore, it can be concluded that the Chinese banking industry being tested is in a long-run equilibrium.

Table 6.3 Test of equilibrium of Chinese banking competition (Return on Assets (ROA) as dependent variable in the reduced-form equation)

	Coefficient	T-statistic
Constant		
LnW1	−0.007	−0.815
LnW2	0.005	0.628
LnW3	−0.029**	−2.22
LnAssets	0.025*	1.88
LnEQUAST	0.008	1.373
LnNPLTL	−0.05**	−2.578
LNNIIGR	0.003	0.18
LNLATA	0.37**	2.93
Adjust R square	0.515	
H-statistic	−0.03***	−2.57
Wald test: $H = 0$	5.83	
P Value	0.21	

*, **, *** denote significant at 10%, 5%, and 1% levels, respectively.
W1: input price 1 (price of fund) which is measured by the ratio of interest expenses to total funding; W2: input price 2 (price of capital) which is measured by the ratio of other non-interest expenses to fixed assets; W3: input price 3 (price of labour) which is measured by the ratio of personnel expenses to total assets; Assets: bank size which is measured by the natural logarithm of total assets; EQUAST: bank capitalization which is measured by the ratio of shareholder's euqity to total assets; NPLTL: bank risk which is measured by the ratio of non-performing loans to gross loans; NIIGR: bank diversification which is measured by the ratio of non-interest income to gross revenue; LATA: bank liquidity which is measured by the ratio of liquid assets to total assets.

Table 6.4 reports the results of Panzar–Rosse H-statistic in the Chinese banking industry on an annual basis as well as the whole examined period. The table shows that in general, the Panzar–Rosse H-statistic kept increasing and reached the highest figure in 2013. This finding suggests that

Table 6.4 Competitive condition in the Chinese banking industry under the Panzar–Rosse H-statistic

Year	H-statistic
2003	0.456
2004	0.527
2005	0.581
2006	0.633
2007	0.648
2008	0.652
2009	0.669
2010	0.734
2011	0.777
2012	0.789
2013	0.883
2003–2013	0.82

the competitive condition in the Chinese banking industry has increased over the examined period and that over the whole examined period, the Panzar—Rosse H-statistic for the Chinese banking industry is 0.82. In other words, the Chinese banking industry is operated under the monopolistic competition as discussed previously, which is very near to the state of perfect competition. The increase in the competition in the Chinese banking industry was mainly attributed to the Chinese banking sector reforms, for instance, the entry of foreign banks in the domestic Chinese banking markets, the exact same treatment between foreign banks and domestic banks in providing financial products and services, the attraction of foreign strategic investors, the IPOs of Chinese commercial banks, the increase in the offering of nontraditional business (ie, investment products); the development of internet finance; the approval from Chinese government with regard to the establishment of private banks in China, as well as the liberalization of the loan interest rate.

6.2.3.4 The Competitive Condition in the Chinese Banking Industry—Boone Indicator

Figs. 6.11—6.13 report the findings with regard to the competitive conditions in different markets in the Chinese banking industry. More specifically, using the Boone indicator, Fig. 6.11 reports the results of competitive condition in the loan market in the Chinese banking industry, Fig. 6.12 reports the findings in terms of the competition in the deposit market in the Chinese banking industry, and Fig. 6.13 shows the findings with regard to the competition among Chinese commercial banks in the noninterest income-generating activities. Starting from the loan market, Fig. 6.11 shows

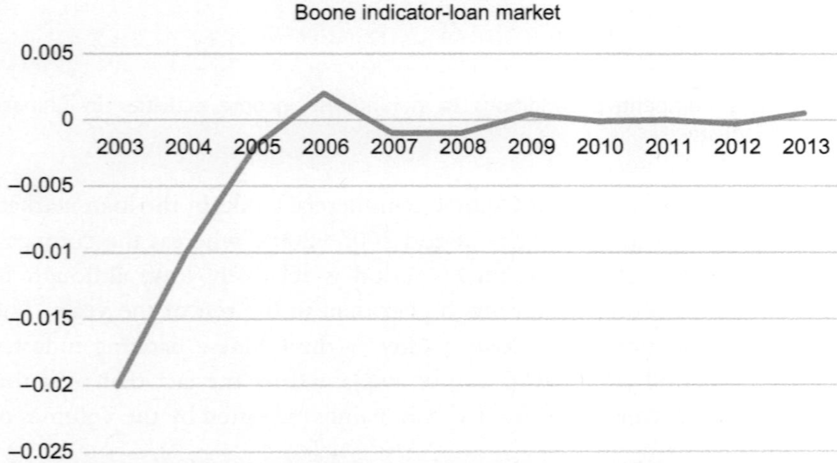

Figure 6.11 Competitive conditions in loan market in Chinese banking industry.

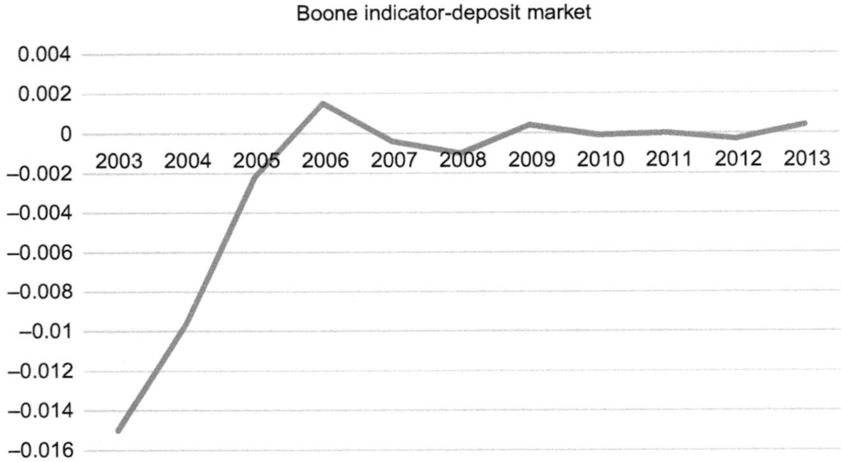

Figure 6.12 Competitive conditions in deposit market in Chinese banking industry.

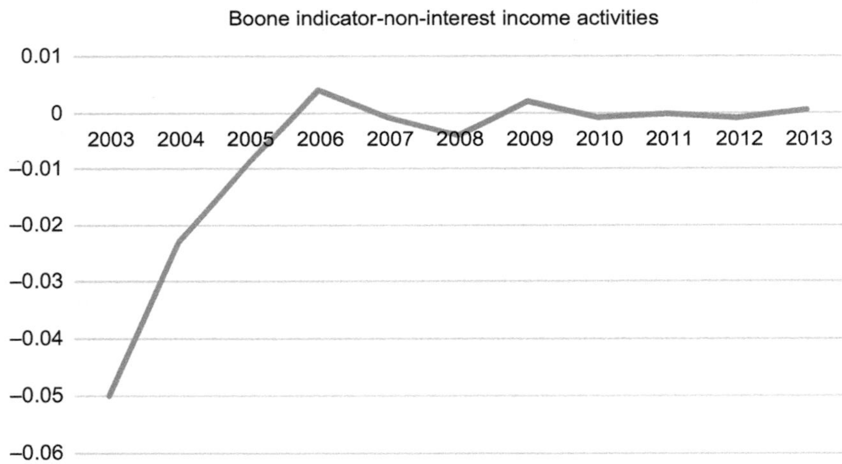

Figure 6.13 Competitive conditions in noninterest income activities in Chinese banking industry.

that the competition among Chinese commercial banks in the loan markets was relatively stronger over the period 2003–2005, whereas the competition for the rest of the examined period is relatively low, although in 2007–2008, the competition was higher than in the rest of the years. The stronger competition in the loan market in the Chinese banking industry during the period 2003–2005 can be explained by the fact that over this period, the performance of the staff was mainly measured by the volumes of loans attracted; therefore, all the staff concentrated on the volumes rather than the quality of loans attracted. This is also the reason for the large volumes of nonperforming loans in the Chinese banking industry. The staffs from different banks compete with each other on the loan business which is the main reason for the highest competition in 2003. The establishment of the China Banking Regulatory Commission together with the capital injection to state-owned enterprises in 2003 strengthen the risk monitoring of loan business not only for the state-owned commercial and but all the commercial banks within the Chinese banking industry. This led to Chinese commercial banks making loan business in a more rational way rather than purely focusing on the quantity but the quality of loans has been emphasized. This behavior reduced the competition among banks in the loan market in 2004 and 2005. The competition during the period 2006–2013 was relatively more stable in the Chinese banking industry, although it is noticed that in 2007 and 2008 the competitive is relatively strong which is mainly attributed to the fact that by the end of 2006, the foreign banks started to be treated exactly the same as the domestic banks; this preceded an increase in bank competition. The competition in the loan market in the Chinese banking industry was quite stable after 2009. This is mainly attributed to the fact that the loan market in China had not been liberalized. On 20 July 2013, the loan interest rate in China was liberalized, in other words, it is supposed that this will increase in the competition among Chinese banks and the effect will start to appear in the coming years.

Fig. 6.12 shows the competitive condition of deposit market in the Chinese banking industry. The pattern is very similar to the one for the competitive condition of the loan market as reflected in Fig. 6.11. Starting from 2003, the competition of the deposit market is the stronger over the examined period. This can be explained from the perspective of the loan market. In 2003 and before, Chinese commercial banks purely focused on the quantity of loan business made and, to provide the funds for the loan business, all the banks made the effort to attract deposits from individuals as well as from different companies, leading to an increase in competition in the deposit market. The declining competitive condition in the following two years in 2004 and 2005 can be mainly attributed to the fact that Chinese commercial banks made loans in a more rational way and proper screening and credit checking procedures had been implemented, and the loan demand was lower than previously which alleviated the pressure of attracting deposits. Although a relatively more stable competitive condition of prevailed in the deposit market over the period 2006–2013, it is still noticed that the competition was relatively stronger in 2007 and 2008. This is mainly attributed to the competition from foreign banks.

Fig. 6.13 shows the competitive condition of noninterest income-generating activities among Chinese commercial banks. The figure reports that the competition in the noninterest income-generating activities among Chinese commercial banks was relatively much stronger between 2003 and 2005 compared to the rest of the period examined. This can be explained by the fact that at 2003, the number of banks offering noninterest income products to customers were very few. In addition, the types of noninterest income products offered to customers were quite limited. The few banks offering the product tried to establish their relationship with customers to obtain higher volumes of customers; this significantly increased the competition among commercial banks. In the following year, the number of banks offering the products as well as the types of noninterest income-generating products increased. All the banks normally provided this kind of noninterest products to their own depositors, this reduces the competitive condition in this market. Same as the competitive condition in the loan and deposit markets, relatively higher competitive conditions in 2007 and 2008 were attributed to the competition from foreign banks offering noninterest-generating products to customers.

Compared to the competitive condition among the above three different banking markets, it is noticed that over the period 2006–2013, the competitive condition for these three different markets was the same, the main difference was noticed during the period 2003–2005. Fig. 6.14 shows that the competitive condition in the noninterest-generating market is the

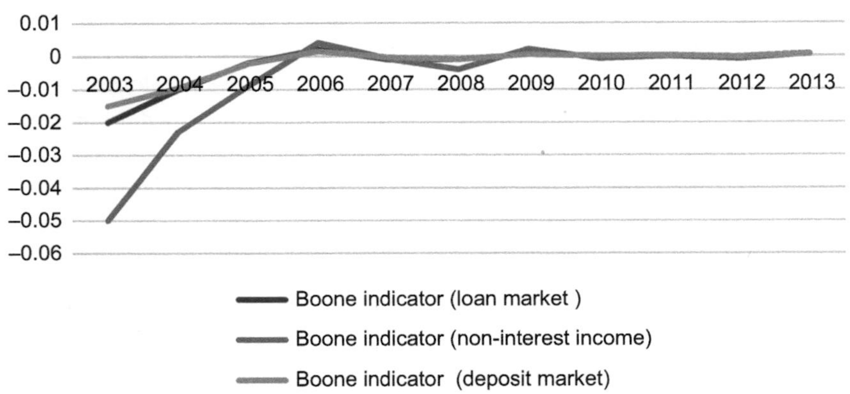

Figure 6.14 Competitive conditions of different banking market in China over 2003–2013.

highest in general between 2003 and 2005 compared to the other two markets, whereas the competitive conditions for the loan and deposit markets were the same over the same period.

6.3 THE IMPACT OF COMPETITION ON EFFICIENCY IN THE CHINESE BANKING INDUSTRY

Tables 6.5–6.7 report the results with regard to the impact of competition on efficiency in the Chinese banking industry using different competition indicators such as three-bank concentration ratio, Panzar–Rosse H-statistic, and Lerner index under the Bootstrapped truncated regression. In addition, one of the main contributions of this book is the use of the Boone indicator to investigate the competitive condition of different banking markets in China and further examine their impacts on efficiency in the Chinese banking industry. More specifically, using the Boone indicator, this book examines the competition of loan, deposit, and noninterest income markets and further test their impact on different types of bank efficiency, ie, technical, cost, revenue, and profit efficiencies of Chinese commercial banks, the results of which are reported in Tables 6.8–6.10.

Using the three-bank concentration ratio as the competition indicator, the results show that bank size is significantly and negatively related to technical efficiency of Chinese commercial banks, indicating large Chinese commercial banks have lower technical efficiency. This finding suggests that large Chinese commercial banks such as SOCBs should have better control in input investment in the production process. Bank diversification is found to be significantly and positively related to technical efficiency of Chinese commercial banks. This can be explained by the fact that Chinese commercial banks can benefit from economies of scope, which precede an improvement in technical efficiency. Bank profitability is found to be significantly and positively related to technical efficiency of Chinese commercial banks. This can be explained by the fact that banks with higher profitability have higher ability and skill in manage the input and output in the production process, which leads to an improvement in technical efficiency. In addition, it is found that bank risk is significantly and positively related to profit and revenue efficiencies of Chinese commercial banks.

With regard to the impact of competition on efficiency, the results show that the impacts are significant but not consistent across different efficiency measures. More specifically, it is found that competition is significantly and negatively related to technical efficiency, but significantly and positively

Table 6.5 Results of Bootstrap truncated regression on the impact of competition on bank efficiency (three-bank concentration ratio as the competition indicator)

	Technical efficiency		Cost efficiency		Revenue efficiency		Profit efficiency	
	Coefficient	**T-statistic**	**Coefficient**	**T-statistic**	**Coefficient**	**T-statistic**	**Coefficient**	**T-statistic**
Bank size	−0.06***	−16.03	−0.0007	−0.89	0.004	1.22	0.002	0.87
Bank capitalization	0.002	1.23	0.00004	0.16	−0.0004	−0.45	0.001	0.61
Bank diversification	0.001***	4.05	−0.00002	−0.29	−0.0002	−0.63	0.0001	0.26
Bank profitability	0.77*	1.85	−0.12	−1.35	−0.26	−0.54	0.16	0.54
Bank risk	−0.0001	−0.09	−0.0001	−0.70	0.002**	2.59	0.001*	1.68
Competition	0.002*	1.64	−0.002***	−7.35	−0.02***	−19.78	−0.02***	−20.02
Banking sector development	0.27***	8.11	−0.2***	−32.6	−0.38***	−15.33	−0.4***	−28.74
Stock market development	−0.0002	−1.53	0.001***	37.61	−0.0004***	−4.39	0.0001	0.89
Inflation	0.006***	2.63	−0.002***	−5.13	−0.02***	−15.96	−0.03***	−37.61
GDP growth rate	0.009**	2.33	−0.03***	−40.28	0.003	1.22	0.001	0.37
Constant	0.36***	0.001	1.53***	80.16	2.31***	29.51	2.35***	44.86
No. of observations	488		539		539		539	
Log likelihood	687.58		1459.92		751.74		903.53	
Wald chi square	459.18***		9594.08***		834.62***		4796.68***	

*, **, *** denote significance at 10%, 5%, and 1% levels, respectively.

Table 6.6 Results of Bootstrap truncated regression on the impact of competition on bank efficiency (Panzar–Rosse H-statistic as the competition indicator)

	Technical efficiency		Cost efficiency		Revenue efficiency		Profit efficiency	
	Coefficient	T-statistic	Coefficient	T-statistic	Coefficient	T-statistic	Coefficient	T-statistic
Bank size	−0.06***	−15.99	−0.0004	−0.56	0.005	1.29	0.004	1.37
Bank capitalization	0.002	1.33	0.0001	0.36	0.002	1.01	0.001	1.25
Bank diversification	0.001***	4.06	−8.54e-06	−0.14	9.19e-06	0.03	0.0002	0.59
Bank profitability	0.77*	1.86	−0.08	−0.79	0.44	0.53	0.6	1.01
Bank risk	−0.0004	−0.69	−0.0002	−0.87	−0.001	−1.56	0.0003	0.37
Competition	−0.3***	−3.07	0.16***	5.34	0.62***	6.16	1.41***	8.80
Banking sector development	0.36***	7.44	−0.23***	−17.15	−0.27***	−6.46	−0.61***	−9.92
Stock market development	−0.0004***	−3.80	0.001***	63.27	0.001***	9.21	0.002***	17.05
Inflation	0.008***	3.51	−0.002***	−4.15	−0.009***	−4.43	−0.03***	−15.46
GDP growth rate	0.016***	5.05	−0.04***	51.49	−0.03***	−9.59	−0.05***	−15.22
Constant	0.37***	4.25	1.45***	79.25	1.13***	14.96	1.46***	20.12
No. of observations	448		539		539		539	
Log likelihood	689.88		1449.55		605.86		745.75	
Wald chi square	462.95***		6579.85***		318.59***		763.48***	

*, **, *** denote significance at 10%, 5%, and 1% levels, respectively.

Table 6.7 Results of Bootstrap truncated regression on the impact of competition on bank efficiency (Lerner index as the competition indicator)

	Technical efficiency		Cost efficiency		Revenue efficiency		Profit efficiency	
	Coefficient	T-statistic	Coefficient	T-statistic	Coefficient	T-statistic	Coefficient	T-statistic
Bank size	−0.06***	−16.64	−0.001	−1.15	0.002	0.54	0.002	0.61
Bank capitalization	0.001	0.69	0.0004*	1.71	0.002*	1.83	0.004***	2.99
Bank diversification	0.001***	5.95	0.00003	0.44	0.002	0.64	0.0003	1.03
Bank profitability	−0.11	−0.18	−0.07	−0.63	0.46	0.51	1.11	1.28
Bank risk	0.0003	0.57	−0.0005**	−2.14	−0.002***	−2.68	−0.003***	−3.37
Competition	0.48***	5.27	0.05**	1.97	0.17	1.57	−0.05	−0.58
Banking sector development	0.25***	9.40	−0.16***	−25.6	−0.006	−0.21	−0.02	−0.69
Stock market development	−0.0004***	−4.00	0.001***	57.16	0.001***	7.96	0.001***	12.93
Inflation	0.004***	2.69	−0.0002	−0.84	−0.001	−0.50	−0.009***	−7.34
GDP growth rate	0.013***	4.15	−0.03***	−56.97	−0.022***	−5.85	−0.03***	−7.22
Constant	0.06	0.57	1.34***	45.97	0.71***	5.65	0.9***	7.24
No. of observations	435		507		507		507	
Log likelihood	680.35		1347.77		565.42		617.27	
Wald chi square	492.69***		5403.76***		227.75***		341.76***	

*, **, *** denote significance at 10%, 5%, and 1% levels, respectively.

Table 6.8 Results of Bootstrap truncated regression on the impact of competition on bank efficiency (Boone indicator loan market)

	Technical efficiency		Cost efficiency		Revenue efficiency		Profit efficiency	
	Coefficient	**T-statistic**	**Coefficient**	**T-statistic**	**Coefficient**	**T-statistic**	**Coefficient**	**T-statistic**
Bank size	−0.06***	−15.93	0.00001	0.02	0.005	1.22	0.004	1.11
Bank capitalization	0.001	1.17	0.0001	0.22	0.002	1.43	0.003**	2.46
Bank diversification	0.001***	3.99	−1.54E-06	−0.02	0.0001	0.20	0.0003	1.00
Bank profitability	0.67	1.55	−0.04	−0.43	0.64	0.71	1.06	1.34
Bank risk	−0.0001	−0.22	0.00003	0.14	−0.002**	−2.46	−0.002**	−2.32
Competition	−1.7**	−2.14	2.27***	6.52	1.81**	2.33	4.34***	3.98
Banking sector development	0.25***	9.49	−0.18***	−36.06	−0.03	−0.85	−0.06**	−2.05
Stock market development	−0.0003***	−3.56	0.001***	68.87	0.0009***	8.25	0.001***	12.85
Inflation	0.004**	2.22	−0.0001	−0.57	−0.001	−0.87	−0.009***	−7.88
GDP growth rate	0.013***	4.25	−0.03***	−68.91	−0.02***	−6.30	−0.03***	−8.12
Constant	0.45***	5.42	1.44***	108.18	0.92***	10.12	0.97***	10.60
No. of observations	448		539		539		539	
Log likelihood	687.72		1478.41		595.09		664.29	
Wald chi square	462.45***		6868.40***		263.65***		412.48***	

*, **, *** denote significance at 10%, 5%, and 1% levels, respectively.

Table 6.9 Results of Bootstrap truncated regression on the impact of competition on bank efficiency (Boone indicator deposit market)

	Technical efficiency		Cost efficiency		Revenue efficiency		Profit efficiency	
	Coefficient	**T-statistic**	**Coefficient**	**T-statistic**	**Coefficient**	**T-statistic**	**Coefficient**	**T-statistic**
Bank size	−0.06***	−15.94	0.0001	0.09	0.005	1.28	0.004	1.21
Bank capitalization	0.001	1.18	−7.52E-06	−0.03	0.002	1.35	0.003**	2.28
Bank diversification	0.001***	4.00	−7.24E-06	−0.12	0.0001	0.17	0.0003	0.95
Bank profitability	0.67	1.57	−0.05	−0.56	0.63	0.70	1.03	1.34
Bank risk	−0.0001	−0.19	0.0001	0.61	−0.002**	−2.31	−0.001*	−1.90
Competition	−2.13***	−2.09	3.33***	8.05	3.44***	3.29	7.47***	5.37
Banking sector development	0.25***	9.48	−0.19***	−38.25	−0.04	−1.22	−0.08***	−2.81
Stock market development	−0.0003***	−3.41	0.001***	68.47	0.001***	7.91	0.001***	12.22
Inflation	0.003**	2.20	−0.0001	−0.32	−0.001	−0.80	−0.009***	−7.77
GDP growth rate	0.01***	4.27	−0.03***	−70.70	−0.02***	−6.55	−0.03***	−8.62
Constant	0.45***	5.30	1.46***	112.58	0.95***	10.56	1.04***	11.52
No. of observations	448		539		539		539	
Log likelihood	687.69		1496.03		596.62		672.09	
Wald chi square	462.62***		7022.53***		284.78***		456.97***	

*, **, *** denote significance at 10%, 5%, and 1% levels, respectively.

Table 6.10 Results of Bootstrap truncated regression on the impact of competition on bank efficiency (Boone indicator noninterest income market)

	Technical efficiency		Cost efficiency		Revenue efficiency		Profit efficiency	
	Coefficient	T-statistic	Coefficient	T-statistic	Coefficient	T-statistic	Coefficient	T-statistic
Bank size	−0.06***	−15.93	−0.00005	−0.06	0.005	1.22	0.004	1.18
Bank capitalization	0.001	1.17	0.0001	0.30	0.002	1.42	0.003**	2.35
Bank diversification	0.001***	3.99	−6.56E-07	−0.01	0.0001	0.20	0.0003	0.99
Bank profitability	0.67	1.55	−0.05	−0.45	0.64	0.71	1.04	1.34
Bank risk	−0.0001	−0.25	−0.00003	−0.12	−0.002**	−2.46	−0.002**	−2.05
Competition	−0.76**	−2.23	0.89***	5.98	0.78**	2.37	2.22***	4.22
Banking sector development	0.25***	9.51	−0.19***	−34.30	−0.03	−0.93	−0.07**	−2.51
Stock market development	−0.0003***	−3.29	0.001***	64.28	0.001***	7.98	0.001***	12.32
Inflation	0.004**	2.21	−0.0001	−0.49	−0.001	−0.86	−0.009***	−7.76
GDP growth rate	0.01***	4.26	−0.034***	−68.46	−0.02***	−6.34	−0.03***	−8.36
Constant	0.45***	5.31	1.44***	100.64	0.92***	10.20	1.01***	11.09
No. of observations	448		539		539		539	
Log likelihood	687.82		1468.95		595.08		668.13	
Wald chi square	461.97***		7000.47***		268.16***		420.06***	

*, **, *** denote significance at 10%, 5%, and 1% levels, respectively.

correlated with cost, revenue, and profit efficiencies of Chinese commercial banks. In other words, it is suggested that higher competition leads to lower technical efficiency, but higher cost, revenue, and profit efficiencies of Chinese commercial banks. In terms of two other industry-specific determinants of efficiency, the results show that there is a significant and positive impact of banking sector development on technical efficiency; however, the impact is significant and negative for cost, revenue, and profit efficiencies. It is found that a higher developed stock market leads to higher cost efficiency but lower revenue efficiency of Chinese commercial banks. Finally, the macroeconomic variables show that inflation precedes an improvement in technical efficiency but a decline in cost, revenue, and profit efficiencies of Chinese commercial banks. Chinese commercial banks have higher technical efficiency and lower cost efficiency during periods of economic boom as reflected by the significant GDP growth.

Table 6.6 reports the results with regard to the impact of competition on efficiency of Chinese commercial banks using Panzar—Rosse H-statistic as the competition indicator. Some of the findings are in accordance with the one in Table 6.5 such as: (1) large Chinese commercial banks have lower technical efficiency; (2) Chinese commercial banks engaging in more diversified activities have higher technical efficiency. (3) Chinese commercial banks with higher profitability have higher technical efficiency; (4) bank competition is significantly and negatively related to technical efficiency; however, it is significantly and positively related to cost, revenue, and profit efficiencies of Chinese commercial banks. (5) Higher developed banking market leads to an improvement in technical efficiency but a decline in cost, revenue, and profit efficiencies of Chinese commercial banks; (6) higher developed stock market precedes an improvement in cost efficiency of Chinese commercial banks. (7) During periods of inflation, Chinese commercial banks have higher technical efficiency but lower cost, revenue, and profit efficiencies; (8) Chinese commercial banks have higher technical efficiency but lower cost efficiency during periods of economic boom.

Table 6.7 reports the results with regard to the impact of competition on efficiency in the Chinese banking industry using the Lerner index as the competition indicator and, compared to Tables 6.5 and 6.7, the results confirm the following findings: (1) there is a significant and negative impact of bank size on technical efficiency of Chinese commercial banks; (2) bank diversification is significantly and positively related to technical efficiency of Chinese banks; (3) Chinese commercial banks have higher technical efficiency in a lower competitive environment; (4) higher banking sector development leads to an improvement in technical efficiency but a decline in cost efficiency of Chinese commercial banks; (5) higher developed stock market precedes an improvement in cost efficiency of Chinese commercial banks; (6) inflation is significantly and positively related to technical efficiency but significantly and negatively related to profit efficiency of Chinese commercial banks; (7) higher economic growth leads to an improvement in technical efficiency but a decline in cost efficiency of Chinese commercial banks. In contrast with the findings reported in Tables 6.5 and 6.6, Lerner index results show that Chinese commercial banks with higher levels of capital have higher cost, revenue, and profit efficiencies, whereas bank risk is significantly and negatively related to cost, revenue, and profit efficiencies of Chinese commercial banks.

Using the Boone indicator as the competition measurement, Tables 6.8–6.10 report the finding with regard to the impact of competition on efficiency in the Chinese banking industry in three different banking markets, namely, loan, deposit, as well as the noninterest income markets. With regard to the impact of competition on efficiency in Chinese loan market, the results in Table 6.8 show that large Chinese commercial banks have lower technical efficiency and those with more diversified activities have higher technical efficiency. Banking sector development is found significantly and positively related to technical efficiency but significantly and negatively related to cost efficiency of Chinese commercial banks. Stock market development is found significantly and positively related to cost efficiency of Chinese commercial banks, whereas with regard to the macroeconomic variables, the findings suggest that higher inflation leads to a higher technical efficiency but a lower profit efficiency of Chinese commercial banks. However, during periods of economic boom, Chinese commercial banks have higher technical efficiency but lower cost efficiency. In terms of the impact of competition in the loan market on efficiencies of Chinese commercial banks, the results indicate that higher competition in the loan market leads to higher technical efficiency, but lower cost, revenue, and profit efficiencies of Chinese commercial banks. Same as Table 6.7 shows that bank risk is significantly and negatively related to revenue and profit efficiencies of Chinese commercial banks, and Chinese commercial banks with higher levels of capital have higher profit efficiency.

With regard to the impact of competition in the deposit market on the efficiency of Chinese commercial banks, Table 6.9 confirms the findings reported from the previous tables as follows: (1) bank size is significantly and negatively related to technical efficiency of Chinese commercial banks; (2) Chinese commercial banks with more diversified businesses have higher technical efficiency; (3) higher developed banking market in China leads to higher technical efficiency but lower cost efficiency of Chinese commercial banks; (4) higher developed stock market precedes an improvement in cost efficiency of Chinese commercial banks; (5) higher inflation leads to higher technical efficiency but lower profit efficiency of Chinese commercial banks; (6) higher GDP growth rate leads to higher technical efficiency but lower cost efficiency in the Chinese banking industry. In particular, the findings of this table are in accordance with the results reported in Tables 6.7 and 6.8 as follows: (1) Chinese commercial banks with higher levels of capital have higher profit efficiency; (2) Chinese commercial banks with higher levels of risk have lower revenue and profit efficiencies. Finally, with regard to the impact of competition in the deposit market on the efficiency of Chinese commercial banks, it is suggested that higher competition leads to higher technical efficiency, but lower cost, revenue, and profit efficiencies of Chinese commercial banks.

Table 6.10 reports the results with regard to the impact of competition in the noninterest income market on efficiency in the Chinese banking industry. The findings confirms the significance of the variables as reported previously including bank size, bank diversification, banking sector development, stock market development, inflation, and GDP growth rate. In particular, the findings are in line with the results reported in Tables 6.7–6.9 in terms of the variables such as bank capitalization and bank risk. Same as for the impact in the loan and deposit markets, the findings show that the higher competition in the noninterest income market leads to higher technical efficiency, but lower cost, revenue, and profit efficiencies of Chinese commercial banks.

To check the robustness of the results, two different modern econometric techniques are used which include the Tobit regression analysis and ordinary least square analysis. Two sets of corresponding results are reported which are shown in Tables 6.11–6.16 using Tobit regression and Tables 6.17–6.22 using ordinary least square. With regard to the impact of competition on efficiency using three-bank concentration ratio as the competition indicator under the Tobit regression analysis, Table 6.11 confirms the findings compared to the competition indicator under the Bootstrapped truncated regression with regard to a number of variables including bank size, bank diversification, bank risk, bank competition,

Table 6.11 Results of Tobit regression on the impact of competition on bank efficiency (three-bank concentration ratio as the competition indicator)

	Technical efficiency		Cost efficiency		Revenue efficiency		Profit efficiency	
	Coefficient	**T-statistic**	**Coefficient**	**T-statistic**	**Coefficient**	**T-statistic**	**Coefficient**	**T-statistic**
Bank size	−0.06***	−16.26	−0.001	−1.04	0.005	1.41	0.002	0.95
Bank capitalization	0.0001	0.05	0.0001	0.15	−0.001	−0.52	0.001	0.69
Bank diversification	0.0008***	3.05	−0.00004	−0.43	−0.0002	−0.79	0.000002	0.09
Bank profitability	0.3	0.66	−0.18	−1.28	−0.32	−0.62	0.15	0.39
Bank risk	−0.001	−1.42	−0.0003	−1.24	0.002**	2.33	0.002**	2.40
Competition	0.004***	3.55	−0.001***	−3.97	−0.02***	−17.92	−0.02***	−25.65
Banking sector development	0.34***	11.35	−0.24***	−25.38	−0.45***	−12.91	−0.47***	−18.79
Stock market development	−0.00002	−0.21	0.001***	28.94	−0.0001	−0.62	0.0004***	4.11
Inflation	0.013***	6.79	−0.005***	7.54	−0.03***	−12.64	−0.04***	−21.98
GDP growth rate	0.005	1.56	−0.04***	−30.86	−0.008**	−2.26	−0.009***	−3.14
Constant	0.18*	1.75	1.66***	48.73	2.66***	21.35	2.66***	29.18
No. of observations	506		539		539		539	
Log likelihood	537.31		971.54		370.4		592.49	
LR chi square	335.96***		1036.34***		416.75***		757.24***	

*, **, *** denote significance at 10%, 5%, and 1% levels, respectively.

Table 6.12 Results of Tobit regression on the impact of competition on bank efficiency (Panzar–Rosse H-statistic as the competition indicator)

	Technical efficiency		Cost efficiency		Revenue efficiency		Profit efficiency	
	Coefficient	T-statistic	Coefficient	T-statistic	Coefficient	T-statistic	Coefficient	T-statistic
Bank size	−0.06***	−16.55	−0.001	−0.89	0.007	1.39	0.005	1.35
Bank capitalization	0.0002	0.17	0.00003	0.07	0.002	1.02	0.002	1.32
Bank diversification	0.0008***	3.04	−0.00003	−0.38	−0.00003	−0.07	0.0002	0.53
Bank profitability	0.28	0.61	−0.16	−1.19	0.62	0.90	0.76	1.46
Bank risk	−0.001*	−1.85	−0.0003	−1.09	−0.002	−1.26	0.0003	0.30
Competition	−0.48***	−4.52	0.13***	4.11	0.49***	3.06	1.5***	13.08
Banking sector development	0.47***	9.50	−0.27***	−18.19	−0.25***	−3.37	−0.67***	−12.63
Stock market development	−0.0003***	−3.32	0.001***	38.21	0.001***	10.11	0.002***	18.11
Inflation	0.014***	7.42	−0.005***	−7.73	−0.01***	−4.11	−0.03***	−14.94
GDP growth rate	0.017***	5.24	−0.04***	−35.49	−0.05***	−9.15	−0.06***	−15.86
Constant	0.26***	3.11	1.63***	55.64	1.31***	10.20	1.68***	17.84
No. of observations	506		539		539		539	
Log likelihood	541.16		972.28		250.39		453.09	
LR chi square	343.66***		1037.81***		176.72***		478.44***	

*, **, *** denote significance at 10%, 5%, and 1% levels, respectively.

Table 6.13 Results of Tobit regression on the impact of competition on bank efficiency (Lerner index as the competition indicator)

	Technical efficiency		Cost efficiency		Revenue efficiency		Profit efficiency	
	Coefficient	**T-statistic**	**Coefficient**	**T-statistic**	**Coefficient**	**T-statistic**	**Coefficient**	**T-statistic**
Bank size	−0.06***	−17.35	−0.002	−1.41	0.004	0.73	0.003	0.58
Bank capitalization	−0.0006	−0.51	0.0004	0.94	0.003*	1.72	0.004***	2.93
Bank diversification	0.001***	4.28	0.00001	0.15	0.0002	0.49	0.0003	0.90
Bank profitability	−0.41	−0.93	−0.18	−1.27	0.56	0.78	1.4**	2.19
Bank risk	−0.0002	−0.28	−0.0004*	−1.95	−0.002**	−2.03	−0.003***	−3.37
Competition	0.48***	5.76	0.07**	2.41	0.21*	1.65	−0.04	−0.36
Banking sector development	0.27***	12.27	−0.22***	−25.85	−0.04	−1.20	−0.06*	−1.90
Stock market development	−0.0003***	−3.32	0.001***	36.09	0.001***	9.48	0.002***	15.05
Inflation	0.009***	6.24	−0.004***	−6.20	−0.006**	−2.36	−0.02***	−7.83
GDP growth rate	0.01***	3.68	−0.04***	−34.12	−0.04***	−8.38	−0.054***	−9.87
Constant	0.04	0.39	1.52***	42.13	0.9***	5.68	1.1***	8.11
No. of observations	491		507		507		507	
Log likelihood	553.16		916.79		238.63		361.27	
LR chi square	347.63***		958.77***		160.42***		307.62	

*, **, *** denote significance at 10%, 5%, and 1% levels, respectively.

Table 6.14 Results of Tobit regression on the impact of competition on bank efficiency (Boone indicator loan market)

	Technical efficiency		Cost efficiency		Revenue efficiency		Profit efficiency	
	Coefficient	**T-statistic**	**Coefficient**	**T-statistic**	**Coefficient**	**T-statistic**	**Coefficient**	**T-statistic**
Bank size	−0.06***	−16.34	−0.0003	−0.28	0.006	1.28	0.005	1.08
Bank capitalization	−0.0003	−0.29	−0.0002	−0.45	0.002	1.42	0.003**	2.33
Bank diversification	0.0008***	2.86	−0.00003	−0.40	0.00002	0.05	0.0003	0.86
Bank profitability	0.12	0.26	−0.15	−1.18	0.82	1.16	1.37**	2.25
Bank risk	−0.001	−0.86	0.0002	0.80	−0.003**	−2.19	−0.002**	−2.15
Competition	−1.54	−1.57	2.71***	10.41	0.03	0.02	4.55***	3.82
Banking sector development	0.28***	11.77	−0.24***	−29.97	−0.05	−1.34	−0.1***	−3.30
Stock market development	−0.0003***	−2.81	0.001***	38.62	0.001***	9.79	0.002***	−8.36
Inflation	0.009***	5.76	−0.003***	−6.54	−0.007***	−2.81	−0.02***	−8.36
GDP growth rate	0.01***	3.69	−0.04***	−37.64	−0.04***	−8.48	−0.04***	−10.81
Constant	0.42***	5.63	1.65***	60.11	1.11***	9.44	1.19***	12.14
No. of observations	506		539		539		539	
Log likelihood	532.28		1014.05		245.8		386.99	
LR chi square	325.9***		1121.34***		167.55***		346.24***	

*, **, *** denote significance at 10%, 5%, and 1% levels, respectively.

Table 6.15 Results of Tobit regression on the impact of competition on bank efficiency (Boone indicator deposit market)

	Technical efficiency		Cost efficiency		Revenue efficiency		Profit efficiency	
	Coefficient	**T-statistic**	**Coefficient**	**T-statistic**	**Coefficient**	**T-statistic**	**Coefficient**	**T-statistic**
Bank size	−0.06***	−16.33	−0.0002	−0.25	0.007	1.32	0.005	1.17
Bank capitalization	−0.0003	−0.27	−0.0002	−0.66	0.003	1.37	0.003**	2.19
Bank diversification	0.0008***	2.87	−0.00004	−0.50	0.00002	0.04	0.0003	0.82
Bank profitability	0.12	0.27	−0.16	−1.30	0.81	1.15	1.33**	2.21
Bank risk	−0.001	−0.85	0.0002	1.12	−0.002**	−2.03	−0.002*	−1.79
Competition	−1.96	−1.57	3.78***	11.82	1.02	0.54	7.67***	5.12
Banking sector development	0.28***	11.64	−0.24***	−31.25	−0.06	−1.52	−0.12***	−3.94
Stock market development	−0.0002***	−2.65	0.001***	38.97	0.001***	9.56	0.002***	14.69
Inflation	0.009***	5.74	−0.003***	−6.38	−0.007***	−2.80	−0.02***	−8.33
GDP growth rate	0.01***	3.70	−0.04***	−39.11	−0.41***	−8.58	−0.04***	−11.20
Constant	0.42***	5.43	1.67***	62.25	1.13***	9.48	1.26***	12.72
No. of observations	506		539		539		539	
Log likelihood	532.28		1026.24		245.95		392.55	
LR chi square	325.9***		1145.73***		167.85***		357.36***	

*, **, *** denote significance at 10%, 5%, and 1% levels, respectively.

Table 6.16 Results of Tobit regression on the impact of competition on bank efficiency (Boone indicator noninterest income market)

	Technical efficiency		Cost efficiency		Revenue efficiency		Profit efficiency	
	Coefficient	**T-statistic**	**Coefficient**	**T-statistic**	**Coefficient**	**T-statistic**	**Coefficient**	**T-statistic**
Bank size	−0.06***	−16.36	−0.0003	−0.35	0.006	1.28	0.005	1.17
Bank capitalization	−0.0003	−0.27	−0.0001	−0.33	0.003	1.42	0.003**	2.23
Bank diversification	0.0008***	2.86	−0.00003	−0.37	0.0002	0.05	0.0003	0.85
Bank profitability	0.12	0.27	−0.15	−1.16	0.82	1.16	1.35**	2.22
Bank risk	−0.001	−0.94	0.0001	0.46	−0.003**	−2.17	−0.002*	−1.82
Competition	−0.76*	−1.79	1.05***	9.16	0.05	0.07	2.49***	4.88
Banking sector development	0.29***	11.72	−0.24***	−29.24	−0.05	0.07	−0.12***	−3.84
Stock market development	−0.0002**	−2.50	0.001***	37.17	0.001***	9.57	0.002***	14.45
Inflation	0.008***	5.73	−0.004***	−6.47	−0.007***	−2.80	−0.02***	−8.33
GDP growth rate	0.01***	3.73	−0.04***	−36.98	−0.04***	−8.51	−0.04***	−11.05
Constant	0.41***	5.38	1.65***	58.73	1.11***	9.30	1.25***	12.55
No. of observations	506		539		539		539	
Log likelihood	532.65		1003.52		245.81		391.5	
LR chi square	326.63***		1100.29***		167.56***		355.26***	

*, **, *** denote significance at 10%, 5%, and 1% levels, respectively.

Table 6.17 Results of ordinary least square regression on the impact of competition on bank efficiency (three-bank concentration ratio as the competition indicator)

	Technical efficiency		Cost efficiency		Revenue efficiency		Profit efficiency	
	Coefficient	**T-statistic**	**Coefficient**	**T-statistic**	**Coefficient**	**T-statistic**	**Coefficient**	**T-statistic**
Bank size	−0.05***	−16.87	−0.0007	−0.84	0.004	1.25	0.002	0.89
Bank capitalization	0.0004	0.38	0.00004	0.15	−0.0004	−0.41	0.0005	0.63
Bank diversification	0.0008***	3.22	−0.00002	−0.26	−0.0002	−0.68	0.0001	0.33
Bank profitability	0.17	0.44	−0.12	−1.10	−0.25	−0.64	0.16	0.53
Bank risk	−0.001	−1.20	−0.0001	−0.74	0.002**	2.34	0.001**	2.58
Competition	0.003***	3.11	−0.002***	−7.83	−0.02***	−20.54	−0.02***	−28.28
Banking sector development	0.3***	11.14	−0.2***	−28.05	−0.38***	−13.94	−0.4***	−19.85
Stock market development	−0.0001	−0.61	0.001***	35.04	−0.0004***	−3.88	0.0001	1.04
Inflation	0.01***	6.08	−0.002***	−5.52	−0.02***	−13.46	−0.03***	−25.14
GDP growth rate	0.006*	1.94	−0.03***	−38.95	0.003	1.21	0.001	0.43
Constant	0.28***	2.93	1.53***	59.79	2.31***	24.27	2.35***	32.79
No. of observations	506		539		539		539	
Adjusted *R* square	0.4872		0.8529		0.5478		0.7545	
F-test	48.98***		312.91***		66.18***		166.38***	

*, **, *** denote significance at 10%, 5%, and 1% levels, respectively.

Table 6.18 Results of ordinary least square regression on the impact of competition on bank efficiency (Panzar—Rosse H-statistic as the competition indicator)

	Technical efficiency		Cost efficiency		Revenue efficiency		Profit efficiency	
	Coefficient	**T-statistic**	**Coefficient**	**T-statistic**	**Coefficient**	**T-statistic**	**Coefficient**	**T-statistic**
Bank size	−0.05***	−17.15	−0.0004	−0.53	0.005	1.29	0.004	1.38
Bank capitalization	0.0005	0.52	0.0001	0.31	0.002	1.08	0.001	1.28
Bank diversification	0.0008***	3.22	−8.54E-06	0.13	8.77e-06	0.03	0.0002	0.68
Bank profitability	0.17	0.44	−0.08	−0.76	0.43	0.83	0.6	1.51
Bank risk	−0.001	−1.63	−0.0002	−0.96	−0.001	−1.20	0.0003	0.41
Competition	−0.4***	9.19	0.16***	6.25	0.62***	4.92	1.41***	14.54
Banking sector development	0.41***	9.19	−0.23***	−19.20	−0.27***	−4.56	−0.61***	−13.47
Stock market development	−0.0003***	−3.41	0.001***	49.67	0.001***	8.63	0.002***	18.08
Inflation	0.012***	6.74	−0.002***	−4.70	−0.008***	−3.75	−0.03***	−14.95
GDP growth rate	0.015***	5.18	−0.04***	−43.24	−0.03***	−8.03	−0.05***	−15.56
Constant	0.33***	4.39	1.45***	69.55	1.13***	11.33	1.46***	18.93
No. of observations	506		539		539		539	
Adjusted R square	0.4947		0.8471		0.2222		0.5592	
F-test	50.43***		299.11***		16.37***		69.25***	

*, **, *** denote significance at 10%, 5%, and 1% levels, respectively.

Table 6.19 Results of ordinary least square regression on the impact of competition on bank efficiency (Lerner index as the competition indicator)

	Technical efficiency		Cost efficiency		Revenue efficiency		Profit efficiency	
	Coefficient	**T-statistic**	**Coefficient**	**T-statistic**	**Coefficient**	**T-statistic**	**Coefficient**	**T-statistic**
Bank size	−0.06***	−17.9	−0.001	−1.11	0.002	0.57	0.002	0.62
Bank capitalization	−0.0001	−0.14	0.0004	1.46	0.003**	2.05	0.004***	3.01
Bank diversification	0.001***	4.43	0.00003	0.40	0.0002	0.61	0.0003	1.00
Bank profitability	−0.4	−1.05	−0.07	−0.64	0.45	0.84	1.1**	2.28
Bank risk	−0.0001	−0.20	−0.0005**	−2.54	−0.002**	−2.52	−0.003***	−3.61
Competition	0.43***	5.73	0.05**	2.20	0.17*	1.68	−0.05	−0.58
Banking sector development	0.25***	12.30	−0.16***	−27.74	−0.006	−0.22	−0.02	−0.83
Stock market development	−0.0003***	−3.39	0.001***	46.15	0.001***	7.85	0.001***	14.22
Inflation	0.007***	5.58	−0.0002	−0.60	−0.001	−0.38	−0.009***	−5.69
GDP growth rate	0.01***	3.80	−0.03***	−43.10	−0.02***	−6.18	−0.03***	−8.03
Constant	0.12	1.32	1.34***	50.19	−0.71***	5.68	0.9***	7.98
No. of observations	491		507		507		507	
Adjusted *R* square	0.5096		0.8362		0.1951		0.3800	
F-test	51.92		259.3***		13.26***		32.02***	

*, **, *** denote significance at 10%, 5%, and 1% levels, respectively.

Table 6.20 Results of ordinary least square regression on the impact of competition on bank efficiency (Boone indicator loan market)

	Technical efficiency		Cost efficiency		Revenue efficiency		Profit efficiency	
	Coefficient	T-statistic	Coefficient	T-statistic	Coefficient	T-statistic	Coefficient	T-statistic
Bank size	−0.05***	−16.96	0.00001	0.02	0.005	1.23	0.004	1.11
Bank capitalization	0.0001	0.10	0.00006	0.21	0.002	1.57	0.003**	2.39
Bank diversification	0.0007***	3.05	−1.54E-06	−0.03	0.0001	0.19	0.0003	1.01
Bank profitability	0.05	0.12	−0.04	−0.44	0.63	1.20	1.04**	2.28
Bank risk	−0.001	−0.78	0.00003	0.15	−0.002**	−2.19	−0.002**	−2.22
Competition	−1.41	−1.57	2.27***	10.16	1.81	1.57	4.34***	4.29
Banking sector development	0.26***	11.85	−0.18***	−33.11	−0.03	−0.89	−0.06**	−2.38
Stock market development	−0.0002***	−2.89	0.001***	50.49	0.001***	7.95	0.001***	14.24
Inflation	0.007***	5.16	−0.0001	−0.43	−0.001	−0.66	−0.009***	−6.05
GDP growth rate	0.01***	3.81	−0.034***	−49.58	−0.02***	−6.52	−0.03***	−9.10
Constant	0.47***	6.82	1.44***	81.53	0.91***	10.04	0.97***	12.11
No. of observations	506		539		539		539	
Adjusted *R* square	0.4798		0.8626		0.1904		0.4035	
F-test	47.58***		338.88***		13.65***		37.39***	

*, **, *** denote significance at 10%, 5%, and 1% levels, respectively.

Table 6.21 Results of ordinary least square regression on the impact of competition on bank efficiency (Boone indicator deposit market)

	Technical efficiency		Cost efficiency		Revenue efficiency		Profit efficiency	
	Coefficient	T-statistic	Coefficient	T-statistic	Coefficient	T-statistic	Coefficient	T-statistic
Bank size	−0.05***	−16.96	0.0001	0.08	0.005	1.28	0.004	1.22
Bank capitalization	0.0001	0.12	−7.52E-06	−0.03	0.002	1.48	0.003**	2.23
Bank diversification	0.0007***	3.06	−7.24E-06	−0.12	0.0001	0.17	0.0003	0.96
Bank profitability	0.05	0.14	−0.05	−0.55	0.61	1.17	1.02**	2.25
Bank risk	−0.0005	−0.77	0.0001	0.62	−0.002**	−1.96	−0.001*	−1.79
Competition	−1.79	−1.56	3.33***	12.08	3.44**	2.35	7.47***	5.87
Banking sector development	0.26***	11.70	−0.19***	−34.72	−0.04	−1.25	−0.08***	−3.19
Stock market development	−0.0002***	−2.73	0.001***	50.32	0.001***	7.59	0.001***	13.60
Inflation	0.007***	5.14	−0.0001	−0.25	−0.001	−0.60	−0.009***	−6.00
GDP growth rate	0.01***	3.82	−0.034***	51.58	−0.02***	−6.72	−0.03***	−9.62
Constant	0.46888	6.60	1.46***	83.76	0.95***	10.25	1.03***	12.86
No. of observations	506		539		539		539	
Adjusted R square	0.4798		0.8713		0.1950		0.4206	
F-test	47.58***		365.34***		14.03***		40.05***	

*, **, *** denote significance at 10%, 5%, and 1% levels, respectively.

Table 6.22 Results of ordinary least square regression on the impact of competition on bank efficiency (Boone indicator noninterest income market)

	Technical efficiency		Cost efficiency		Revenue efficiency		Profit efficiency	
	Coefficient	**T-statistic**	**Coefficient**	**T-statistic**	**Coefficient**	**T-statistic**	**Coefficient**	**T-statistic**
Bank size	−0.05***	−16.99	−0.00005	−0.06	0.005	1.23	0.004	1.18
Bank capitalization	0.0001	0.12	0.00008	0.29	0.002	1.57	0.003**	2.31
Bank diversification	0.0007***	3.05	−6.56E-07	−0.01	0.0001	0.19	0.0003	1.00
Bank profitability	0.05	0.13	−0.05	−0.45	0.62	1.19	1.03**	2.26
Bank risk	−0.0006	−0.85	−0.00003	−0.13	−0.002**	−2.19	−0.002**	−1.96
Competition	−0.69*	−1.76	0.89***	9.02	0.78	1.56	2.22***	5.12
Banking sector development	0.26***	11.78	−0.19***	−32.09	−0.03	−0.95	−0.07***	−2.88
Stock market development	−0.0002**	−2.58	0.001***	47.50	0.001***	7.58	0.001***	13.30
Inflation	0.007***	5.13	−0.0001	−0.37	−0.001	−0.64	−0.009***	−5.99
GDP growth rate	0.01***	3.85	−0.034***	−48.53	−0.02***	−6.51	−0.03***	−9.30
Constant	0.46***	6.57	1.44***	78.93	0.92***	9.95	1.009***	12.50
No. of observations	506		539		539		539	
Adjusted R square	0.4805		0.8577		0.1930		0.4120	
F-test	47.7***		325.37***		13.65***		38.69***	

*, **, *** denote significance at 10%, 5%, and 1% levels, respectively.

banking sector development, and inflation. In particular, the results are also in accordance with Table 6.5 with regard to other variables such as: (1) stock market development is significantly and positively related to cost efficiency of Chinese commercial banks. (2) Higher GDP growth leads to lower cost efficiency in the Chinese banking industry. Comparing Table 6.12 with Table 6.6 which uses the same competition indicator (Panzar–Rosse H-statistic) under a different econometric estimation, the following variables exhibit the same significances including bank size, bank diversification, bank competition, banking sector development, stock market development, inflation, and GDP growth rate. Comparing Tables 6.13 and 6.7 using Lerner index as the competition indicator, the same findings have been shown on the variables including bank size, bank risk, bank diversification, banking sector development, stock market development, and GDP growth. In particular, these two tables also have the following same findings: (1) bank capitalization is significantly and positively related to revenue and profit efficiencies of Chinese commercial banks. (2) Bank competition is significantly and negatively related to technical and cost efficiencies of Chinese commercial banks; (3) higher inflation leads to higher technical efficiency but lower profit efficiency of Chinese commercial banks. Comparing Tables 6.14 and 6.8, both of which use the Boone indicator to test the impact of loan market competition on efficiency of Chinese commercial banks, they have the same findings with regard to bank size, bank capitalization, bank diversification, bank risk, banking sector development, stock market development, inflation, and GDP growth. In particular, both of these tables show that higher competition in the loan market leads to lower cost and profit efficiencies of Chinese commercial banks. Comparing Tables 6.15 and 6.9, which use the Boone indicator to examine the impact of competition in the deposit market on efficiency of Chinese commercial banks, they report that bank size, bank capital, bank diversification, bank risk, banking sector development, stock market development, and GDP growth have the same significance. With regard to competition, both of them suggest that higher competition in the deposit market leads to lower cost and profit efficiencies of Chinese commercial banks and higher inflation leads to higher technical efficiency but lower profit efficiency in the Chinese banking industry. Finally, comparing Tables 6.16 with 6.10, both of which evaluate the impact of competition in the noninterest income market on efficiency of Chinese commercial banks, both of these two tables have the same significant bank-specific variables including bank size, bank diversification, bank risk, and bank capital. They also exhibit the same significance with regard to banking sector development, stock market development, and GDP growth. With regard to the impact of competition on bank efficiency, both of these tables indicate that higher competition in the noninterest income market leads to higher technical efficiency, but lower cost and profit efficiencies of Chinese commercial banks and higher inflation leads to higher technical efficiency but lower profit efficiency in the Chinese banking industry.

Finally, the robustness of the results has been checked by using the ordinary least square estimator to test the impact of competition on bank efficiency in China. Tables 6.17–6.22 report the findings in terms of the impact of three-bank concentration ratio on different efficiencies, the impact of Panzar–Rosse H-statistic on different efficiencies, the impact of Lerner index on different efficiencies, and the impact of the Boone indicator on different efficiencies. Comparing between Tables 6.17 and 6.5, as well as Table 6.11, all of which use three-bank concentration ratio as the competition indicator, all these three tables show the same significance and impact with regard to bank size, bank diversification, bank risk, bank competition, banking sector development, and inflation. All three tables indicate that a higher developed stock market leads to higher cost efficiency, whereas higher GDP growth rate has a significant and negative impact on the cost efficiency of Chinese commercial banks. Comparing Table 6.18 with Tables 6.6 and 6.12, all of which used Panzar–Rosse H-statistic as the competition indicator, all have the same finding with regard to the significance and impact of the variables including bank size, bank diversification, bank competition, banking sector development, stock market development, inflation, and GDP growth. With regard to using the Lerner index as the competition indicator, Tables 6.7, 6.13, and 6.19 have the same findings in terms of the variables including bank size, bank risk, bank diversification, stock market development, and GDP growth rate. In particular, these three tables also have the same findings as follows: (1) Chinese commercial banks with higher levels of capital have higher profit and revenue efficiencies. (2) Higher developed banking sector leads to an improvement in technical efficiency but a decline in cost efficiency in the Chinese banking industry; (3) Chinese commercial banks have higher technical and cost efficiencies in a lower competitive environment. (4) In a higher inflationary environment, Chinese commercial banks have higher technical efficiency but lower profit efficiency. Comparing Tables 6.8, 6.14, and 6.20, all of which use the Boone indicator to test the impact of loan market competition on efficiency of Chinese commercial banks, the variables exhibiting same significance across these three tables include bank size, bank capital, bank diversification, bank risk, banking sector development, stock market development, and GDP growth. Furthermore, all three tables suggest that higher competition leads to lower cost and profit efficiencies of Chinese banks and higher inflation leads to an improvement in technical efficiency but a decline in profit efficiency in the Chinese banking industry. With regard to competition in the deposit market across different econometric estimations, Tables 6.9, 6.15, and 6.21 have the same findings with regard to the significance of bank size, bank diversification, bank risk, bank capital, banking sector development, stock market development, and GDP growth rate. In addition, it is shown that higher competition in the deposit market leads to lower cost and profit efficiencies of Chinese commercial banks and higher inflation leads to higher technical efficiency but lower profit efficiency in the Chinese banking industry. Finally, comparing across Tables 6.10, 6.16, and 6.22, all of which test the impact of competition in the noninterest income market on efficiency of Chinese commercial banks, all of them have the same findings with regard to bank size, bank risk, bank capital, and bank diversification, with regard to the industry-specific and macroeconomic variables, banking sector development, stock market development, and GDP growth rate have the same significance and impact. It is found that in a more competitive environment, Chinese commercial banks have higher technical efficiency but lower cost and profit efficiencies, and inflation is significantly and positively related to technical efficiency but negatively related to profit efficiency.

In summary, the use of different competition indicators as well as different econometric techniques provide robust results with regard to the impact of competition on efficiency in the Chinese banking industry. It is found that in the Chinese banking industry, technical efficiency is significantly affected by bank size and bank diversification. Cost efficiency in the Chinese banking industry is also found to be significantly affected by stock market development and GDP growth rate, whereas the technical and cost efficiencies of Chinese commercial banks are significantly affected by banking sector development. Inflation is found to be significantly related to technical and profit efficiencies of Chinese commercial banks, whereas with regard to the impact of competition on efficiency in the Chinese banking industry, it is found that a higher competitive environment in the industry leads to a lower technical efficiency of Chinese commercial banks. In particular, the results show that higher competition in the loan market, deposit market, and noninterest income market lead to lower cost and profit efficiencies of Chinese commercial banks, whereas the higher competition in the noninterest income market precedes an improvement in technical efficiency of Chinese commercial banks.

6.4 CONCLUSION

This chapter reports the findings with regard to the efficiency, and competition as well as the impact of competition on efficiency in the Chinese banking industry. More specifically, the first part of this chapter reported the results of different efficiencies of Chinese commercial banks. Using the nonparametric DEA, the findings suggested that SOCBs in China have the highest technical efficiency over the examined period, which is followed by city commercial banks, whereas the JSCBs are found to be least technical efficient. The technical efficiency is further decomposed into another two components which are pure technical and scale efficiencies. The results indicated that SOCBs have the highest pure technical and scale efficiencies, whereas the pure technical and scale efficiencies of JSCBs are the lowest. Comparing between these two components of technical efficiency, scale efficiency is found to be higher than the pure technical efficiency. This finding indicates that scale efficiency contributes more to the overall technical efficiency of Chinese commercial banks, and Chinese commercial banks should better allocate and manage the inputs and outputs in banking operation. It is further argued from the finding that SOCBs in China have a higher ability to manage the resources in banking operations and they benefit from economies of scale as well as economies of scope.

Rather than using the nonparametric DEA, the second part of this chapter analyzes the cost, revenue, as well as profit efficiencies under the parametric stochastic frontier approach. The results indicate that compared between different ownership types of Chinese commercial banks, city commercial banks have the higher cost, revenue, as well as profit efficiencies over the examined period. In general, rather than experiencing a constant increase in trend over the examined period, the current study finds that for all the efficiencies including cost, revenue, as well as profit efficiencies, all three different types of ownership had undergone relative volatility. More specifically, city commercial banks have smaller volatility in cost and revenue efficiencies compared to JSCBs and SOCBs, whereas JSCBs have relatively smaller volatility in profit efficiency compared to the other two ownership types. Finally, it is argued from the results that SOCBs have the strongest volatility in all the efficiencies.

The second part of this chapter concentrated on discussing the results with regard to the competitive conditions of Chinese banking industry using different competition indicators. First, using the Lerner index as the competition indicators, the findings suggest that over the examined period, the competition among SOCBs is lower than that for JSCBs and city commercial banks. Furthermore, it is found that after 2005, the level of competition among city commercial banks is lower than that for JSCBs. Finally, under the Lerner index estimation, it is found that over the period 2005–2013, the level of competition of JSCBs is the highest compared to that among SOCBs and city commercial banks. The three-bank concentration ratio shows the competitive condition of Chinese banking industry on a year-by-year basis. The indicator suggested that the ratio kept declining from 2003 until 2012; in other words, the competitive condition in the Chinese banking industry has significantly improved. This is mainly attributed to several rounds of Chinese banking reforms. However, it is noticed that in 2013, there is a slight increase in the three-bank concentration ratio; in other words, the competition has recently decreased in the Chinese banking industry.

Using the Panzar–Rosse H-statistic as the competition indicator to measure the competitive condition on an annual basis, slightly different from the findings reported from the three-bank concentration ratio, the results show that the competitive condition in the Chinese banking industry kept increasing during the examined period and the competition was the highest in 2013. This was very near to the state of perfect competition, whereas over the period 2003–2013, the results indicate that the Chinese banking industry operated under a state of monopolistic competition. Finally, using the Boone indicator, the competitive conditions of three different banking markets in China, namely, the loan market, deposit market, and noninterest income market have been examined over the period. More specifically, with regard to the loan market, the competition is relatively stronger during 2003–2005 with the rest of the period being relatively more stable, although over 2006–2013, the competition in 2007 and 2008 is stronger than in the rest of the years. In terms of the competitive condition in the deposit market of the Chinese banking industry, the pattern of competitive conditions is quite similar to the one in the loan market. Higher competition has been noticed during 2003–2005, although there is a declining trend in competition over this period, whereas the rest of the years have a relatively more stable competitive condition. With regard to the competition in the noninterest income market, the results suggest that relatively higher competition has been noticed over the period 2003–2005, whereas over this period, the competitive condition declined. This is the same as the trend noticed in the loan and deposit markets over the period 2006–2013, relatively stronger competition has been noticed in 2007 and 2008 compared to the rest of the years. Comparing the competitive condition among the loan, deposit, and noninterest income markets, the findings show that the competition over the period 2006–2013 across these three markets was the same. However, the competition over the period 2003–2005 was the highest for the noninterest income market, and the competition for the loan and the deposit markets was the same over 2003–2005.

Finally, using different competition indicators, this chapter examines the impact of competition on efficiency of Chinese commercial banks using different econometric techniques to check the robustness of the results including the bootstrapped truncated regression, Tobit regression, as well as the ordinary least square estimator. The findings show that a higher competitive environment in the Chinese banking industry leads to lower technical efficiency of Chinese commercial banks. More specifically, with regard to the impact of competition in different banking markets on efficiency of Chinese commercial banks, the results suggest that a higher competitive environment in the loan, deposit, and noninterest income markets lead to declines in cost and profit efficiencies of Chinese commercial banks. It is further argued that in a higher competitive environment of the noninterest income market, the technical efficiency of Chinese commercial banks is higher. In addition, the results show that there are significant impacts of bank size and bank diversification on the technical efficiency of Chinese commercial banks. Stock market development and GDP growth rate are found to be significantly related to technical and profit efficiencies of Chinese commercial banks, banking sector development is found to be significantly related to technical and cost efficiencies of Chinese commercial banks and inflation has a significant impact on technical and profit efficiencies in the Chinese banking industry.

REFERENCES

Ariff, M., Can, L., 2008. Cost and profit efficiency of Chinese banks: a non-parametric analysis. China Economic Review 19 (2), 260–273.

Berger, A.N., Hasan, I., Zhou, M., 2009. Bank ownership and efficiency in China: what will happen in the world's largest nation? Journal of Banking and Finance 33 (1), 113–130.

Ding, N., Fung, H., Jia, J., 2015. What drives cost efficiency of banks in China. China and World Economy 23 (2), 61–83.

Du, J., Girma, S., 2011. Cost economies, efficiency and productivity growth in the Chinese banking industry: evidence from a quarterly panel dataset. Empirical Economics 41 (1), 199–226.
Park, K.H., 2013. Testing for competition in the South Korean and Chinese commercial banking markets. Asia-Pacific Journal of Financial Studies 42, 56–75.
Zhao, H., Kang, S., 2015. Cost efficiency of Chinese commercial banks. International Journal of Finance and Accounting 4 (3), 180–186.

CHAPTER 7

Conclusion

7.1 INTRODUCTION AND SUMMARY OF THE FINDINGS

The world has paid great attention to the Chinese economy during recent decades because its economy has experienced fast growth compared to other countries around the world. According to the statistics provided by the World Bank, the gross domestic product (GDP) growth rate over the period 2003–07 in China kept increasing from 10% in 2003 and reached the highest point in 2007, which was 14.2%; although economic growth decreased slightly over the period 2008–11, the average annual growth was still over 9.2%. In 2012 and 2013, the GDP growth in China was 7.8 and 7.7%, respectively. Compared to some developed countries, such as the United Kingdom and the United States, the GDP growth rate over the same period was less than 3% and during some years, these two countries even experienced negative growth. Without any doubt, the Chinese banking industry has played a vital role in promoting the economic growth in China. In other words, a sustainable, healthy, and well-performed banking industry is very important for the Chinese economy. From this perspective, government officials, banking regulatory authorities, as well as academic researchers have attached great importance to the performance of the Chinese banking industry. Since the establishment of the China Banking Regulatory Authority in 2003, the Authority has published an annual statement every year including all the issues and events in the Chinese banking industry that occurred that year, one aspect of which was the summary of bank performance (bank profitability). In addition, during recent years, the literature reporting on the research investigating the profitability of Chinese banking industry and its determinants using different methods has grown rapidly. Besides profitability, bank efficiency has also been the focus of academic researchers analyzing performance of the Chinese banking industry and most of the research examines either the technical efficiency, or the profit and cost efficiencies in the industry. This book fills a gap in the empirical literature by comprehensively and systematically examining the efficiency in the industry including technical efficiency, cost efficiency, revenue efficiency, and profit efficiency using

Efficiency and Competition in Chinese Banking
ISBN 978-0-08-100074-8

both nonparametric data envelopment analysis as well as parametric stochastic frontier analysis.

Since the third plenary session of the 11th Central Committee of the Chinese Communist Party in 1978, the Chinese government has begun implementing the policies of reform and opening up to the rest of the world. More importantly, the Chinese banking industry started several stages of reforms, the purposes of which were to improve the performance, increase the competitive condition, as well as reduce the risk-taking behavior of Chinese commercial banks. Statistics suggest that the three largest state-owned commercial banks hold more than 50% of the assets of the whole Chinese banking industry in 2003, although the dominance of the state-owned commercial banks reduced somewhat the following years. However, in 2013, the three largest state-owned commercial banks still held nearly 40% of total banking sector assets. In other words, from this perspective, the Chinese banking industry is still insufficiently competitive. Besides considering the assets of the largest state-owned commercial banks as a proportion of the total assets in the banking industry, a growing number of studies are using different methods to examine the competitive condition in the Chinese banking industry, including the Panzar—Rosse H-statistic and the Lerner index. The current book comprehensively analyzes the competitive condition in the Chinese banking industry using the three-bank concentration ratio, Panzar—Rosse H-statistic, the Lerner index, and, more importantly, the Boone indicator. The first two indicators measure competition in the Chinese banking industry on an annual basis, whereas the Lerner index is able to test the competitive condition by ownership types, and the Boone indicator is able to evaluate competition in different banking markets. One of the main contributions of the current book lies in the fact that it analyzes the competition in different banking markets in China such as the loan, the deposit, and the noninterest income markets.

The credit risk (non-performing loans) in the Chinese banking industry has been a historical problem over the decades; however, the situation has significantly improved. According to World Bank statistics, the nonperforming loan ratio in the Chinese banking industry in 2003 was 20.4%; although the trend declined somewhat the following year, it still had a nonperforming loan ratio of over 6% until 2008. In comparison to some developed countries, such as the United Kingdom and the United States, the nonperforming loan ratios of which were lower than 5%, credit risk was a very serious problem in the Chinese banking industry. However, statistics show that the nonperforming loan ratio of the Chinese banking industry kept on declining since 2008 to the lowest point in 2013, the ratio of which was 1%. The substantial decline in the non-performing loan ratio is mainly attributed to the management and supervision efforts made by Chinese government as well as banking regulatory authority.

One interest point and another contribution of the current book is to examine the impacts of competition and risk on efficiency in the Chinese banking industry. Competition, risk and efficiency are three main issues addressed by several rounds of banking reforms in China. When examining this type of relationship, the current study also controlled a number of bank-specific variables, industry-specific variables, as well as macroeconomic variables. The bank-specific variables include bank size, bank capitalization, bank profitability, and bank diversification. Two industry-specific variables were considered in the current book which are banking sector development and stock market development; with regard to the macroeconomic variables, both inflation and GDP growth rates are considered. In terms of the data, the current book uses 100 Chinese commercial banks over the period 2003–13, which include five state-owned commercial banks, 12 joint-stock commercial banks, and 83 city commercial banks. To check the robustness of the results, the current book uses a number of econometric techniques including bootstrapped truncated regression, Tobit regression, as well as ordinary least square estimator.

The findings show that over the examined period, state-owned commercial banks have the highest technical efficiency, which is followed by city commercial banks, with the technical efficiency of joint-stock commercial banks coming in last and lowest. Comparing pure technical efficiency and scale efficiency, the latter is higher which indicates that the Chinese banking industry should improve the allocation of inputs and outputs in the production process. On an annual basis over the examined period, the findings show that state-owned commercial banks have the highest technical efficiency, pure technical efficiency, and scale efficiency, whereas the differences between these three efficiencies among these three different efficiency indicators are relatively small. Different from the results of technical efficiency, the findings of cost efficiency indicate that city commercial banks have the highest cost efficiency, which is followed by state-owned commercial banks, whereas the cost efficiency of joint-stock commercial banks is the lowest. With regard to the cost efficiency of different ownership types of Chinese commercial banks on an annual basis, the results show that there is little difference in cost efficiency among different ownership types; however, stronger volatility characterizes cost efficiency in state-owned commercial banks compared to the other two ownership types. The findings show that over the examined period, city commercial banks have the highest revenue efficiency, which is followed by state-owned commercial banks, whereas the revenue efficiency of joint-stock commercial banks is the lowest. With regard to the revenue efficiency of three different ownership types of Chinese commercial banks on a year-by-year basis, rather than experiencing a constantly increasing trend, the revenue efficiency for all the banks was quite volatile over the examined period. In particular, compared to state-owned commercial banks and joint-stock commercial banks, city commercial banks were relatively more stable in revenue efficiency. Finally, the results of profit efficiency report that city commercial banks have the highest profit efficiency over the examined period, which is followed by state-owned commercial banks, whereas the joint-stock commercial banks have the lowest profit efficiency. Different from cost efficiency and revenue efficiency, the difference in profit efficiency between city commercial banks and state-owned commercial banks is quite small. In terms of the profit efficiency of the three different ownership types of Chinese commercial banks on an annual basis and compared for cost efficiency and revenue efficiency, the findings suggest that stronger volatility attends to profit efficiency. Furthermore, the volatility of profit efficiency in state-owned commercial banks and city commercial banks is stronger compared to that for joint-stock commercial banks.

With regard to the competitive condition in the Chinese banking industry, the three-bank concentration ratio suggests that, over the examined period, the competitive condition kept declining from 2003 until 2013, when a slight increase occurred in the competitive condition. With regard to using the Panzar—Rosse H-statistic to measure the competitive condition in the Chinese banking industry, the results suggest that the competitive condition kept increasing on an annual basis and competition in 2013 reached the highest level which was near the state of perfect competition. For the Chinese banking industry as a whole over the examined period, the findings suggest that the banking industry operated under a state of monopolistic competition. The results of the Lerner index show that, over the examined period, state-owned commercial banks have the highest market power. In other words, compared to joint-stock commercial banks and city commercial banks, state-owned commercial banks have lower competitive condition. The results further argue that over the period 2005–13, city commercial banks have higher market power compared to joint-stock commercial banks; in other words, over the period 2005–13, city commercial banks experienced lower competition than joint-stock commercial banks. Finally, joint-stock commercial banks are characterized as having the highest competition over the period 2005–13 compared to state-owned commercial banks and city commercial banks. With regard to the competitive conditions in different banking markets as reflected by the Boone indicator, the findings suggest that, over the period 2003–05, the competition in these three banking markets was quite volatile, although a declining trend of competition occurred over the period. With regard to the rest of the period, the competitive condition was relatively more stable. One point worth mentioning is that in 2007 and 2008 the Chinese banking industry experienced slightly higher competitive conditions. Compared with the loan, deposit, and noninterest income markets, the competition in the noninterest income market is substantially higher than that for the loan and deposit markets over the period 2003–05; the difference in competition between the loan market and the deposit market over the same period was relatively quite small. It is further argued that the difference in competition among these three different banking markets over the period 2006–13 was very small.

Using bootstrapped truncated regression, together with Tobit regression as well as Ordinary Least Square estimator, to check the robustness of the results, the book tests the impact of competition on efficiency in the Chinese banking industry. The results suggest that Chinese commercial banks have lower technical efficiency in a more competitive environment. More specifically, in terms of the impact of competition on different banking markets on the efficiency of Chinese commercial banks, the results indicate that Chinese commercial banks have lower cost and profit efficiencies if they were operated in a more competitive loan market, a more competitive deposit market, as well as a stronger competitive noninterest income market. However, it is found that in a higher competitive environment in the noninterest income market, the technical efficiency of Chinese commercial banks is higher. The findings show that the technical efficiency of Chinese commercial banks is significantly affected by bank size and bank diversification; the technical efficiency and profit efficiency are found to be significantly affected by stock market development and GDP growth rate. It is further suggested that banking sector development has a significant impact on technical and cost efficiencies of Chinese commercial banks, and technical and profit efficiencies are significantly affected by inflation rate.

Besides the empirical analysis of efficiency, competitive condition, as well as the impact of competition on efficiency in the Chinese banking industry, this book also reviews the Chinese banking sector reforms and structure. More specifically, the current book divides the Chinese banking industry reforms into four stages: that between 1949 and 1978, that between 1978 and 1992, that between 1992 and 2001, and the most recent reform between 2001 and 2013. With regard to the structure of the Chinese banking industry, this book has a detailed introduction on the five large-scale commercial banks,including the Agricultural Bank of China, the Industrial and Commercial Bank of China, the Bank of China, China Construction Bank, as well as the Bank of Communication. In addition, this book also has a detailed introduction on the joint-stock commercial banks on a one-by-one basis, including China Merchant Bank, China Citic Bank, Hua Xia Bank, China Everbright Bank, Shanghai Pudong Development Bank, China Minsheng Bank, Industrial Bank, China Guangfa Bank, Ping An Bank, Zheshang Bank, China Bohai Bank, as well as Evergrowing Bank. Besides the introduction on both the state-owned commercial banks and joint-stock commercial banks, this book also has an introduction regarding city commercial banks. The state-owned commercial banks, joint-stock commercial banks, and city commercial banks are the three largest ownership types of Chinese commercial banks according to the size of the assets. Finally, this book briefly introduces other banks and nonfinancial institutions.

In addition, this book also comprehensively and systematically reviews relevant theories in bank efficiency as well as bank competition. With regard to bank efficiency, this book explains the theories of technical efficiency, cost efficiency, revenue efficiency, as well as profit efficiency. In terms of the theories on the measurement of bank efficiency, this book reviews two main streams of methods, namely, the parametric and the nonparametric methods. More specifically, three approaches have been discussed with regard to the parametric method, which are the stochastic frontier approach, the distribution-free approach, as well as the thick frontier approach. On the other hand, two nonparametric methods have been examined by this book, which are Data Envelopment Analysis and free disposal hull. With regard to relevant theories in bank competition, this book explains and discusses the structure—conduct—performance paradigm, the Lerner index, Panzar—Rosse H—statistic, and the Boone indicator on a one-by-one basis.

7.2 POLICY IMPLICATIONS FOR THE CHINESE BANKING SECTOR

The findings from the book provide valuable policy implications for the Chinese government as well as banking regulatory authorities to improve future efficiency. The policy implications can be summarized as follows:

Better management in the noninterest expenses in Chinese commercial banks: to improve the efficiency of Chinese commercial banks, the cost of banks is the most important factor needing consideration. There are two components with regard to the cost of banks, one is interest expense and the other is noninterest expense. The former mainly means the cost incurred by the banks to pay out the interest to the depositors. From October 2015, the interest rate on deposits has been liberalized in China, which indicates that the interest rate on deposits paid out by banks will be determined by market force, that is, the interest expenses will be determined by the market. However, the commercial banks still have their own control on the noninterest expenses they pay out. There are three main components under the noninterest expenses: (1) salaries paid out to staff and managers; (2) expenses related to rent, utility bills, equipment, etc.; and (3) loan loss provisions. The second expense must be paid by the banks and the commercial banks have little maneuvering room over this type of expense, whereas the Chinese commercial banks should have better control and management on the salary expenses as well as the expenses related to loan loss provisions.

In recent years, the Chinese banking regulatory authorities have put forward relevant policy to reduce the levels of salary to staffs as well as managers working in the banking industry, however, problems remain with regard to this aspect. According to the official statistics, in 2014, the annual salaries offered to the managers in state-owned commercial banks were around RMB 1 million, which was lower than the levels of the previous years. However, for the managers working in the joint-stock commercial banks, their levels of salaries were substantially higher than the ones for state-owned commercial banks. The official statistics show that the higher salary offered to the banking manager in 2014 was over RMB 8.3 million, which was paid to the managers in Ping An bank, whereas the levels of salaries of management personnel working in Mingsheng bank were also more than RMB 4 million in 2014. This large difference in salary levels to management personnel between state-owned commercial banks and joint-stock commercial banks is closely related to the efficiency improvement.

Thus, it is suggested that in future years, Chinese banking regulatory authority should reduce the level of salaries paid to managers in joint-stock commercial banks to further improve the efficiency of Chinese commercial banks, especially the joint-stock commercial banks.

The second aspect that needs great attention paid in terms of controlling the noninterest expenses is to further improve the quality and management of credit risk of commercial banks. According to the regulation with regard to the provision of loan loss in the Chinese banking industry, the amount of provision will be in line with the types of loans made by the banks. There are five types of loans classified in the Chinese banking industry according to the risk, which are normal, special attention, substandard, doubtful, and loss. More specifically, with regard to the special attention loans, the percentage of provision is 2%, whereas with regard to substandard loans, the percentage of provision is 25%, in terms of the doubtful loans, the percentage of provision is 50%, and with regard to the loss loans, the percentage of provision is 100%. In particular, according to the regulation, with regard to the substandard as well as the doubtful loans, the percentage of provision can be fluctuated above or below by 20%. Therefore, to reduce the provision of loan losses which is one category under the noninterest expenses, the Chinese commercial banks should better control the risk of loans being made, which could further reduce the provision of loan losses and lead to a reduction of noninterest expenses to improve the efficiency of Chinese commercial banks.

State-owned commercial banks in China should further improve the credit risk checking and monitoring. According to official statistics, in 2013, the nonperforming loan ratio in state-owned commercial banks was 1% which was higher than the one for joint-stock commercial banks, which was 0.86%. In addition, the official statistics show that the volumes of nonperforming loans in five state-owned commercial banks reached RMB 506.1 billion, which accounted for 60.07% of the nonperforming loans in the whole banking industry. Better control of credit risk in the nonperforming loans will significantly reduce the noninterest expenses for state-owned commercial banks and further improve their efficiency.

Chinese commercial banks should expand their business scope because the results show that bank diversification is significantly and positively related to the technical efficiency of Chinese commercial banks. Therefore, besides the traditional loan and deposit services provided by Chinese commercial banks, other nontraditional activities should be engaged in by Chinese commercial banks. These include (1) domestic and foreign settlement; (2) bill settlement and discount; (3) issuing financial securities; (4) trade in foreign exchange; (5) bank card business; (6) provide letter of credit and guarantee; (7) provide financing products to customers, etc.

Further develop the stock market in China. The results show that stock market development is significantly and positively related to the cost efficiency of Chinese commercial banks. In other words, Chinese commercial banks have higher cost efficiency in a more-developed stock market. Because stock market development is measured by the ratio of market capitalization of stock market to GDP, a higher figure of this ratio indicates higher development of the stock market. To increase the market capitalization of the stock market, there are mainly three ways: (1) improve the performance of the companies listed in the stock market. The share price will increase following the improvement of company performance, with existing shares being issued, the total share value of the company increases and further promotes the increase in the market capitalization of the whole stock market. (2) Issue more shares in the stock market; (3) encourage and reduce the barriers for companies to be listed on the stock exchange. More companies listed will further increase the market capitalization. The requirement for listing on the Chinese stock exchange is still quite difficult compared to developed countries such as the United Kingdom with regard to the initial capital. The initial capital required in China to be listed is over RMB 50 million, whereas in comparison to the United Kingdom, it is around RMB 7 million. In other words, moderately reducing the entry barriers for Chinese companies to be listed on the Chinese stock exchange will further improve the development of the Chinese stock market.

7.3 LIMITATIONS OF THE BOOK AND FURTHER STUDIES

The current book presents a number of limitations. First, as discussed at the beginning of this chapter, the purposes of several rounds of banking reforms in China were to improve the performance, increase the competitive condition, as well as reduce risk-taking behavior in the Chinese banking industry. The current book comprehensively analyzes the competitive condition as well as different types of efficiencies in the Chinese banking industry. It also evaluates the impact of competition on the efficiency of Chinese commercial banks. The credit risk has been considered in the current study and its impact on efficiencies in the Chinese banking industry has been tested. However, some other types of risk indicators are not considered in the current book, such as liquidity risk, capital risk, security risk, as well as insolvency risk. Comprehensive analysis of different types of risk in the Chinese banking industry will provide valuable information to the Chinese government and banking regulatory authorities, and analysis of the impacts of different types of risk on efficiency should provide additional policy implications. Thus, future studies are suggested to examine comprehensive types of risk in the Chinese banking industry and their impacts on different types of efficiencies.

Although this book analyzed three types of the biggest commercial banks in China which are state-owned commercial banks, joint-stock commercial banks, and city commercial banks, foreign banks have been excluded in the current analysis. Future studies can consider the foreign banks and compare their efficiencies and competitive conditions with domestic Chinese commercial banks and see whether the impact of competition on efficiency in foreign banks is similar or different between domestic Chinese commercial banks and foreign banks. This will provide a more general picture on the overall banking industry in China.

INDEX

'*Note:* Page numbers followed by "f" indicate figures, "t" indicate tables.'

L

M

N

O

P

Q

R

S

T